The Hidden Curriculum:
Reproduction in Education,
A Reappraisal

Kathleen Lynch

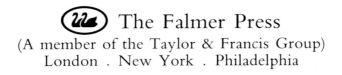 The Falmer Press
(A member of the Taylor & Francis Group)
London . New York . Philadelphia

UK   The Falmer Press, Falmer House, Barcombe, Lewes, East Sussex,
      BN8 5DL

USA   The Falmer Press, Taylor & Francis Inc., 242 Cherry Street,
      Philadelphia, PA 19106–1906

First published 1989

British Library Cataloguing in Publication Data

Lynch, Kathleen
    The hidden curriculum: reproduction in education, a reappraisal
    1. Education. Sociological perspectives.
    I. Title
    370.19

    ISBN 1–85000–573–7
    ISBN 1–85000–574–5 Pbk

Jacket design by Caroline Archer

Typeset in 10½/13 point Bembo by
Alresford Typesetting & Design, New Farm Road, Alresford, Hants.

Printed in Great Britain by
Redwood Burn Limited, Trowbridge, Wiltshire

To John

Contents

Contents

Acknowledgements

As the research for this book began seven years ago there are many people who have contributed to its completion. I am grateful to all of them even though space may not permit me to mention each one by name.

My first vote of thanks is to the school principals who gave of their time to participate in the study. I am deeply indebted to them for the great volume of information they made available to me about their schools. A special thanks also to Sr Mary O'Neill, FCJ who, along with other FCJ sisters, was the very first person to assist me in the pre-pilot stage of the research. I am very grateful too to Ms Lorna Heffernan, Principal of Sallynoggin Community School, for allowing me teaching experience in her school while conducting the study.

Two people who gave me great help in undertaking the interviewing were Gretchen Smyth and Michele Dillon. Sincere thanks to them for their dedicated work.

As much of the research for this book was undertaken while completing my doctoral thesis in the Sociology Department at University College Dublin, there are many people in UCD whom I wish to thank. My thanks firstly, to my colleagues in the Education Department for their support and to the staff of the computer centre and library for their constant help. I am particularly grateful to the staff of the Sociology Department for the many insights and encouragement they provided. Thanks to Conor Ward for his constant encouragement and help and to Mary Kelly for her valuable comments on earlier drafts of the book. I am especially appreciative of the help Pat Clancy gave me; he has provided support and given valuable criticism on the work throughout its development. Teresa Brannick gave me invaluable help with the statistical and computer work; without her help I would have been greatly handicapped. Anne Coogan of UCD's Social Science Department typed the book. The care, competence and expeditious manner in which she completed the task are much appreciated.

While researching the book I spent some time at the University of

Acknowledgements

Wisconsin at Madison. Both Maureen Hallinan and Michael Apple gave me great help and encouragement while I was there. I am especially indebted to Maureen Hallinan for making my stay in Madison such a welcoming one.

Finally, I wish to thank my beloved mother for her unstinting encouragement, and my family and friends for their kindness, support and affection throughout. Many of them have contributed to the development of the ideas within it.

I dedicate the book to John whose untold generosity gave me the time and space to complete the book. His love inspires. And for Nora, our little love, a big hug.

Preface

The role schooling plays in the reproduction of inequalities has been the subject of considerable debate and research in education over the last twenty years. Although neo-Marxists have been the principal contributors to this debate, many other educationalists have contributed to our understanding of how schools at times assuage, but more often exacerbate, class, racial and/or gender inequalities; the latter however, have worked outside the framework of reproduction theory. The relationship between schooling and social inequality is a key issue therefore in educational research, regardless of one's paradigmatic allegiance. It is a complex question in need of continuous research.

This book is set in the context of sociological debates regarding the dynamics of reproduction in education. Using Irish data, we try to unveil some of the complex mechanisms whereby inequalities get reproduced. As Andy Hargreaves (1982) observed some years ago, one of the major lacuna in neo-Marxist writing on education has been the dearth of empirical evidence to substantiate theoretical claims. Through our analysis of detailed evidence (primarily quantitative but also qualitative) on ninety second-level schools in the Republic of Ireland, we supply important evidence substantiating the claims of reproduction theorists. We take issue however, with certain aspects of reproduction theory; in particular, we argue that inequality is reproduced because schools have a variety of universalistic (equalizing) features (at the level of service *provision*) which offset its (inegalitarian) particularistic effects (at the level of service *consumption*). In Chapters 2–4 we present empirical evidence substantiating our universalistic–particularistic model.

The book also suggests that reproduction theorists have been somewhat remiss in underplaying the role of the cultural and historical factors in the reproduction process. Furthermore, we argue that the role of educational mediators (those who administer, manage and deliver educational services on a day-to-day basis) in perpetuating inequalities has not received adequate attention from neo-Marxist scholars. Chapter 5 is devoted to the analysis of the latter two issues. Here we show how the post-colonial context of Irish education has a vital influence on the operation of educational services. Because educational credentials are crucial for the attainment of wealth and power in a way which is not likely to hold true in more powerful industrialized economies (where material capital rather than cultural capital is the more crucial social differentiator), education is a live political issue for all classes. It is especially central however to the political agenda of the propertyless middle classes as schooling is the mechanism by which they maintain and perpetuate privilege.

While we suggest that the propertyless middle classes are key agents in perpetuating inequalities, we also show how those who act as educational mediators (in Ireland this includes the churches, teacher unions, parent organizations, vocational education committees etc.) can perpetuate inequalities by protecting their own status and/or power interests in the educational *status quo*. The mediators can and do act as agents of counter-resistance. To understand how inequalities are reproduced through education therefore, one must take cognizance of how the universalistic and particularistic aspects of schooling interface with each other. Comprehending the universalistic-particularistic balance requires, in turn, that one take account of how unique cultural processes and educational mediators influence the reproduction process.

The book is divided into six chapters opening with a review of the work of reproduction theorists in Chapter 1. In this chapter, we present a detailed analysis of most of the major contributors to the reproduction debate. Our principal contention is that neo-Marxists have tended to underestimate the significance of school's universalizing features in the reproduction of inequality. Chapters 2, 3 and 4 are devoted to the presentation of empirical evidence substantiating our universalistic-particularistic claims. Through the analysis of the knowledge dissemination process in the formal curriculum (Ch. 2) we show how all schools are increasingly concerned in Ireland with the development of a technically competent individual. Regardless of class or gender, technical knowledge is increasingly emphasized in schools. This is not to deny however, that the *form* which the technical takes varies frequently with the class and gender composition of the school as we show in Chapter 4. Chapter 3 examines the relational life of the school — what is most often defined as the hidden curriculum. Here we illustrate the universality of competitive individualism and hierarchical control. We show how the form of competitiveness and control within schools is also influenced by the class and gender composition of the student body. Chapter 4 examines certain particularistic aspects of schooling, using evidence on extracurricular activites to illustrate the case.

The particularistic-universalistic balance which characterizes Irish schools is, we suggest, in part a function of unique cultural and historical processes which have received little consideration to date. Chapter 5 highlights the effects of some of these unique cultural and historical forces, focusing particularly on the impact of post-colonialism on the Irish class structure and relatedly on education. It also examines the role of educational mediators in perpetuating particularistic features of schooling.

The final chapter of the book departs from the reproduction debate *per se* to overview the trends and developments in Irish education identified in Chapters 2, 3 and 4. We show how the rise of technical knowledge does not by any means seem warranted by recent employment patterns, and how the competitive individualism of schooling is strongly anathema to the collectivistic ideals which so many of those involved in education profess to believe in. Finally, we suggest that, as schools are the principal institutions in our society, for both producing and reproducing cultural forms, those skills and knowledge forms which it fails to credentialize become marginalized in the wider sociocultural agenda. Schools only give accreditation to a limited range of mental labours; hence other labour, in particular love labour, is marginalized by the schooling process.

Chapter 1

The Hidden Curriculum: A Reappraisal of Reproduction Theories

Broadly speaking, there are two theoretical approaches to the analysis of the hidden curriculum within the sociology of education, the functionalist and neo-Marxist. As the latter is the predominant one, especially in recent years, most of our attention in this chapter will focus on it. We will begin, however, with a brief review of the functionalists' contribution.

The Functionalist Tradition

While neo-Marxists are by far the most prolific writers on the hidden curriculum, Philip W. Jackson is generally acknowledged as being the first person to use the term in *Life in Classrooms* (1968: 10–33). He identified three features of classroom life as forming the core of the hidden curriculum. Pupils, he claims, must come to terms with these if they are to have a satisfactory passage through the school institution: the crowded nature of the classroom requires the pupils to cope with delays, denial of their desires and social distractions; the evaluative character of the school demands contradictory allegiance to both teachers and peers; the unequal power relations give the teacher authority to command the pupils' attention. What Jackson identifies as the hidden curriculum of the school therefore is the social requirements of its learning situation. The social or institutional requirements of schooling are, he suggests, anathema in many ways to educational goals. It is conformity rather than creativity which bring rewards in school.

What Jackson set out to establish in his analysis therefore was the unexplored social complexity of classroom life. In particular he argued that neither learning theory or human engineering have provided much understanding which is of value to the practising educator. Both perspectives

1

have failed 'to come to grips with the reality of classroom events' (ibid., 59). The focus of his work, therefore, was not just an elaboration of a hidden curriculum thesis but also the presentation of a challenge to existing paradigmatic frameworks explaining the learning process in schools.

While he highlighted the contradictions between the institutional expectations of the hidden curriculum and the requirements of intellectual mastery (ibid., 35–7) his analysis, however, remains broadly functionalist. Although he does not discuss the structural relationship between the school and society *per se* it is clear from his line of argument that a simple consensual relationship is assumed to exist between them.

The other main proponent of the functionalist view of the hidden curriculum is Robert Dreeben. Unlike Jackson, Dreeben is explicit in his functionalism focusing as he does on the structural relationships between the school and the institutions of public life. His main 'contention is that the social experiences available to pupils in schools, by virtue of the nature and sequence of their structural arrangements, provide opportunities for children to learn norms characteristic of several facets of adult public life' (1968: 65). The social life into which people are initiated via school is assumed to be a consensual, socially undifferentiated whole where achievement, independence, universalism and specificity are the required norms of conduct. No attempt is made to analyse how conflicting social class, gender, racial or religious interests might influence the normative climate of schooling. In this respect Dreeben's analysis is similar to Jackson's. While Jackson focuses on the classroom as the core unit for analysing the hidden curriculum, Dreeben focuses, however, on the school itself. The overall school prerequisites of performing alone, of having one's achievements judged by certain standards of excellence, of being treated as a member of a particular category, and of adapting to the experience of casual associations, contribute respectively to the promotion of the norms of independence, achievement, universalism and specificity (ibid., 63–86).

The work of Philip Cusick (1973) is also essentially concerned with the hidden curriculum of school life although he does not use the term in his analysis. Like both Jackson and Dreeben, his work is premised on a consensual understanding of both society itself and of the school's role in relationship to it. His work, however, is different in two other respects. Firstly, his analysis of the school organization and its effects on pupils is based on a participant observation study in a senior class in an American public high school; secondly, his theoretical approach is symbolic interactionist. The main conclusions of Cusick's study relate to the school as an organization. He identified nine 'mutually reinforcing sociocultural characteristics' which have both intended and unintended consequences for pupils. The most significant implication of the social organization of life he suggests (from the pupils' perspective) is that it 'provides an enormous amount of time when students are actually required to do little other than be in attendance and minimally compliant' (ibid., 214). Despite the social latitude allowed (unintentionally) to students, Cusick claims, however, that the school was very successful as a maintenance sub-system of the larger society. His follow-up research on students after they left high school found them to be compliant workers in the various organizations in which they were employed (ibid., 220). Cusick assumes that they would not adapt in this manner to their work roles if they had not attended school. He has, however, no comparative evidence to prove this.

The Neo-Marxist Perspective (US)

Bowles and Gintis

Although the concept of the hidden curriculum originated in the consensualist school of thought, it has been the conflict theorists who have developed it within the sociology of education. This development however, has taken an implicit rather than explicit form, as many of those who contribute to the debate on the unwritten purposes or goals of school life do not use the term 'hidden curriculum'. This is noticeably the case in Bowles and Gintis' work, *Schooling in Capitalist America* (1976). This study, involving an analysis of secondary data on the relationship between norms of schooling and those of work, is, perhaps, one of the most well-known pieces of research pertaining to the unwritten functions of school life. Their correspondence thesis is central to most current debates on the hidden curriculum of schools.

The central tenet of the correspondence principle is that 'a structural correspondence' exists between the social relations of school life and the social relations of production (ibid., 131). Bowles and Gintis suggest that schools reproduce the existing social relations of capitalist society by reproducing the consciousness necessary for such relations. The particular social relations which they deem important in the reproductive process are principally: the hierarchical division of labour between teachers and pupils; the alienated character of pupils' school work itself; and the 'fragmentation in work . . . reflected in the institutionalized and often destructive competition among students through continual and ostensibly meritocratic ranking and evaluation' (ibid.). Beyond the aggregate influence of these sets of relations they also suggest that different levels of schooling 'feed workers into different levels within the occupational structure' (ibid., 132). What Bowles and Gintis are proposing, therefore, is that schools are highly functional for the maintenance of the capitalist system. In particular they suggest that the hierarchical division of labour in school fosters the development of docility and compliance which is functional for capitalist employment later. It is also suggested that the lack of intrinsic rewards in school work prepares students to accept similar types of work relationships, while the constant fragmentation and evaluation of students through streaming and testing fosters status divisions and antagonisms which prepare them for their future stratified work careers. Depending on the level of schooling which one experiences (lower, middle or higher) one also has had exposure to different normative climates. They claim that the lower levels emphasize rule-following, the middle stresses dependability while the higher level expects 'internalization of the norms of enterprise' (ibid., 132).

There is no doubt that Bowles and Gintis' work is important in the development of a theory of the hidden curriculum. First of all, they locate the debate on the nature of the hidden curriculum in the context of the larger social system, as they define school as an integral part of the latter. Understanding of the hidden curriculum of schools cannot be provided by focusing purely on the internal dynamics of the classroom, as Jackson did, for example. The complexities of classroom life are fully comprehensible only when one takes cognizance of the structural forces outside of schools which Bowles and Gintis identify.

Bowles and Gintis' work also highlights the socially differentiated character of the students' hidden curricular experience. The students' social class, race, and/or gender all have significance in determining what kind of social experience s/he may have in school. To speak therefore of a unitary, undifferentiated entity called a hidden curriculum as Dreeben (1968) does (in terms of the four universal norms he identifies) is to assume falsely that all students are exposed to a similar normative climate in schools. As Bowles and Gintis point out, both divisions within schools (such as streaming, grading and testing) and between schools (arising from the social composition of intake or the level at which schooling is directed) result in considerable variability in the school's normative climate for a given type of pupil. In other words, the conflicting interests arising from the social relations of production in our capitalist society have daily significance for the social organization of school life.

Although Bowles and Gintis' work is (as we shall see shortly) open to certain criticism on empirical grounds the work was, when published, and still is, one of the few works pertaining to the hidden curriculum which bases its claims on anything other than small ethnographic studies. While the works of Cusick (1973), Everhart (1983), Willis (1977) and McRobbie (1978) all provide ethnographic insight into the dynamics of the hidden curriculum, it is difficult to make generalizations from their studies to unrelated school or work contexts. The data analysed by Bowles and Gintis enable us to draw tentative conclusions about relationships between the educational system and the occupational structure of society.

Finally, their book was important in providing a framework for the analysis of the relationship between the economy and the classroom. Whether one agrees with their interpretation or not, one must allow that *Schooling in Capitalist America* provided educationalists with a model of schooling which highlighted the ways in which the relations of production can influence life in classrooms.

Schooling in Capitalist America, however, can be subjected to criticism on a number of grounds. Firstly, as Karabel and Halsey (1977: 37) and Bills (1983: 185–210) have noted there is a tendency to put forward, as established scientific fact, propositions that are only equivocally supported by available evidence. Not unrelated to this is their tendency to generalize from apparently atypical samples and to be remarkably selective in their reporting of secondary evidence (Olneck and Bills: 1980, 31; Bills, 1983: 188). In terms of providing an understanding of the dynamics of the hidden curriculum in schools, their work is also far from adequate. There is no specific data which is based directly on evidence from schools; only the study reported on the personality traits rewarded and penalized in a New York high school (p. 137) is based directly on school evidence, and this tells us nothing about how school processes and practices actually operated to achieve their ends.

This leads us to the other major criticism of this book, namely that Bowles and Gintis fail to explain how the structural correspondence between schools and the capitalist economy actually occurs (Demaine, 1981: 105). A highly mechanistic and deterministic relationship is assumed to exist between the economy and the school system. This both ignores the complexities of the class structure and class interests in contemporary capitalist society, and the fact that schools as organizations are dynamic and self-interested social entities in themselves. One cannot assume that a singular dominant class interest exists and that this is the prime mover in the school system as even within the middle class itself there are economic, political and social divisions leading to tensions and conflicts (Abercrombie and Urry, 1983). Furthermore, schools and those who manage and administer the educational service (what we call educational mediators) generate their own interests as social organisms. The social class demands placed on schools may or may not accord with the interests of the latter. Whether they do or not depends on the unique historical and cultural contexts of a given system. What Bowles and Gintis seem to have ignored therefore is:

> that most institutions not only came about because of conflict, but are continuously riven by conflicts to-day. Furthermore, people employed in these institutions at all levels often have their own

interests they try to pursue based on their own material circumstances and histories. Many times, these interests will cohere with those of dominant groups...At times, though, these same people will mediate, transform and attempt to generally set limits on what is being imposed from the outside (Apple, 1988: 120).

What we are suggesting therefore is that the educational system is a distinctive 'site of production' in its own right with its own 'intrinsic principles and possibilities' (Moore, 1988: 75).

A theme that runs throughout Bowles and Gintis' work too is the attribution of inequalities in education and the hierarchical division of labour to capitalism. This is, as Karabel and Halsey observe a gross over-simplification, because 'an equally hierarchical organization of work is...compatible with Soviet-style socialism' (1977: 39). While educational inequality may persist as long as capitalism exists, this is no guarantee that its abolition will herald the end of a hierarchical school system as Bowles and Gintis imply.

The evaluation of *Schooling in Capitalist America* presented here is itself, of course, limited in scope. Our main concern is the adequacy of the work in terms of hidden curriculum theory; the book itself addresses a variety of historical, social policy and educational issues which do not pertain directly to this theme and which are therefore ignored. In no way, therefore, can our assessment of the work claim to be a comprehensive one. Furthermore, it must be pointed out that Bowles and Gintis have taken note of their critics as they published short papers in 1980 and 1988 which show that they have modified the more mechanistic and deterministic elements of their reproductive thesis considerably.

In their 1980 paper, they admit that their earlier work suffered from 'an inadequate treatment of the systemic contradictions of advanced capitalism' (p. 51) and they proceed to develop a theory of society 'as an ensemble of structurally articulated sites of social practice' (p. 55). The school system is defined 'by and large'....as 'a subsite of the state', the family and capitalist production being the other two sites. As a subsite, however, they admit it can develop according to its 'own internal principles' and thereby 'undermine the reproduction processes of other sites' (p. 57). The processes involved are rather elaborately labelled by Gintis and Bowles as 'contradictory delimitation' and 'contradictory transportation' (pp. 57, 58). The principal reason why the school is likely to be involved in undermining the reproductive processes of other sites, is, they claim, because of its contradictory position. As a general subsystem of the state it 'is directly subject to the principle of rights vested in persons' yet it also 'plays a central role in reproducing the political structure of the capitalist reproduction process', and is thereby involved in perpetuating rights 'vested in property'. In other words, 'education reproduces rights vested in property while (it) itself (is) organised in terms of rights vested in persons' (p. 62).

The article (1980) in which Gintis and Bowles outline their modified reproduction thesis is, however, rather brief. Consequently, we are given little insight, even in hypothetical terms, as to how they perceive the contradictions of capitalism working out in schols. The fresh insight they provide on social reproduction requires considerable theoretical and empirical elaboration.

The Work of Apple

Within the conflict perspective one of the most prolific writers on the hidden curriculum has been Michael Apple. His work, however, differs considerably from that of Bowles and Gintis although both are within the neo–Marxist tradition. Apple focuses his analysis on the formal curriculum and the role of teachers. Bowles and Gintis did not address these issues at all. Apple's work differs also from that of Bowles and Gintis in being almost entirely theoretical, and, in more recent times, focused increasingly on issues within Marxist theories of education and reproduction generally, rather than the hidden curriculum *per se*.

Any comment on Apple's work must be prefaced with a recognition of the shift which has occurred in his work between the 1970s and the 1980s. His earlier work, *Ideology and Curriculum* (1979), was, in Apple's own words, simply concerned with reproduction: 'It saw schools, and especially the hidden curriculum, as successfully corresponding to the ideological needs of capital' (1982: 23). It presented a rather economically deterministic view of the school system. What Apple claims was lacking in his earlier analysis, and what he claims to provide in *Education and Power*, is a more developed notion of determination, one which takes account of 'contradictions, conflicts, mediations and especially resistances' (1982: 24). We will begin our analysis of Apple's contribution to hidden curriculum theory, however, by firstly examining *Ideology and Curriculum*.

The difficulty of evaluating this book (and indeed *Education and Power*) is that it is really a series of articles on closely related themes rather than a work which presents an elaborated theory of the hidden curriculum. Because of this, there is considerable overlap between chapters. It is also rather difficult to decipher a clear line of argument although the basic reproduction thesis is evident throughout. Despite these limitations it is clear, in particular from Apple (1979: Ch. 2), that Apple regards the manner of distributing high-status curricular knowledge as a core element of the hidden curriculum of reproduction. Within a capitalist economy, he claims 'what is actually required is not the widespread distribution of high status knowledge to the populace in general' but rather the maximization of its production. Consequently, low levels of achievement on the part of the poor, minorities etc. can be tolerated because they are of less consequence to the economy 'than is the generation of the knowledge itself' (1979: p. 37). Apple also claims that the exclusion of certain groups from high-status knowledge is made possible by its 'technical' character. The class-biased nature of school curricula, therefore, makes it 'a device or filter for economic stratification' (ibid., 38). While Apple makes frequent reference throughout the book to the importance of technical knowledge and technical modes of evaluation in schools, the precise dynamics of the relationship between the production and distribution of technical knowledge in schools and social reproduction, are not fully explicated. Neither are the issues raised in Apple (1979: Ch. 2) followed through systematically throughout the work.

The content of the curriculum is, however, discussed again in Apple (1979: Ch. 5) although here Apple is principally concerned with noting the neglect of conflict themes in both the curricula of the natural and social sciences. It is his contention he says 'that the schools systematically distort the functions of social conflicts in collectivities' and this in turn 'may contribute significantly to the ideological underpinnings that serve to fundamentally orient individuals towards an unequal society' (ibid., 101–2). No evidence is presented however, to support this claim. The evidence which he does have relates to the content of a limited range of texts in the natural and social sciences. He gives no indication, however, as to the representativeness of these texts. What is notable here also is Apple's failure to explain the relationship between the social reproduction which occurs through the production and distribution of curricular knowledge (as specified in Apple, 1979: Ch. 2) and the reproduction that occurs through the propagation of a consensualist perspective within particular disciplines (Apple, 1979: Ch. 5). Presumably these processes are related yet no analysis of their interrelationship is provided.

While Apple's Chapters 2 and 5 deal with the reproductive impact of formal curricular content, his Ch. 3 (written with Nancy King) addresses the reproductive effects of the form in which knowledge is presented. Using evidence drawn from just one particular kindergarten, Apple identifies a number of normative practices to which the children are exposed (ibid., 53–7). He draws on the work of Sharp and Green (1975) in his interpretation of these normative practices, defining them principally as the outcome of the larger structural relationships within which schools are located (Apple, 1979: 59). Unfortunately, he does not explain the dynamics of the interrelationship between normative practices and structural forces.

Apart from the discussion of the content and form of curricular knowledge, Apple also addresses the question of the reproductive effects of teachers' common-sense presuppositions for schooling. These are defined also as being largely determined by structural forces outside of schools.

Although *Ideology and Curriculum* offers a number of insights into hidden curriculum theory, it does not offer a cogent theoretical model which could be empirically assessed. Even more so than in the work of Bowles and Gintis, there is a clear void at times between the claim that schools are socially reproductive and the evidence available both to support this claim and to explain how it occurs.

While Apple's earlier work is notable for its deterministic view of the educational system, his later work, exemplified in particular in *Education and Power* (1982) and *Teachers and Texts* (1986) is characterized by its emphasis on the 'relative autonomy' of the school system (1982: 17, 58, 91, 96, 143, 165; and 1986: 22, 131) as a particular cultural and superstructural entity. Influenced by the work of Paul Willis in particular, Apple devotes much of *Education and Power* to arguing that schools are not just distributors but also producers of culture (p. 22). Consequently, reproduction does not occur in the simple functionalist manner outlined in 1979 but rather through processes of contradiction, contestation and mediation. Pupils, he holds, engage in informal resistances to the school system, yet their resistance is contradictory as it results in both partial penetration of the system on the one hand, and reproduction of existing class relations on the other (1982: 27).

The other major theme in *Education and Power* also pertains to social reproduction but from a different angle, namely, that of the state. By subsidizing the production of technical/administrative knowledge, he claims that the state underwrites the class interests of the new petty bourgeoisie as it is this class which is most suitably poised to use this knowledge to reproduce itself (1982: 54–5). In particular, Apple claims that curricular knowledge is presented in a form which is amenable to the cultural practices of the career-oriented petty bourgeoisie. It is organized according to the principles of possessive individualism (pp. 152–5). He goes on to point out that 'when it finally reaches the school it is again mediated and transformed by teachers and children of those very same workers and employees who have historically confronted technical/administrative knowledge in their own workplaces' (p. 169).

Apple's most recent work, *Teachers and Texts* (1986), examines the ways in which reproduction occurs through the control of teachers and textbooks in schools. Taking up the proletarianization thesis introduced in *Education and Power*, he argues that teachers are being deskilled through the introduction of curriculum packages and the increasing demands of test requirements (1986: 32). He suggests that deskilling is facilitated by the fact that teaching is a predominantly female occupation (pp. 31–78). The production and control of textbooks is also defined as a key issue in the reproduction of inequalities and Apple devotes the second part of the book to outlining the various vested interests in text publishing in the United States.

There are a number of questions left unresolved by Apple's more recent works (1982, 1986). Hargreaves, for example, has challenged both the ideas of 'resistance' and 'relative autonomy' in the context of a critique of Marxist analyses of education. The 'movement from correspondence to resistance', he suggests, was 'born less out of scholarly interest in the open and exploratory quest for knowledge about the schooling process, than out of the academic left's political conscience about the revolutionary (or rather non-revolutionary) implications of its own theorising' (1982: 111). In addition, Hargreaves claims that the emphasis on the relative autonomy of schools has merely led to 'incoherent and contradictory accounts of the determination of schooling' (ibid., 116). Finally, he suggests that the work of Apple is weak at the theoretical level: 'it is frequently characterised', he suggests, 'by a type of mystification in which style substitutes for substantative and meticulous argument' (1984: 208–9).

Hargreaves' criticisms of Apple and other neo-Marxists are not without foundation, although I see little point in questioning the legitimacy of authors' motivations. Certainly, it is difficult at times to see how the mechanics of reproduction actually operates on a daily basis; a preoccupation with certain limited theoretical issues seems to substitute for detailed inspection of the education system. I also believe that the work of Apple suffers from its indifference to empirical research — be that research historical, ethnographic or statistical. One cannot arrive at an understanding of the relations between social classes, schools, the labour market etc., without systematically testing and retesting one's hypotheses against empirical reality. This is something neo-Marxists rarely do. In Apple's case, empirical evidence is used both sparingly and selectively.

For example, in *Teachers and Texts* (1986: 48), Apple uses material from interviews with teachers to support his claim that women teachers resist the controls being imposed on them, albeit sometimes in a manner that is reproductive of patriarchal relations. We are not informed however, as to when or where the teachers were interviewed, how many there were or how representative they were of teachers generally. The same problem occurs in relation to the use of unpublished material by Gitlin (ibid., pp. 44–6). Equally, coming away from the chapters on texts and publishing one has no idea as to how representative or comprehensive a picture one has seen. We are not suggesting here that the type of material used by Apple to substantiate his theoretical claims is either inaccurate or unacceptable. Rather, the problem is one of mode of presentation. Because empirical material is not presented in a systematic and contextualized manner, one is left with serious doubts as to the authenticity of claims based upon it.

Apple's work is important, however, in highlighting the varied and complex processes by which reproduction occurs. He has demonstrated how the form and content of the formal curriculum influences the reproduction process. His more recent work also focuses attention on the need to understand the role of publishers, teachers and students as producers of culture, if one wishes to understand the complex social dynamics of the hidden curriculum (Apple and Weis, 1983; Apple, 1986). Also through his mediation and development of Willis' work he has helped redirect the research of American sociologists of the curriculum from their concern with economic reproduction to an analysis of processes of cultural reproduction in schools. By highlighting the importance of cultural processes in explaining how reproduction occurs, therefore, Apple has drawn attention to the importance of agency and process in the reproduction debate in the USA.

Anyon, Giroux and Others

Evidence of Apple's influence on North American hidden curriculum theory is very clear from an analysis of the work of two of its widely published contributors, Jean Anyon, and Henry Giroux. Robert Everhart's work (1983) is also clearly located within the cultural reproduction mould which takes account of resistance, as is the work of McLaren (1986) in Canada.

Anyon focuses considerable attention on the latent agenda of the formal curriculum in schools. Her analysis of US history textbooks (1979) and of curriculum in use (1981) are now widely cited in the literature on the hidden curriculum. These studies are also important in themselves as they are among the first research studies undertaken in the USA to support the reproduction thesis with respect to the curriculum (the 1979 study) and to lend support to the resistance thesis (the 1981 study). Anyon's study (1984) of the interface between gender and class, and between accommodation and resistance, represents an extention of her earlier work on resistance.

Anyon's analysis of the history texts adds a new dimension to our understanding of curriculum. She presents evidence from seventeen US textbooks which highlights the class–biased nature of curriculum selections. However, some of the conclusions which she draws from her findings are not warranted by the evidence presented. In her conclusion, for example, Anyon claims that 'The school curriculum has contributed to the formation of attitudes that make it easier for powerful groups, those whose knowledge is legitimized by school studies, to manage and control society' (1979: 382).

She supplies no evidence in her own study, however, to support this contention regarding the effects of the curriculum on attitudes. Neither does she attempt to provide such evidence from other sources. Related to this issue is her claim, in the closing stages of the article, regarding the 'resistance' potential of the curriculum. 'Perhaps', she says, 'the most important conclusion to be drawn from the point of view expressed here is that the school curriculum as a major contributor to social attitudes can be used to change those attitudes' (ibid., 385). We are not informed, however, as to why or how such changes are likely to occur.

In her article, 'Social Class and School Knowledge' (1981), Anyon presents ethnographic evidence from five schools differentiated by social class. Her principal claim is that 'What counts as knowledge in the schools differs along dimensions of structure and content' (p. 31), depending on the social class composition of the school. The most substantive criticism of this work comes from New Zealand and the work of Peter Ramsay. Ramsay's study (1983) is based entirely on a sample of thirty working–class schools while Anyon's study was of two working–class, one middle-class, one 'affluent professional', and an 'executive elite' school. Ramsay's wider sample, however, led him to find much greater variability between working–class schools than Anyon suggests. Though Ramsay does not tell us how he discriminates between 'successful' and 'unsuccessful' working–class schools, it is clear from his evidence and that of Reynolds (1976), Rutter (1979), Coleman (1982) and others such as Hannan and Boyle (1987) that the ethos of a school is not simply determined by its class composition, but also by the policy of its management and the attitudes of its principal and teachers. Not only is there variability between schools with a similar class intake as Ramsay notes, but there is also likely to be great cross-cultural variability between schools which in itself impinges on the possibility of curriculum variability between schools. In a country like the Republic of Ireland, for example, there is a highly centralized system of control of school curricula (especially at second level). Consequently, teachers are not free to present children in working-class areas with the type of knowledge they deem suitable for their perceived social-class needs.

Anyon's second major explanatory concept is that of pupil resistance. Unfortunately as Hargreaves observes, her use of this concept is rather 'indiscriminate' (1982: 113). We are given no indication as to how the author discriminated between resistance and other modes of pupil response. Consequently, almost every act of non-compliance is defined as resistance. It is highly doubtful, as Hargreaves notes, that rebellious acts such as arson or vandalism are qualitatively of the same order as retreatist actions such as daydreaming or 'failing to respond to teachers' questions' (ibid.). Likewise, other social-scientific evidence suggests that passive forms of withdrawal are unlikely to provide a platform for the social transformation that Anyon seems to desire (Goffman, 1962).

While Anyon's work is open to criticism, therefore, on the grounds of its uncritical approach to the data collected, it must also be appreciated for its strengths. Anyon, unlike so many neo-Marxists, goes beyond the level of mere assertion in making claims regarding the hidden curriculum. While her work may suffer from some methodological flaws, it does indicate that there is a vast social world pertaining to the content and teaching of school curricula which is as yet unexplored in social science.

Everhart's study *Reading, Writing and Resistance* (1983) is quite different from Anyon's work. Though also concerned with how student resistance leads to the reproduction of existing social relations, it focuses on students' non-academic life rather than their curricular experiences. The latter was, of course, Anyon's concern. An ethnographic study undertaken over a two-year period in a predominantly blue-collar junior-high school (12–16-year-olds), *Reading, Writing and Resistance* is, in broad outline, a replica of Willis' work. Indeed, the author himself admits that 'it is in the tradition of the works of Cusick, Willis and Larkin' (p. 20). His main concern is to provide an understanding of the hidden curriculum from the students' perspective.

One of the most significant findings to emerge from his study pertains to the use of time in school. Like Cusick, Everhart also observed that a large proportion of student's time was spent on 'maintenance' rather than instructional activities: 'overall only slightly more than half of the time a student spends in school is occupied by instructional activities' (p. 84). The significance of this finding arises from the manner in which students utilize the time which is free of instructional demands. Everhart claims that students perceive the instructional business of school (learning reified knowledge) as an alienating activity, consequently, any time which is free of instructional demands is used to produce 'regenerative knowledge', that is knowledge 'which is imbedded in the constitutive processes that make history and, in opposition to reified knowledge, is generated by social groups as a natural process' (p. 125). Regenerative knowledge, therefore, is an attempt by pupils to reappropriate their labour from its estranged state (p. 194). Students do not actually succeed in their attempt at reappropriation, however, although their activities of 'goofing off' are a constant challenge to the organization of reified knowledge (p. 195). The reason, Everhart suggests, that their activities such as skipping classes, smoking, answering back, etc. do not seriously challenge the social relations within the school is 'because any collective self-consciousness of how reified knowledge ultimately leads to estranged labour is absent'. Their resistance is more 'a reaction' rather than a 'conscious opposition' to basic social relations (p. 229).

Everhart's study is important in so far as it replicates Willis' findings in a different cultural context. It does also, however, add another dimension to our understanding of the hidden curriculum in its own right. In his interpretation of the findings Everhart draws on the work of Habermas. He points out how the conflict between the 'formal culture' of the school and the informal culture of friendship groups, may itself represent a conflict between two knowledge systems; the school's 'reified knowledge' which is based on 'technical interest' and is directed to 'instrumentally' controlling the environment (p. 239), and the pupils' regenerative knowledge arising from practical interests and primarily serving communicative purposes within the group (p. 243). Although Everhart does not go on to say this, it is obvious from his interpretation of the evidence that 'resistance' in school is not only likely to occur among Willis' lads or among working-class youths. Conflict would seem endemic to all schools, in so far as they are cultural sites within which two very different sets of interests are being pursued within both limited time and space: the pupils' regenerative knowledge interest which emphasizes 'reciprocity and mutuality of interaction' (p. 244) (regardless of pupils' social class, gender or race, I might add), and the school's technical knowledge interest which 'pertains to the manipulation of a given environment so as to control that environment in the terms that the environment defines' (p. 239).

Unfortunately Everhart makes no reference to Willis (or any other hidden curriculum theorists) when interpreting his data so one cannot be sure as to how he views his findings in relation to other writers in the field. Beyond his short, and generally descriptive account of other works in the introduction to the book, no other substantive comments are made. Everhart gives no clear indication either as to whether he regards the reproductive effects of the pupils' regenerative culture as being class-specific, or indeed gender-specific (only the boys of Harold Spencer were studied in detail). In spite of these omissions, one does come away from reading *Reading, Writing and Resistance* with an awareness that conflict may be an endemic feature of all school life regardless of its social class composition, and that the byproduct of this conflict, cultural reproduction, may be a far more complex process than it was originally thought to be.

To complete our review of the American conflict theorists of the hidden curriculum it is necessary finally to make some comment on the work of Henry Giroux.

Henry Giroux's work (1981, 1983a, 1983b, 1983c, 1984) tends to focus on the hidden curriculum indirectly, through commentaries on resistance theory within Marxism, rather than directly through the analysis of the school system itself. Indeed his more recent work (1985, 1986) has been primarily concerned with the dynamics of critical pedagogy and making teachers into 'transformative intellectuals'. It has presented prescriptions for schools rather than an analysis of how they work.

Giroux has, however, identified a number of problems in resistance theory which do have a bearing on our understanding of the hidden curriculum. Firstly, he observes accurately that resistance theory 'is missing. . . analyses of those historically and culturally mediated factors that produce a range of oppositional behaviour, some of which constitute resistance and some of which do not' (Giroux, 1983a: 285). In other words, resistance theorists fail to inform us as to how we can discriminate between the social conditions that generate resistance and those which do not. Related to this is their failure also to provide a theory of resistance which enables one to discriminate between deviant behaviour which is 'resistant' and that which may be retreatist or rebellious. Secondly, Giroux points out that what resistance theory defines as resistance behaviour in schools may not be behaviour which is trying to challenge the 'dominant ideology of the school' at all; rather, 'it may be fueled by ideological imperatives that signify issues and concerns that have very little to do with school directly' (ibid., 286). To interpret all acts of opposition to school authority as generating within the school is, therefore, to ignore much of the evidence available from psychological theory, and to underestimate the importance of sites of cultural practice outside school for what goes on within them. Resistance has indeed been most commonly defined as a working-class male response to schooling: the way in which gender, race and ethnicity interact with social class in generating resistance is largely ignored.

Giroux's third criticism of resistance theory pertains to its focus on overt acts of rebelliousness. He notes that some students are able to penetrate 'the lies and promises of the dominant school ideology but decide not to translate this insight into extreme forms of rebelliousness' (ibid., 288) for very pragmatic reasons. Resistance theory fails to explain this type of accommo-dation within the school system. The penetrating speculative awareness of such accommodators (many of whom remain silent in order to succeed within the system) is surely potentially as politically explosive as the more overt resistances. If social transformation is an aim among resistance theorists, and it certainly seems to be at present, they must, therefore, look beyond those who overtly resist as potential agents of social change.

Finally, Giroux is critical of the resistance theorists because of their failure to explain fully, why and how pupils who 'resist' in school eventually become compliant members of society. He suggests that resistance theory will only be complete when it is integrated with a 'critical psychology' which explains 'how domination reaches into the structure of personality itself' (ibid.).

Giroux's critique of resistance theory is valuable as it highlights aspects of the theory in need of further development. He remains loyal, however, to the resistance thesis himself. It provides, he holds, 'the necessary connection between structure and human agency' (ibid., 292) which other concepts lack. Like both Anyon and Apple he is primarily concerned with education as a socially transforming process. He does not call for the abandonment of the notion of resistance. His major work *Theory and Resistance in Education* (1983c), portrays an even stronger belief than some of his earlier articles that the possibilities for emancipatory practice exist within schools. Furthermore, he has tried in recent times to identify the ways in which emancipatory education might develop (Giroux, 1985; 1986; and Arnowitz and Giroux, 1985).

At the personal level I adhere strongly to the ideals presented in Giroux's work (which he acknowledges are influenced by the work of Paulo Freire and critical theory generally) yet, as a sociologist, I have serious reservations about them. While it may be highly desirable that teachers become transformative intellectuals (Giroux and McLaren, 1986) the likelihood of this happening is greatly attenuated by the sociopolitical status of teachers. Although teachers may have experienced a certain proletarianization (Apple, 1986; Ozga and Lawn, 1981) in recent years, this process has by no means been universal across cultures, as I will show in Chapter 5. Also, even if teachers are proletarianized, this does not guarantee their allegiance to socialist or emancipatory ideals. Indeed, research on trade unions would show that at times of threat, retrenchment rather than rapprochement is the order of the day (McCarthy, 1973; Kelly, 1980). The tendency to idealize the transformative role of teachers, as Giroux, Arnowitz and others such as Carlson (1987) tend to do, is, in my view, an exercise in Hegelian idealism. Solutions to real material inequalities are presented at the level of the ideal. There is little or no reference to the real material circumstances of teachers as collective entities whose historical and cultural circumstances vary considerably. Teachers' potential as educational emancipators needs to be empirically established in different contexts; it cannot be assumed.

While Giroux and other critical theorists are justified in their claim that theory should be a transformative activity (1983c: 19) which highlights the 'centrality of human agency and struggle' (ibid., 36) in the development of history, this does not warrant a theoretical analysis which is indifferent to empirical evidence. To be transformative in education, we need to confront reality as it is (and that means fully recognizing the interests, forces and structures established to maintain the status quo) not as we would like it to be. What seems to have been happening is that, in eschewing the determinism of earlier reproduction theorists, critical theorists have emphasized the power of human agency despite empirical evidence to the contrary, at least in certain societies. Furthermore, there seems to be a belief in much of their work that the 'agent' is invariably of a radical or left-wing persuasion. This is by no means the case. The agents who confront structures are not only those who resist them but also those who wish to reinforce and strengthen existing patterns of educational consumption. There are agents of counter-resistance as well as agents of resistance.

Whether one is in accord with the 'education as social transformation' thesis or not, one must allow that Giroux is attempting to analyse its feasibility and identify some of its pitfalls. There are times indeed when Giroux (1984: 133) seems to be keenly aware that the radical potential of education is seriously circumscribed by the controlling interests within it. For my part, I tend to concur with Ramsay; if there is to be a challenge to 'the prevailing meritocratic ideology' it will 'be deliberate and intentional and not an accidental result of the hidden curriculum' (Ramsay, 1983: 313).

Neo-Marxism in Britain

The Work of Paul Willis

In our review of theories of the hidden curriculum, our focus so far has been entirely on American research. While the early proponents of the hidden curriculum thesis there were clearly structural-functionalists, the late 1970s and 1980s have witnessed the emergence of a strong conflict perspective. There is probably no more conspicuous influence on this conflict perspective than Paul Willis' work, *Learning to Labour* (1977). It is necessary, therefore, to examine his work in a little more detail. It must also be examined in its own right because of its considerable influence on the sociology of education as a whole.

The main tenets of Willis' thesis are now well-known. I will, therefore, only summarize them here. The school's role in social reproduction, Willis claims, resides not merely in some dominant and invincible institutional determinants, but also in the cultural forms produced by the 'lads' in their resistance to the authority of the school system. The pupils' resistance, although it is a form of educational and occupational self-damnation, is experienced paradoxically as true learning, affirmation, appropriation and as a form of resistance (1977: 3). It is the fact that it is experienced as such which facilitates social reproduction in schools. In other words pupils, such as the 'lads' who 'see through' or 'penetrate' the arbitrariness of the exchange relationship between teacher and pupil, and who give expression to this penetration in forms of resistance, actually experience a sense of power themselves within the school system. Their penetration enables them to differentiate between themselves, the 'ear 'ole' conformists, the teachers and girls. This differentiation is not without evaluation; drawing from the sexism, racism and distrust of mental labour found in the shop-floor culture, they can define themselves as superior according to the shop-floor norm. Within a particular frame of (male working-class) reference, therefore, the 'lads' can legitimately feel superior to the 'ear 'oles' and to girls, in school. However, in producing their culture of masculine superiority they are reproducing their own class position. In other words they bind themselves daily to a future subordinate social position by producing cultural practices of resistance in school.

It is not, therefore, according to Willis, the hidden curriculum of school structure which is most important in determining the reproduction of class relations in schools; rather, it is the hidden curriculum of pupil resistances (cultural production) which must be understood if the dynamic of social and cultural reproductionism is to be explained. That is to say, understanding the clash between the formal school culture and the informal culture of the working-class 'lads' provides the key to explaining the latter's opposition to school, and their reproduction of their own class position (ibid., 22–3).

That Willis' work has had considerable influence on both the methodology and content of contemporary sociology of education is now widely recognized (Gordon, 1984). Although there is little doubt that many were aware of the inadequacy of large-scale inequality studies to explain social reproduction in terms of school processes, it was Willis' work which metamorphized this movement and presented an alternative mode of analysis. His work heralded both a shift from quantitative towards qualitative ethnographic research methods within the sociology of education as a whole, and a shift, within the Marxist perspective, from highly deterministic accounts of social reproduction towards an appreciation of the role of cultural processes.

Willis' work has been subjected to considerable criticism. One of the most persistent criticisms pertains to the adequacy of his sample. Twelve 'lads' are not regarded by several commentators as a representative sample for examining pupil responses to schools. To criticize Willis purely on this account, however, is to apply survey research standards to an ethnographic study. Willis does not, after all, suggest that the 'lads' are representative of all pupils in school. As Gordon observes, Willis did not claim that the counter-school culture which he examined was the only form of such a culture, nor that forms of resistance in other sites are the same as those of the 'lads'. There are many cultures and many forms of resistance. What Willis offers therefore is 'a set of analytic tools and a research methodology which can be employed to seek out and understand forms of cultural resistance' (1984: 110).

Where *Learning to Labour* is open to criticism in terms of its representativeness is in Willis' failure to explain the differential response of *all* the working-class youth he actually included in his study. Few working-class pupils within a school resist in the overt ways the 'lads' did (his own evidence even suggests this), yet they too go on to become the conformists on the shop floor. In a sense they 'reproduce' their own class position without resisting the way the lads did. Willis fails to explain how this process occurs, and whether or not it is different in kind from the lads' reproduction of their own class position *via* their production of oppositional cultural practices. If Willis' aim in *Learning to Labour* was to explain processes of cultural production among pupils, as a later paper suggests (Willis, 1981), then he should have given some attention to those cultural modes of production in school which are not oppositional. As Woods notes in his work, *The Divided School* (1979: 71–2), there are many modes of pupil adaptation to be found in schools — conformity, ritualism, retreatism, colonization, intransigence and rebellion being the major ones. To focus only on resistance as a form of cultural production is to ignore much of what happens even among working-class pupils in school. Woods has suggested, for example, that 'colonization' may be the most typical mode of pupil response in a compulsory institution such as school. There is certainly plenty of empirical evidence in the social sciences which lends support to this contention. The work of Hammersley (1974), Furlong (1976), and Reynolds (1976) all cast doubts on the 'applicability of the category of "resistance" to vast and diverse areas of pupil conduct' (Hargreaves, 1982: 112). Willis, however, does not address this literature. To posit a theory of cultural production among school pupils solely on the notion of resistance, therefore, is to oversimplify the complexity of pupil response to school, even the response of working-class pupils.

In terms of its adequacy in explaining the hidden curriculum processes of schooling, Willis' work also suffers from its failure to utilize theories of socialization or learning. While mainstream sociological theories of socialization may lack explanation of 'the tension and uncertainty' involved in learning (Willis, 1977: 183), this does not mean that the influence of structural processes on learning does not need to be explained. Willis' claim that the 'macrodeterminants . . . pass through the cultural milieu to reproduce themselves' (ibid., 171) does not tell us, however, how structural definitions and understandings are actually learned so that they are resisted by some but accepted by others. Without such an explanation one cannot comprehend why it is that learning processes (admittedly involving contradiction, contestation etc.) seem to vary within the working-class group itself, i.e. between the 'lads' and the 'ear 'oles'. After all, Willis claims that the distinguishing factor between these two groups is the fact that the 'ear 'oles' have no informal culture like the lads (ibid., 23). This implies that they cannot 'produce' culture and create meaning and learning in the way the 'lads' do. The question which is left unanswered then is: how do they learn to conform, or at least not to resist? The most obvious explanation here is that learning, even of the unwritten curriculum, is not confined to participation in an informal group network. The structuralist argument that school organization itself plays a role in perpetuating a particular normative order must be taken into account in understanding this process. Willis ignores this. His focus on the informal group as the centre of meaning and locus of learning leads him, therefore, to underestimate the role played by other powerful socializing agents, the school itself with its rules, regulations, teachers etc., the media and the family.

As a theory of social reproduction, Willis' work is also open to criticism. While he adverts 'to the existence of objective structures and determinants of social reproduction, at no point does he elucidate the nature of these forces or explain their impact on the job choices of working-class students' (Burris, 1980: 525). Consequently, both the educational system itself, and the hierarchical occupational system which it services, are inadvertently absolved from direct responsibility for the reproduction of class inequality.

In spite of its shortcomings, *Learning to Labour* remains one of the more original and provocative works published in education in recent times. It has rightly redirected the attention of Marxist scholars in education to the analysis of what goes on within school itself, in their attempts to understand inequality. As such, it has added a microscopic dimension to what was traditionally a purely macroscopic perspective. As an empirical study the work provides both exciting ethnographic evidence and insightful analysis into the dynamics of counter-school cultures. It also offers an analytical and methodological framework by which others can examine sub-cultural processes.

Pierre Bourdieu

While Willis' work redirected hidden curriculum theory from deterministic to more activistic theories of reproduction, he is not alone in propagating a culturalist approach to educational reproduction. The work of Pierre Bourdieu is also clearly within this tradition. His understanding of how cultural processes influence reproduction in schools, however, is very different from that of Willis.

Bourdieu's interest in education forms part of his wider sociological interest in delineating the mechanism of symbolic domination and control by which the existing social order is maintained. The school system is, according to Bourdieu and Passeron, involved in 'pedagogic action'. As such, it is engaged in an act of 'symbolic violence' as it imposes the particular 'cultural arbitrary' of the dominating groups in society on other groups (Bourdieu and Passeron, 1977: 5). The school is, in their view, only one of a number of pedagogical bodies involved in such a process. It is, however, a powerful and influential one as it is a 'relatively autonomous' institution and thereby is able to serve 'external demands under the guise of independence and neutrality' (ibid., 178). The principal external purpose which the school serves is cultural and social reproduction (ibid., 57). Bourdieu sees the schooling system, therefore, as being directly involved in the perpetuation of class inequalities. His primary concern is to explain the objective processes by which this occurs.

To proceed with his explanation Bourdieu invokes the ideas of 'cultural capital' and 'habitus'. The pedagogic work involved in schooling is, he claims, undertaken within a particular habitus, that is, 'a system of schemes of thought, perception, appreciation and action' which reflects the material and symbolic interests of the dominant groups or classes (ibid., 40–1). Because, Bourdieu holds, different social classes vary in the nature of their primary socialization, then each class has its own characteristic habitus with individual variations. The habitus of working-class life, therefore, is quite different from that of the middle and upper classes. It does not, however, generate the kind of 'cultural capital', (i.e. 'instruments for the appropriation of symbolic wealth', Bourdieu, 1973: 73) necessary for success in schools. Schools in their turn, do not give such pupils the means of appropriating this capital either. 'By doing away with explicitly giving to everyone what it implicitly demands of everyone, the educational system demands of everyone alike that they have what it does not give' (Bourdieu and Passeron, 1977: 494). The fact that certain pupils do not have the cultural capital to succeed, and that schools do not provide it, leads to a further development within the educational process. Pupils from lower income background learn very quickly in school that their objective chances of success (being members of a particular class category) is low. Consequently, they lower their aspirations in line with their objective changes of success as members of a class category. Their subjectively expressed 'low aspirations' therefore are no more than objective chances intuitively perceived and gradually internalized (Bourdieu, 1974: 33–5). Finally, like Willis, Bourdieu argues that it is the seemingly neutral position of the school, combined with the self-elimination of large numbers of working-class children, which ultimately grants the school legitimacy.

Bourdieu's writings in the sociology of education are but part of his wider sociological interest in the means by which systems of domination persist and reproduce themselves without conscious recognition by a society's members. It follows from this that Bourdieu eschews sociological methods which focus either solely on the subjective perceptions of individuals, or on common sense classifications of social groups. These perceptions and classifications being of the very stuff of which domination is made. What Bourdieu does, therefore, is to focus on the 'unseen' structures, though he does allow a role for purposive and reasoning actors within them. His object of analysis becomes 'the production of the habitus, that system of dispositions which acts as a mediation between structures and practice' (1977: 487). His mode of analysis becomes a relational one. Analysis of

> the receivers of a pedagogic message [can only be meaningful, he claims, if it involves] the construction of the *system of relations* [my emphasis] between, on one side, the school system conceived as an institution for the reproduction of legitimate culture . . . and, on the other side, the social classes (ibid., 101).

He is, in fact, strongly critical of traditional methodologies in the sociology of education (for what he calls 'substantialist atomism' (ibid., 487) because they treat the school population, the organization of the school and its values as if they were autonomous entities whose characteristics pre-existed their interrelation. This Bourdieu holds to be untenable, as it involves the use of 'reifying abstractions' in conceptualizing and defining issues (ibid., 102).

Just as Willis has offered a set of analytical tools and a research methodology, which can be employed in understanding pupils' interpretative resistance to the structural constraints of the hidden curriculum, so Bourdieu has presented us with a new mode of analysis for understanding the hidden curriculum itself. The focus in the latter's case is neither solely on structures or on individual practice but rather on the interrelationship between the two at different points along the communicative relations ladder — the essence of pedagogic work involving communicative relations according to Bourdieu (ibid., 102).

In spite of the richness of Bourdieu's thought there are features of his work that are open to question. The complexity of his linguistic style, the ambiguity of much of his conceptual apparatus and his rather careless treatment of survey material are particular cases in point (Di Maggio, 1979: 1466–9). More substantively, Bourdieu has been criticized for his 'overly deterministic view of human agency' (Giroux, 1983a: 271). Kennett (1973) and Willis (1983) concur with Giroux in this evaluation. However, as Harker (1984) has noted, these critics have tended to examine Bourdieu's work apart from his sociological theory in general, and, in particular, have ignored some of his other studies including *Algeria 1960* (1979) and *Outline of a Theory of Practice* (1977). Consequently, they have not fully comprehended Bourdieu's dialectical concept of 'habitus'. Bourdieu sees habitus as mediating between objective structures and practice. It is something which is constantly changing owing to its dialectical character. The kernel of the problem seems to be, therefore, not that Bourdieu failed to use the concept of habitus in his educational work, as he did; rather, that his use of the concept of habitus in his educational analysis tends to underestimate the role of human agency. At no point in his major educational work, *Reproduction in Education* (1977), does he explicate clearly how the social actor acts back upon the structure even within the context of the habitus. The criticisms of educationalists such as Giroux, therefore, have some legitimacy though their evaluations may not be applicable to the whole of Bourdieu's work.

Although Bourdieu does provide us with a form of conceptual apparatus for analysing the dynamics of the hidden process of reproduction, he supplies very little empirical evidence for his assertions. For example, he alleges that the habitus of different social classes are fundamentally different yet he does not establish empirically what relationship exists between social class and early childhood experience in the first place. Likewise, he gives us very little concrete evidence on the actual nature of cultural capital or class habitus. While he asserts that the culture of the elite differs in 'style, taste, wit' and language from that of the working class, we are not informed as to how the clash of these two cultures in school actually precipitates the elimination of the working class from the educational system. Indeed, Bourdieu's claim that the pupils' subjective internalization of their objective chances (as members of particular class categories) has a major role to play in their self-elimination (1974: 39–40) is not easily reconcilable with his more persistent thesis that it is a 'lack' of cultural capital on behalf of the working class which accounts for class reproduction through education. Part of the problem may lie in what, at times, appears to be a tautological definition of cultural capital. As stated already, cultural capital is defined, at least once, by Bourdieu as those 'instruments for the appropriation of symbolic wealth' (1973: 73). Defining cultural capital as the instruments for appropriating symbolic wealth, and telling us that working-class pupils lack cultural capital and thereby fail in school, begs the question as to what the 'instruments' of symbolic wealth are in the first place.

One of the most persistent claims throughout Bourdieu's work is also that schools are 'relatively autonomous'. However, he supplies no evidence in proof of this either. His critical antipositivist method is useful, therefore, in generating hypotheses. It is not so effective in confirming them.

Another, and perhaps rather major, problem with Bourdieu's work arises from his use of cultural capital as an explanatory variable. As Halsey *et al.* (1980: 199) have noted, a small but significant proportion of working-class children have succeeded within the educational system. The cultural capital thesis does not provide explanation for this. Undoubtedly, as Harker (1984: 124) observes, Halsey *et al.* did not construct their study to investigate the cultural capital thesis. Consequently they did not have adequate information on the cultural capital of the students they studied. The generalizations which they make about the irrelevance of cultural capital 'after selection for secondary school' (Halsey *et al.*, 1980: 200) seem unwarranted therefore. This does not take away from the fact, however, that some working-class children have succeeded. Appeal to the cultural capital thesis alone will not explain their success. Bourdieu's idea that pupils subjectively internalize their objective class chances does help explain it, but neither this nor the cultural capital thesis explains why it is that certain working-class children succeed while others do not. Within-class cultural variability is left unexplored.

Not unrelated to this is the problem arising from the variability within any given culture, irrespective of its class origins. While Bourdieu alludes to this issue in his discussion of the difference between the 'content' of a culture and the 'style' or 'manner' of acquiring it (1974: 45), the discussion is within a footnote. He does not examine the implications of this distinction with respect to schooling. If it is the style or manner of acquiring culture which forms the crucial barrier to educational success, as he suggests, does this mean that the content of the curriculum itself is not a barrier? Does it mean that it is not part of cultural capital? Does it imply that the content of a curriculum can be examined apart from the mode or style of its presentation? All these questions are left unanswered, though they have serious implications for the explanation of Bourdieu's central reproduction thesis.

It is clear from the foregoing discussion, therefore, that Bourdieu's work does suffer from a number of conceptual and empirical weaknesses. These limitations, however, do not take away from either the originality of his insights or the innovativeness of his methodology. His identification of the importance of symbolic systems in both creating and reproducing the present system of class relations is of considerable significance for educationalists. It shows that a purely economically deterministic view of the process of class reproduction is inadequate. Education must be seen therefore as relatively autonomous, both as a determining and determined social agency. Methodologically his work is simultaneously a practical attempt to avoid both the extreme subjectivism of ethnomethodology, while retaining the idea of the purposeful social actor, and an attempt to avoid a purely structuralist view, while recognizing the importance of structural forces. Though the dynamism of this methodological model is lost at times in his educational analysis it does represent a unique approach within reproduction theory.

The Neo-Weberian Perspective of Randall Collins

Bourdieu's influence on reproduction theory in education has not been commensurate with the volume of his publications. Undoubtedly, as Di Maggio noted (1979), this is partly due to the difficulty of his linguistic style, both in the French original and in the English translation. One writer who has been noticeably influenced by Bourdieu's work, however, is the

American, Randall Collins. His major educational work, *The Credential Society* (1979), relies heavily on the idea that cultural capital is a prerequisite for obtaining educational credentials. In the opening pages of his work, however, Collins clearly points out that he regards Bourdieu's thesis as a necessary but not sufficient basis for explaining the role schools play in the stratification process. The 'larger mechanism explaining the macro pattern of educational stratification and its historical development' is, he claims, 'obscure in Bourdieu's model' (ibid., 10). As Collins goes on to present his own cultural explanation of reproduction, it is important to review his work here.

In the realm of conflict theory, Collins is within the neo-Weberian camp; his central thesis is based on the idea of cultural and material markets. The schools, he claims, are involved in the distribution of educational credentials; these credentials then become a form of cultural currency which can be used for negotiating acess to occupational positions. Education, therefore, is seen as 'part of a system of cultural stratification' (ibid., 192).

It produces and distributes culture; credentials are awarded to certify cultural acquisition. However, Collins argues, it is not because of the technical skills they certify that credentials are used increasingly for occupational selection. Rather, the available evidence suggests that 'the lengthy courses of study required by business and professional schools exist in good part to raise the status of the profession and to form the barrier of socialization between practitioners and laymen' (ibid., 17). Educational credentials have, therefore, a normative rather than a technical value. They certify one's possession of that type of middle- and upper-class cultural capital desired in particular by white-collar professions and occupations (ibid., 31–48). Although Collins does not discuss the issue in detail, it is clearly implied in the book that acquiring cultural capital in school is contingent on being predisposed towards it from one's primary socialization in the home. This line of argument is similar to Bourdieu's claim that schools only distribute cultural capital to those who have the means of receiving it.

Collins' primary interest, however, is not in explaining why cultural capital or educational credentials cannot or are not acquired by some pupils in school. Rather, his concern is with showing how educational credentials are utilized in the marketplace as a way of justifying privilege. He shows how certain occupations through their 'political labour' have built educational requirements into the definition of certain positions, thereby consolidating their status and ensuring the exclusion of others from the attendant privileges and powers. It is because there are a variety of occupations struggling 'to gain control over their own positional property' (ibid., 179) that Collins rejects an analysis of social conflict along Marxist lines.

Collins has little to say on the internal dynamics of the school itself. His work, therefore, does not give any fresh insight into the hidden curriculum at that level. However, in so far as he highlights the role played by professional and occupational groups in determining the usage of educational credentials, he adds an important dimension to the debate. Unlike Bourdieu, Bowles and Gintis or Willis he shows that the concept of class is highly problematic in present-day society. There are within-class as well as between-class divisions; both of these are further confounded by issues of gender, race and ethnicity. His work highlights the limitations of using a dominant–subordinate class model in educational analysis.

Overall, Collins' work is probably more useful for helping us understand the relationship between professional occupations and the educational system rather than in explaining the internal dynamics of the school system itself. In so far as the former process impinges on the latter, however, his analysis is relevant for understanding what happens in schools.

If Collins' work suffers from any weakness it must be its tendency towards unwarranted generalizations. Undoubtedly, as Collins alleges, the technocratic educational model does not represent accurately all that is learned in schools. However, this does not mean that no technical skills are learned within them as he seems to imply (Vogt, 1981: 135–51). One would require much more evidence than Collins (or indeed anyone else) has supplied to prove that schools do not teach technical skills.

Secondly, one of Collins' principal claims is that two types of labour exist, political and productive: 'The distinction separates the two major social classes: the working class engaged in productive labor, and the dominant class engaged in political labor' (Collins, 1979: 52). This is a highly debatable generalization. Many workers are not engaged in material production (e.g. service workers such as bus conductors, refuse collectors etc.) but this does not mean that they are part of the 'sinecure sector' who are largely engaged in domination. Furthermore, he would need to distinguish much more clearly between those white-collar jobs which are primarily sinecures and those which are not, and between those jobs in which there is a high level of 'political labour' and those in which there is very little. Such refinements would add great lucidity to his arguments.

Other Issues in the Reproduction Debate

Both functionalists, and a large number of conflict theorists, have ignored issues of gender and race in their analysis of the school's hidden curriculum. These two themes have also been given little attention hitherto in this discussion. Their exclusion here, however, is a conscious choice rather than an unconscious omission. It does not occur because the author regards the reproduction of gender and race relations as minor compared to those of class. Rather, it arises from the character of the analysis undertaken in these two fields. The examination of gender and race in the hidden curriculum has drawn heavily on existing reproduction and resistance theories. Consequently, at the theoretical level, it can generally be regarded as a school of thought within reproduction theory rather than a distinctive area of research outside of it. The work of Anyon (1984), McDonald (1980), McRobbie (1978), Spender and Spender (1980) and Stanworth (1981) can clearly be located within reproduction theory. Indeed a number of these authors regard class and gender, and/or class and race, as interacting forces in the reproduction process (see Anyon's, McDonald's and McRobbie's work for example). Mainstream reproduction theory has, of course, been influenced by these secondary developments in the field. Apple's more recent work (1982, 1986) is a clear attempt to explain reproduction in education in terms of class, gender and race interacting together; Willis' publication in Dale's book (1981b: 257–73) seems intent on highlighting those aspects of *Learning to Labour* which examine the relationship between patriarchy, race and labour. In view of this incorporation of gender and race issues into mainstream thought, and the paradigmatic allegiance of the many of those who write of gender and race reproduction to a neo-Marxist model, it did not seem necessary to review the work of the latter separately here. Many of the strengths and weaknesses of mainstream reproduction theorists also hold true for those analysing gender and race reproduction in schools.

In the concluding part of this chapter we will introduce our own theoretical model for the analysis of the hidden curriculum. This model will attempt to show how neither neo-Marxist or functionalist explanations of the hidden curriculum are entirely adequate in their explanation of social reproduction. We will focus especially on why the neo-Marxist model fails to explain fully why inequality persists. We will argue that it fails to explicate fully the universalistic dimensions of school life and the legitimating effects of these on the educational system. Our basic proposal is, therefore, that the hidden curriculum of schools is simultaneously universalistic and particularistic. Social inequalities are reproduced through schools because schools are universalistic in their *provision relations*, and particularistic in their *consumption relations*. Central government control of the provision of basic educational services ensures universality in certain aspects of school life. However, powerful mediating groups — on whom central government is heavily dependent for its survival — exercise considerable control over the consumption relations of education. These groups perpetuate particularistic practices as these practices help consolidate their own interests and influence.

A more detailed analysis of our theoretical approach will be presented in Chapter 5. For example, discussion on the precise role of the mediating groups is reserved mostly for this chapter. Empirical data demonstrating how the hidden curriculum of school life is simultaneously universalistic and particularistic is presented in Chapters 2, 3 and 4.

Conclusion: An Outline of the Particularistic–Universalistic Model of Reproduction

Thought on the hidden curriculum has been dominated throughout the 1970s and 1980s by the reproduction and resistance theories of the neo-Marxists. While a number of weaknesses in this model have already been identified in the foregoing discussion of individual authors, there are two interrelated issues which have not been analysed, namely, the assumption that socialization into the hidden curriculum of school life is primarily particularistic in character (i.e., that it is entirely class, race or gender specific) and the relationship between this phenomenon and the reproduction of inequality. Undoubtedly there is a growing body of research evidence to support the particularistic contention: the class and racial biases known to exist in streaming/tracking (Lunn, 1970; Shavit, 1984); the gender specific character of subject provision in many schools (Byrne, 1978; Council of Europe, 1982; Hannan *et al.*, 1983), and the class and gender biases which influence teachers' expectations and practices in classrooms (Becker, 1952; Goodacre, 1968; Rist, 1970; Davies and Meighan, 1975; Spender and Spender, 1980). That schools are particularistic therefore in the treatment of certain social groups there can be no doubt. To say this, however, leaves another related and very important question unanswered. If schools, through their hidden curriculum, are as reproductive of inequalities as neo-Marxists suggest why has their legitimacy not been seriously challenged? This becomes an even more serious question when one considers the huge volume of reports published since the 1960s highlighting schools' failure to eliminate social-class inequalities in any basic way.

Certain neo-Marxists have recognized the importance of the school's universalistic façade in determining the legitimacy of the educational system and thereby in reproducing inequality. Bowles and Gintis (1976) emphasize the significance of the school's meritocratic façade in legitimating inequalities while Bourdieu (1977) regards the school's relative autonomy as a crucial factor in creating an aura of impartiality around education and thereby in concealing its negative reproductive outcomes. While recognizing the importance of Bourdieu's and Bowles and Gintis' observations, where we dissent from their views is in their assertion that the universalism of school is merely a façade. Schools are universalistic (i.e. are equalizers) in very definite ways as the following chapters will show. The problem is that universalism is only evident in the *provision relations* of educational services not in the *consumption relations*. The reasons why this is the case are elaborated on later.

Most reproduction theorists, however, give little attention to the universalistic dimensions of schooling. They tend to regard schools as purely particularistic in class, race and/or gender terms. This, we will argue, is by no means the case. Schooling could be classified on an ideal type universalistic-particularistic continuum, some aspects of it being classified as highly particularistic, while others are principally universalistic. The plausibility of such a model becomes evident when we examine the rules and regulations governing second-level schools in more detail.

Universalism

Second-level schools in the Republic of Ireland[1] are characterized by a range of organizational features which are identical for all pupils. The first dimension of universality which one can identify is within what Cusick (1973: 214) calls the *productive sub-system* — that is, in the realm of the formal curriculum where knowledge is selected, organized, evaluated and distributed in a particular way. The manner in which knowledge is selected, and the ways in which it is organized and evaluated, are largely identical in all schools. The content of syllabi is similar as it is specified annually by a centralized government authority, the Department of Education. The practice which prevailed in Anyon's (1981) study in the USA therefore, cannot prevail in Ireland. The content of what is taught in a given subject cannot be social-class specific (cf. Department of Education, *Rules and Programme for Secondary Schools* 1984/85 for example). The universalistic character of syllabus determination is reinforced by the character of subject organization and presentation. Knowledge systems in all schools are compartmentalized, taught by subject specialists and distributed to pupils in batches. The specialists, in turn, are all required to have some third-level certification before they are legitimated as distributors. Finally, within the school's productive subsystem, the procedure for knowledge evaluation further reinforces the universalism of both knowledge selection and organization. All major examinations are public and centrally controlled by the state. The time allotted for each examination, the age and conduct of examinees and the procedures for marking are identical for all classes and gender groups.

To make the productive system effective, schools must also operate a system of *maintenance and procedural activities* (Cusick, 1973: 47–9) which create the conditions of learning. Because schools are required to transmit knowledge efficiently and effectively to large groups within a limited time, all pupils are 'processed' in 'batches' (ibid., 56) ('crowds' as Jackson calls it) and 'banking' (Freire, 1972: 45–9) characterizes pedagogic relations. In addition, it is also mandatory for schools to promote hierarchical relations between teacher and taught (which Cusick calls 'the doctrine of adolescent inferiority' and what P. Jackson terms 'unequal power relations') within the classroom; without this vertical organization of relations the passing on of knowledge to large groups could not be realized within the time specified. Batch processing, banking and hierarchical relations are all therefore universalistic features of the school's maintenance subsystem. They lead in turn to other universalistic practices, such as the routinization of everyday life, the fragmented mode of presenting knowledge (usually 40- or 45-minute periods), and a future-oriented reward system.

The third area in which one can identify universalistic qualities in school is in their *external relations*, in particular with parents. Because schools undertake the socialization of all children for a larger proportion of their waking-day, parents (of all classes and genders) are freed from the responsibility of caring for them. They can pursue work or leisure activities which would be either impractical or impossible without a custodial institution such as school. The custodial function of education therefore is a significant factor in contributing to the universality of schooling in its present form.

Particularism

Just as one can identify universalistic qualities in the school's productive system, in its maintenance activities and in its external relations, one can also identify particularistic practices in these spheres. In the production sphere, schools, through their administrators and pedagogues, act as mediators of state policy. The simple mechanistic relationships, which both functionalists such as Dreeben and neo-Marxists such as Bowles and Gintis claim exists between schools and the economic system do not obtain: school administrators, teachers, and pupils mediate the application of state educational policies to themselves. Consequently, schools cannot be regarded as solely and successfully imposing a middle-class patriarchal system of education on all pupils as many neo-Marxists suggest; neither can they be regarded as being devoid of class and gender interests in their hidden curriculum as the functionalists suppose. Certain aspects of school organization and practice are primarily universalistic while others take particularistic forms. The mediators of educational services (i.e. those who manage and administer them) play a key role in determining the particularistic–universalistic balance in a given area.

Returning to the question of knowledge transmission, one can identify clear particularistic practices in the manner in which knowledge is distributed. Both within-school and between-school streaming are the most obvious examples of this. Firstly, streaming and banding are common features of Irish second-level schools (Hannan *et al.*, 1983; Lynch, 1988). This results in variability in the type of knowledge distributed to upper and lower streams and/or bands (the basic higher and ordinary syllabus divisions are the most obvious examples of this). Because working-class pupils are disproportionately over-represented in the lower streams (Hannan and Boyle, 1987), one can clearly see that schools are class particularistic in their ability-grouping. In an educational system such as Ireland's where between-school streaming (between public schools which cannot select and private schools which can) exists as well, one can once again see particularism in evidence. Working-class pupils are disproportionately over-represented in the non-selective schools (Breen, 1984). For a variety of reasons the non-selective schools (in particular the vocational schools)[2] are less likely to offer both types and grades of subjects which are necessary for entering higher education (Hannan *et al.*, 1983). This reproduces existing social class divisions.

It is not only the system of streaming/tracking which determines the particularistic character of knowledge distribution but also the timetabling practices schools adopt. As Hannan *et al.* (ibid.) and the DES (1975) have shown, the range of subjects made available and the level at which these are then offered, is frequently dictated by gender stereotypes rather than by any theory of education. Reinforcing this process are the attitudes and dispositions of those who have a major say in translating policy into practice, the teachers. As already pointed out above, teacher attitudes and their expectations of pupils are clearly influenced by the latter's social class and gender. (The pupils' so-called 'ability' also influences teachers' expectations and attitudes (Moore, 1984), an issue which is ignored entirely by neo-Marxists, and almost entirely by functionalists). This is especially noticeable in the realm of career guidance, where, as Willis (1977) observed, the socialization models offered by teachers to pupils are those which they deem congruent with their anticipated sex roles and class position. The materials available to career guidance teachers reinforce this process in turn.

Finally, with regard to teachers, it is clear that the character of their rewards system and the means by which status is attained among peers, each encourages them to be particularistic in their classroom practice. Because of the career structure of their occupation, the only variable rewards open to teachers are the psychic ones (Lortie, 1975). Consequently, teachers are likely to concentrate efforts on those pupils from whom psychic rewards are most forthcoming. While the feeling of having 'got through' to pupils is likely to be experienced with all pupils at different times, the work of Sharp and Green (1975) and Keddie (1971) would suggest that it is work with pupils who are most receptive to learning, and who share the teacher's values and attitudes, which is most likely to increase the flow of psychic rewards to the teacher at any given time. Furthermore, it is likely that the teacher's peers and principal would reinforce this. Teachers (especially in second level) must be seen to get results if they are to have professional credibility — the most visible results are the grade levels attained in public examinations. Good grades (and the social recognition which accrues to the teacher from them) are most forthcoming from the 'good pupils' or the upper streams who are more often middle-class than working-class.

In their mediation of state policies, therefore, both teachers and school administrators engage in particularistic practices. In Ireland, the universalistic character of knowledge selection, organization and evaluation is counterbalanced by the particularism of knowledge distribution and consumption.

A similar pattern emerges when one examines the school's external relations system. Although all schools engage in custodial functions for parents, certain schools have discretionary powers in the exercise of their custodial duties. A majority of second-level schools in the Republic of Ireland are secondary. All secondary schools are private institutions and are free therefore to use selection procedures.[3] Consequently, the climate for learning will vary considerably between schools (McDill and Rigsby, 1973; Rutter *et al.*, 1979; and Coleman *et al.*, 1982). The right to be selective or not also affects what one might call the ancillary learning process: that is to say, it affects the extracurricular activities offered; friendship choices; and the linguistic patterns, mannerisms, tastes, styles of dress, and political knowledge of all kinds to which one is exposed in a school. In Ireland therefore, while universalism characterizes the centrally controlled formal knowledge system to a large degree, as we will show in the following chapter, the ancillary and informal knowledge systems are highly particularistic in character.

Just as one can identify particularistic dimensions to the school's productive and external systems, one can identify similar patterns in its maintenance and procedural practices. While the 'doctrine of adolescent inferiority' dictates the pattern of teacher–pupil relations in general this doctrine does not apply equally to all pupils. As pupils grow older they become less 'inferior' (Cusick, 1973: 207). Related to this is the issue of individual autonomy. The level of autonomy granted to pupils is influenced by one's position within a streamed school which, in turn, is contingent on one's so-called ability (Hargreaves, 1967). Likewise, class and gender intervene at times in determining pupil autonomy. Dress, for example, is traditionally more tightly circumscribed in girls' schools than in boys'; expression of individual interest is more likely to be facilitated in schools that can afford to offer a wide range of extracurricular interests than in those which cannot.

Concluding Remarks

It is clear from the foregoing discussion, therefore, that in their analysis of the hidden curriculum both functionalists and neo-Marxists are open to criticism; the former for ignoring the particularistic, the latter for underplaying the universalistic aspects of the hidden curriculum. Neo-Marxists' general indifference to the universalistic practices of schooling helps explain the inadequacy of their theory in accounting for the school's role in reproducing inequality. If schools were purely particularistic in their hidden curriculum practices they would face constant crises of legitimation. This is clearly not the case for the majority of schools. Schools tend to be universalistic in their more visible provision aspects — syllabi, evaluation systems, teacher training, hours and days of schooling, buildings etc. — consequently they appear the same, and are the same, in certain basic ways. The outer coating of universalistic *provision* conceals the not-so-visible inner core of particularistic *consumption*. The visibility of the former and the lack of immediate visibility of the latter is therefore one factor facilitating the reproduction of inequality.

Undoubtedly consumption patterns are not entirely concealed from public view. Parents who have had lengthy exposure to second- and/or third-level education know full well the ramifications of the streaming system, for example. Likewise, teachers and educational administrators are wise to the effects of variables such as teacher expectations and competence, or the importance of subject choice at an early age. However, there is no reason for the wise to inform the innocent. In the case of parents, the advantages they can attain for their children vis-à-vis others is itself conditional on 'knowing the system' better than others and maximizing advantages accordingly. This is not to suggest that some parents deliberately exclude information from others in a conspirational manner. We are suggesting, rather, that the wise, in the pursuit of self-interest, (which is defined as natural in our society) try to maximize the benefits of their own knowledge. They are aware of the need to outperform others in a competitive situation. Gaining control in the credential market is no different, therefore, to gaining control in other markets in a capitalist world.

Teachers and educational administrators also form part of the wise. In their capacity as parents they are no different to others who are informed. As professionals they have little incentive either to make innocent parents wise. To inform parents of the effects of teacher expectations would be to encourage teacher and school accountability which has long been resisted by teachers themselves. It would increase pressure on teachers which is anathema to their desire for autonomy (Lortie, 1969). Because problems in the consumption of educational services are primarily visible to the educationally wise, there is less political pressure on the central state system to initiate change.

The lack of challenge to the reproduction of inequality through the hidden curriculum, therefore, is in part the outcome of two forces interacting together: the fact that schools have universalistic (provision) qualities which are both highly visible and widely publicized to all sectors of society; and the fact that the schools' particularistic (consumption) processes are primarily visible to those who both understand them and are capable of managing them in their own interests.

Notes

1 All references to Ireland in this book refer to the Republic of Ireland only unless otherwise stated.
2 There are four separate types of second-level schools in the Republic of Ireland — secondary schools, vocational schools and community and comprehensive schools. Secondary schools are privately owned and managed (generally by Catholic religious orders or diocesan clergy) but almost entirely state financed for both their current and capital expenditures. Almost all of them have their origins in the nineteenth century or earlier. Most secondary schools do not charge fees, however, so within the secondary sector one must bear in mind that fee-paying secondary schools are quite distinct from non-fee-paying secondary schools. The latter are known in Ireland as 'free scheme' schools. Secondary schools have traditionally been the most academic schools, although there is considerable variability among them. The student composition of secondary schools tends to be the most middle-class of all school types (Breen, 1984).

   Vocational schools were introduced in 1930. They are administratively controlled by county-based vocational educational committees (VECs). These schools are directly controlled, therefore, by local elected representatives. They are funded by central government via the local VEC. Although vocational schools did not originally offer a broad-ranging academic curriculum this changed in the early 1970s and now all four types of schools can offer a full range of subjects. Vocational schools still tend to offer more technical subjects on their curriculum, however, than secondary schools. Vocational schools have a larger proportion of working-class pupils than either secondary or community/comprehensive schools.

   Comprehensive schools were initiated in the late 1960s under the direct control of the state Department of Education. They offer a wide-ranging technical and academic curriculum. For a variety of political reasons, the comprehensive school idea was superseded by the community-school concept in the early 1970s. Community schools are jointly owned and controlled by the local VEC, religious orders and the state Department of Education. Community and comprehensive schools offer a full range of academic and technical subjects. Like the vocational, comprehensive and most secondary schools, they are non-fee-paying. The distribution of students between the various types of schools is as follows: secondary schools, 67.5%; vocational schools, 22.2%; community and comprehensive schools, 10.3% (Dept. of Education, *Statistical Report*, 1982/83: 9. 10).

3 All secondary schools being legally defined as private institutions can select pupils at entry. Neither vocational, community or comprehensive schools have this freedom.

Chapter 2

Knowledge Dissemination in Second-Level Schools: The Case for Universalism

Before we present our empirical evidence substantiating our theoretical claims, it is necessary to present a brief outline of how the research was undertaken.

Research Methodology

At the time this study was undertaken there were 816 second-level schools in the 26 counties of the Republic of Ireland. As a pilot study of 8 schools was undertaken in one county, this county (N = 27 schools) was subsequently excluded from the main study. The final proportional stratified random sample of 90 schools therefore was drawn from a population of 789 schools. The response rate was 96 per cent (N = 86) and this represented 11 per cent of the population. The sample was stratified on the basis of school size, gender composition, and administrative type.

A variety of research techniques were employed in the collection of data about the hidden curriculum of the schools, including the analyses of school timetables, prospectuses, annual reports, magazines and any other documents available on the schools. The main data base, however, was the detailed interviews with school principals based on a questionnaire with a large proportion of open-ended questions. In Ireland, principals are key informants about schools as they are responsible for their day-to-day management and administration, hence the reason for their selection.

As the interviews took place in schools and lasted on average for one and a half hours each, we got an opportunity in many cases to meet other staff members and even pupils in some cases. Through the visits to the schools we got an insight into the school ethos which would not have been possible with postal questionnaires.

Finally, while undertaking the research the author taught two classes weekly in a second-level school for two consecutive years. This experience proved invaluable when examining and interpreting the evidence. It gave the author an insider's view on the school world.

While there is no doubt that a study such as this would benefit greatly from interviews with pupils and teachers as well as more direct observational work, such was not possible given the limited resources and finance available. The material collected however, was extremely detailed and accurate. The questionnaire comprised almost 250 questions which yielded 924 variables of information. While it may not complete the picture on the hidden curriculum we hope it goes some way towards it.

In the preceding chapter we identified three major areas in the school's organizational life where the universalism–particularism continuum could be examined: the school's productive sub-system, its maintenance and procedural system and its external relations systems. In this chapter we will focus our attention on how the first two of these are increasingly concerned with the development of a technically competent individual. Our attention will focus on how the dissemination of technical knowledge (and by technical we mean scientific, technological and commercial) is an increasingly important preoccupation in all types of schools. We will begin our analysis by showing how external organizations (as part of the school's external relations system) actually operate in controlling the school's productive and maintenance systems.

Universalism as a Product of State Control and Third-Level Entry Requirements

The Productive Sub-system

The production sub-system of the school refers to the process of selecting, organizing, evaluating and distributing the formal knowledge systems of the curriculum. The type of knowledge selected, and the way it is organized and evaluated, gives us a clear indication as to the concept of the ideal person informing educational practice. In other words, those aspects of a society's cultural tradition which it elects for mandatory transmission in schools inform us as to the priorities accorded to particular cultural practices within it: they inform us as to its underlying value-orientations.

The content of the formal knowledge systems which is transmitted in Irish second-level schools is tightly controlled by a central organization, the state Department of Education: the content of what is taught, therefore, is highly universalistic in character. To understand it, it is necessary, however, to examine the nature of the control system in more detail. The state regulations governing curriculum provision are specified in detail in *Rules and Programme for Secondary Schools* published annually, and in *Rules and Programmes for the Day Vocational Certificate Examinations* (Document/ Memorandum V50). As yet no published rules exist for community schools, though they are being developed by the Department of Education. The former document outlines the programme and procedures pertaining to the two major public examinations in the state, the Leaving Certificate Examination and the Intermediate Certificate Examination;[1] the latter provides similar information on the Group Certificate course and examination. These official rules and regulations would be of little significance if they were not adopted in practice. As has been noted elsewhere (Coolahan, 1981: 199; Raven, 1975) however, such is not the case in Ireland. Owing to the widespread use of public examination certificates (especially and increasingly the Leaving Certificate) by employers, and their universal use by third-level educational institutions in selecting intake, second-level teachers must adhere closely to the prescribed courses. Indeed, the structural constraints imposed by departmental regulation, and underwritten by the processes of social selection and allocation, are numerous.

All pupils in the junior cycle of second-level schools undertaking the Intermediate Certificate Examination are required to study Irish, English, mathematics, and civics (not for examination).[2] Students in *secondary* schools[3] are required to study history and geography as well, and at least two other subjects from the list of twenty recognized examination subjects.[4] Furthermore, to be recognized as a secondary school by the Minister of Education, the school must also offer science; or a language other than Irish or English; or commerce; or a subject from the business studies group. Students in vocational, community or comprehensive schools may complement their compulsory study of Irish, English, mathematics and civics in the junior cycle, with either mechanical drawing, art, home economics or commerce, instead of history and geography. Like secondary school students, they must also study at least two other recognized subjects if they are to be eligible to sit the Intermediate Certificate (ICE) examination (Department of Education, 1984/85: 11–13; Department of Education, Memo V50). Because there is no definite limit to the number of subjects pupils may take for the ICE and because pupils take eight subjects on average (Hannan *et al.*, 1983: 92) it is clear that there is a considerable choice open to students — only four subjects being compulsory. However, as Hannan *et al.* have shown, and as we will see later in this chapter, pupils' real choice is, on average, much more limited than it appears. The tradition of the school; its location geographically and vis-à-vis others; the availability of staff; the capital costs involved in a subject; the preferences and prejudices of principals; and perhaps, most of all, the market viability (both perceived and real) of a given subject, all operate in limiting choices.

With thirty subjects[5] recognized for the Leaving Certificate Examination (LCE), and only Irish being compulsory, a wide range of options would appear to exist, thus permitting highly particularistic practices in the diffusion of knowledge in the senior cycle. However, while schools vary considerably in the type of science, applied science or business studies subjects they offer, external structural constraints (principally in the form of third-level requirements and points awarded) force schools to offer a fairly similar range of subject types. The reality of these constraints becomes evident when one examines matriculation requirements.

The four colleges of the National University of Ireland (NUI) require all students to have Irish, English and another language. In addition, students in certain faculties are required to have mathematics and a science subject (Coolahan, 1981: 212). Students who wish to keep their future occupational options open therefore, in terms of university entrance, must do the five subjects mentioned above. The impact of structural constraint on pupil choices at second level becomes increasingly evident when one examines the higher education system in detail. The character of the national certificates, diplomas and degrees currently approved by the National Council of Education Awards (NCEA) (the validating body for the non-university higher education colleges) also shows how this quickly expanding section of higher education imposes further constraints on second-level schools. The university and colleges of education requirements for English, Irish, mathematics and/or a foreign language are complemented by the technological sector's requirements for science, applied science or business type subjects as well as mathematics. Of the 247 national certificate, national and graduate diploma and degree courses offered, 60.7 per cent are in science or technology (mostly engineering) and 21.2 per cent are in business studies (NCEA, 1983: 104–12). Given the fact that half the entrance places in higher education are in the technological sector *per se* (Clancy, 1982: 10, 11) pupils must take Irish, English, mathematics, a foreign language, a science or applied-science subject or a business-type subject if they are to have any real occupational choices after school. As the university points system only relates to six subjects, and as it is 'strongly recommended' that students do not take more than seven (Department of Education, 1984/1985: 27), one can see that choice is much more limited than it might first appear.

In summary, therefore, it is clear that two major structural forces operate in maintaining universalistic practices in the *selection* and *diffusion* of formal *knowledge* systems in second-level schools: Department of Education regulations and the requirements of third-level educational institutions. Analysis of Departmental regulations governing the presentation and evaluation of curriculum knowledge in schools adds further weight to the universalistic argument.

Firstly the Department of Education has very clear specifications as to the type of people who can legitimately present curricular knowledge: Memorandum No. Reg. 002 outlines in detail the credentials required for secondary school teachers, while Memorandum V7 provides similar type information for vocational schools. Although slightly different in the past the conditions of entry to teaching in secondary, community and vocational schools have become increasingly standardized in recent years. All intended teachers must now pursue a basic third-level course in teaching subject(s) of their choice and a course in education. In presenting their certified knowledge the teachers are not, however, free agents: the content of each syllabus is clearly delineated in the Department of Education's regulations. It permits only limited choices in the themes covered and in the materials used. When choice does exist it is between similar type knowledge systems. For example, in Intermediate Certificate English (Higher Course, Literature Section) all the prose, poetry and short stories are determined by the Department; the only choice is between one of two novels, *Men Withering* and *Huckleberry Finn* and one of two plays, *King Richard II* and the *Merchant of Venice* (Dept of Education, 1984/85). The syllabi in Intermediate Certificate Irish, history and geography offer similar limited choices, though a large number of intermediate courses seem to offer no choice; science, mathematics, mechanical drawing, commerce, Latin, home economics, are all cases in point (ibid., 48–144). The lack of choice, or the imposition of severe restrictions on choice of theme also exist in the Leaving Certificate courses (ibid., 150–353). Compounding the lack of choice is the system of differentially distributing marks (awards) to various sections of the course, thereby rein-forcing the importance of particular sets of knowledge within a given subject.

To understand the character of the knowledge systems credentialized in schools, one must analyse the procedures for selecting them. Those who select the knowledge (syllabi) for the school curricula obviously determine the character of what is transmitted to a large degree. John Coolahan provides a succinct account of the process up to the formation of the new National Council for Curriculum and Assessment in 1987[6]. There is, as yet, no indication that the character of the personnel involved in syllabus selection hitherto will change, or that the role of the Minister or universities will be radically different. Hence, past procedures may still have relevance:

> The syllabuses for the various examination subjects are devised by syllabus committees. The syllabus committees are chaired by a departmental inspector and are composed as follows: one represen-tative of each of the two teacher unions (ASTI and TUI), two

representatives of the managers of schools, one representative of the chief executive officers of the vocational educational committees. At Leaving Certificate level one representative from each university (NUI and TCD) sits on the committees... (Coolahan, 1981: 208).

Two factors can be noted here: (a) the character of the personnel on the syllabus committees, and (b) the power of the Minister and universities. With regard to the former it is clear that the key post of chairperson is held by a staff member from the Department of Education. Secondly, all representatives are persons with third-level education, and finally, the committee (in the case of the Leaving Certificate) has a significant lobby from the university sector. In composition, therefore, syllabus committees (especially the more important Leaving Certificate one) are composed of people who have been highly successful within the educational system themselves. They are not likely to challenge, nor indeed have they done so in practice, the strongly academic orientation which has dominated the second-level syllabi since their inception. With the exception of four subjects in both senior and junior cycles (home economics, woodwork, metalwork and mechanical drawing in junior; and home economics (general) engineering, construction studies and technical drawing in senior) courses in the 20 junior and 30 senior programmes are almost entirely designed to test intellectual skills.

Because syllabus committees are ultimately subject to the Minister *de jure* and to the universities *de facto* they are not free agents anyhow. The structural forces will influence the diffusion of knowledge in school and also determine its selection at the pre-school stage. The bias of the universities toward intellectual knowledge is inevitably reflected, therefore, in the syllabi and school curricula.

Through the analysis of the operational procedures of the syllabus committees one sees, therefore, how external bodies influence the content of what is taught. The influence of external bodies occurs both at input and output level. In terms of specifying who can be taught what, when, where and how (input–level–influence), control is exercised by the Department of Education; with regard to determining what constitutes a valid credential for the purposes of social allocation and selection (output–level–influence), control is exercised by the Department of Education, third-level institutions, and indeed increasingly, employers.

The control of syllabus *content* is but one area of control within the productive sub-system; curriculum provision is another. In this regard the expanding technological sector exercises considerable indirect influence. Approximately 70 per cent of new entrants to higher education are in what might broadly be called the commercial–technological sector (Clancy, 1988: 15), consequently student uptake of these subjects has increased dramatically in recent years. This expansion of interest in the scientific, commercial and technological fields has been offset by a decline in the uptake of traditionally popular humanities subjects, such as art, history and geography (Lynch, 1982). Thus, the intellectual orientation of education is increasingly occurring in the technological and commercial spheres. As it has been central government policy which led to the expansion of the technological sector in the first place (Wickham, 1981: 321–34), the influence of the latter on second level is itself a product of government policy also.

The mode of *evaluating* curriculum knowledge also witnesses strongly to the importance of central government control. Assessment in public examinations is almost entirely by means of written assessment in terminal examinations. The time, materials used, location and eligibility of students to participate in these examinations are all specified by the Department of Education. Written, as opposed to oral, manual or other, abilities are emphasized. The ability to perform alone and under time-pressures is also an unwritten determinant of success.

We can see therefore, through the analysis of the school's productive sub-system, how schools are structurally controlled (directly by government regulation and indirectly by third-level entry requirements) and, thereby, how particular cultural practices are both disseminated and legitimated through the educational system. We shall now proceed to overview the structural constraints in the maintenance and procedural, and external relations sub-systems of the schools to see how they reinforce the practices in the productive sub-systems. Some of these have been identified already above; therefore discussion here will be brief.

The Procedural and Maintenance Sub-System

The Department of Education lays down a number of regulations governing teacher-pupil ratios which ensure the perpetuation of batch-processing at second level.[7] Batch-processing, in turn, necessitates hierarchical control by teachers. As Jackson observed, the teacher is the pupil's first boss; he/she controls his/her attention while in school. In this situation pupils experience subjection to authority; they learn to pursue tasks which are dictated to them by persons in authority regardless of their personal interest.

It is not only the control exercised by teachers that requires pupils to pursue topics which, at times or always, are of little interest to them. This is necessitated also by the process of credentialization for the purposes of social allocation and selection. As pointed out in the previous section, both government regulation and occupational selection procedures (mediated in particular through third-level institutions) determine to a large degree the

Knowledge Dissemination in Second-Level Schools

type of interests (subjects) pupils may pursue in school. Thus, courses are pursued very often for the credentials they offer (Raven, 1975; McDonnell, 1988) and a banking mentality is facilitated among pupils. The banking mentality is also facilitated by the mode of organizing curriculum knowledge (the collection code (Bernstein, 1975)), and by the principal modes of assessing it, terminal examinations. Finally, one can see how regulations pertaining to the use of time also encourage such an orientation to learning. The length of the school day and year are both clearly specified for schools. Consequently, time has to be rationed between subjects, and within subjects between various aspects of the syllabus. There is little scope for the pursuit of voluntaristic interests which are not credited in public examinations.

The maintenance and procedural system of schools can be seen to operate in schools, therefore, for two interrelated purposes: the transmission of selected knowledge systems and the related attainment of credentials in public examinations on the one hand; and the maintenance of social order in the school on the other. Without a system of batch-processing, commodification of knowledge, hierarchical relations and time rationing, the school's productive sub-system could not function. Cumulatively these processes foster the development of selective cultural attributes at the expense of others. Given the universality of the practices outlined, these attributes are not exclusively transmitted to any particular social group; this is not to say, of course, that the form which they take will not vary with the particularistic feature of certain groups.

The external control systems of the school's productive sub-system, *viz.* the Department of Education, the employer sector and the third-level education sector (especially and increasingly its technological wing), currently ensure that intellectual learning is the primary focus of the second-level system. In particular they foster intellectual learning in the technological, commercial and scientific spheres. The procedural and maintenance systems necessary to realize these ideals in schools also foster particular cultural attributes. The banking approach to learning, the commodification of both subject content and time itself, and the rewarding of the entire process with marketable credentials, are all a highly individualistic affair. It is the individual who must accumulate the knowledge, ration time between themes and subjects and between the acquisition process of school and other commitments.

Finally, it is the individual who is credentialized. The entire process rewards egocentricism highly and sanctions altruism severely. It imposes penalties on co-operative effort at times of evaluation. One is likely to suffer a grade loss should time be devoted to activities or relationships which are not open to credentialization. Indeed the logical outcome of assisting others, legitimately in preparation for evaluations, is self-loss. Time devoted to others

43

is at the expense of one's own credential acquisition. Furthermore, assisting others increases their chances of success and thereby reduces one's own. In a competitive situation the gain of one can only be at the loss of another. Schools do not, of course, prescribe these ideals; they are however, the logical outcome of their major procedural and maintenance systems.

The procedural and maintenance structures of school life, therefore, foster a set of relations in which one works for extrinsic gain rather than for intrinsic value or interest in the task itself: work relations in school have all the attributes of alienated labour (Marx, 1975: 322–4). Thus, while the school rewards the individualistic principle of (egocentric) self-development, especially in terms of intellectual development in the technical sphere, through its hierarchical procedures it violates the principle of autonomy in some very fundamental ways. The pursuit of the former aspect of individualism seems at variance with the latter (for a discussion of the various aspects of individualism, cf. Lukes, 1973).

Having shown how external agencies exercise control over schools, and thereby ensure a certain universalism in educational provision, our next task is to present statistical data highlighting the dynamics of universalism within the school's productive sub-system. Initially, we will show how universalism is evident in the forms of knowledge provided in different types of second-level schools. Then we shall examine the changes that have occurred in recent years in curriculum provision. Here we will be focusing on the universal shift towards technical–intellectual knowledge in all types of schools. Finally, we shall examine the time-allocation practices within schools. We will show here how certain forms of technical knowledge are given priority in terms of time vis-à-vis other formal curriculum subjects. It will also be shown how the non-examination subjects occupy a marginal status on the timetable.

Empirical Evidence of Universalism in the Content and Organization of the Formal Curriculum

The Junior Cycle

Studies, such as those of Hannan *et al.* (1983) are important in so far as they highlight the particularistic character of subject provision within and between schools. However, as the authors themselves observe: 'What is perhaps most striking about the Intermediate Certificate curricula of schools. . .is the high similarity between them' (ibid., p. 157). There is, in other words, a universalistic quality to subject provision. When we analyse the pattern of subject provision at the Intermediate level in this study, this becomes very evident. As can be seen from Table 1 there is a core group of six subject

Table 1. *Proportion of schools offering the various Intermediate Certificate courses on the timetable*

Subject	Provided on timetable	
	N	%
Irish (Higher)	83	(96.5)
Irish (Lower)	83	(96.5)
English (Higher)	84	(97.7)
English (Lower)	84	(97.7)
Mathematics (Higher)	79	(91.9)
Mathematics (Lower)	86	(100.0)
History and Geography	84	(97.7)
French	84	(97.7)
Commerce	76	(88.4)
Science (A)	75	(87.2)
Science (E)	26	(30.2)
Home economics	63	(73.3)
Art	63	(73.3)
Mechanical drawing	54	(62.8)
Woodwork	54	(62.8)
Music (A)	39	(45.3)
Music (B)	22	(25.6)
Metalwork	37	(43.0)
German	24	(27.9)
Latin	12	(14.0)
Spanish	10	(11.6)
Italian	3	(3.5)
Greek	1	(1.2)
Hebrew	0	(0.0)
Classical studies	0	(0.0)

areas (eight subjects according to Departmental classification) — Irish, English, mathematics, history, geography and French — which are available in almost every school in the country. Commerce and science (A) are almost on a par with these, being available in almost 90 per cent of schools. At the other extreme one finds another group of six subjects which are characterized by their almost universal absence from the timetables of schools: Latin, Spanish, Italian, Greek, Hebrew and classical studies are not provided in 85 + per cent of schools. While there are clear differences in the provision of the nine remaining subjects, two are, in fact, available in almost three-quarters of the schools, namely, art and home economics. Therefore, although considerable variability exists in subject provision in the junior cycle, one must bear in mind that it occurs in a minority of junior cycle subjects. It occurs mostly in woodwork, metalwork, mechanical drawing, music, science and German.

Even when one controls separately for gender, size, location and administrative type (i.e. whether secondary, vocational or community/comprehensive) the patterns identified above persist. The popular core of Irish, English, French, mathematics, history and geography are available in over 90 per cent of schools irrespective of their size, gender composition, location or administrative character (Tables A10–A13).[8] The only exceptions to this are higher- and lower-level courses: higher-level Irish being provided in slightly under 90 per cent of vocational schools and higher mathematics being provided in 84 per cent, 74 per cent and 83 per cent of small schools, vocational schools and rural schools respectively. No great variability is found either at the other end of the continuum, that is in the provision of the least popular subjects. The size, location, administrative character or gender composition of the school have little bearing on the provision of the marginal subjects identified already; Spanish, Italian, Greek, Hebrew or classical studies are not present in approximately 80 per cent of all school types. Latin is somewhat of an exception in that the size of the school and its gender composition both have a statistically significant ($P < 0.01$ and $P < 0.05$, respectively) impact on its provision (large male schools are most likely to offer it).

As pointed out above, commerce and science (A) are both subjects which tend towards the popular end of the provision continuum. When we control separately for gender, size, administrative type and location (the 4 major independent variables) it is clear that there is variability between small and large schools and between vocational and secondary schools in particular (Tables A11, A12). However, even allowing for this, it must be borne in mind that both subjects are available in over 60 per cent of all types of schools. Art occupies a similar type position being available in over 50 per cent of each type; home economics is also available in well over 50 per cent of all schools with the exception of all-male schools from which it was totally absent (at least among the schools in this sample).

In summary, therefore, one can identify definite universalistic trends in the distribution of different types of knowledge within the junior phase of second-level education. Firstly, the knowledge systems themselves could be classified broadly into six classes as outlined in Table 2. When we review our data on provision in the light of these classifications we can see that all *classes* of knowledge are widely distributed throughout the system with the exception of the practical/technical types. Of the six subject-areas in which there is highest variability three are of a practical/technical kind (woodwork, metalwork and mechanical drawing). The remaining three represent the arts/humanities group (music), the science group (science) and the modern languages group (German). However, while the latter three areas are already well represented within the system by other subjects of the same class, the same does not hold true for the practical/technical subjects. The only subject representing this group is home economics, the provision of which is highly contingent on the gender composition of the school.

Table 2.   Six classes of knowledge in the junior cycle

Class	No. of subjects	Title	Names of subjects
I	2	Native languages	Irish and English
II	7	Modern and ancient languages	French, German, Spanish, Italian, Greek, Hebrew, Latin
III	4	Arts and humanities	History and geography, art, music, classical studies
IV	4	Practical/technological subjects	Woodwork, metalwork, home economics, technical drawing
V	1	Business studies	Commerce
VI	2	Sciences	Science, maths
	20		

What is being suggested therefore is that the school's productive sub-system, in the junior cycle, displays highly universalistic features in its provision. With the exception of one area of knowledge — the practical/technical — the type of knowledge provided in schools is very similar in most: approximately 80 per cent or more of all schools, irrespective of their size, location, gender or administrative character, offer subjects in five of the six knowledge areas outlined above. The lack of universality in the practical/technical sphere is explicable in terms of the low status of the knowledge system itself within the educational sphere, and, indeed ultimately, in terms of the relatively low status of incomes accorded to the labour associated with it outside schools. The low status of this knowledge area–as reflected in its irrelevance for attaining higher educational credentials in particular — eliminates any legitimation problems which might arise due to its absence from a large number of schools. As it is largely irrelevant for the attainment of high status, schools are not delegitimized or discredited by its absence.

The Senior Cycle

When one examines the pattern of knowledge distribution at Leaving Certificate level, universalistic patterns are also evident (Table 3). They are not, however, quite as consistent as those in the junior cycle, reflecting the greater range of choice in this sector. As in the junior cycle though, there is a core group of six subjects which are found in approximately 90 per cent

Table 3. Proportion of schools offering the various Leaving Certificate courses

Subject	Provided on timetable N	%	Subject	Provided on timetable N	%
Irish	84	(97.7)	Construction		
English	84	(97.7)	studies	30	(34.9)
Mathematics	84	(97.7)	Music	28	(32.6)
French	80	(93.0)	German	26	(30.2)
Biology	77	(89.5)	Physics and		
Geography	77	(89.5)	chemistry	16	(18.6)
History	74	(86.0)	Applied		
Business			mathematics	13	(15.1)
organisation	62	(72.1)	Agricultural		
Accounting	59	(68.6)	science	12	(14.0)
Art	55	(64.0)	Spanish	12	(14.0)
Chemistry	54	(62.8)	Latin	10	(11.6)
Home economics			Economic history	7	(8.1)
(scientific and			Italian	4	(4.7)
social)	51	(59.3)	Mechanics	1	(1.2)*
Technical drawing	50	(58.1)	Greek	1	(1.2)
Physics	49	(57.0)	Agricultural		
Economics	39	(45.3)	economics	0	(0.0)
Engineering	31	(36.0)	Hebrew	0	(0.0)
Home economics					
(general)	31	(36.0)			
N = 86**					

*Mechanics is no longer a senior cycle subject.
**Two schools had no senior cycle but % are calculated on the total N = 86.

of all schools—namely Irish, English, mathematics, French, biology and geography. We can see, therefore, that four of the major knowledge classes are represented in the vast majority of schools; native languages, modern languages, sciences and humanities. The practical/technological subjects are again absent from the most popular core, as indeed are the business studies group. However, while there is great variability in the provision of all practical/technological subjects—for example, 80 per cent, 100 per cent and 80 per cent of vocational schools offer engineering, technical drawing and construction studies respectively, compared with 13 per cent, 37 per cent and 11.1 per cent of secondary schools (Table A15); 95 per cent of girls' schools offer home economics (scientific and social), while no boys' schools do (Table A14)—variability in at least two of the most popular business studies subjects is not nearly so dichotomized. In fact, apart from the consistently popular core outlined above (plus history, which is in 86 per cent of schools) business organization and accounting are the next most popular subjects being available respectively, in 72 per cent and 69 per cent of all schools.

At the other end of the popularity continuum one also finds fairly universal patterns. While there were 6 of the junior subjects which were not available in 85 per cent of schools, the same holds true for 10 of the 31 senior cycle subjects. At both junior and senior levels, therefore, there is almost one-third of the curriculum which is largely ignored in the provision procedures of schools. When one examines the 10 least popular subjects at senior level one finds that 5 of them are those same subjects (all languages) which were least popular at junior level already, namely, Latin, Greek, Hebrew, Spanish and Italian. The remaining five are in the business studies and applied science spheres—economic history, agricultural economics, agricultural science, applied mathematics and mechanics.

When we examine subject provision controlling separately for the gender, size, location and administrative character of the school, universal patterns of inclusion and exclusion at both ends of the continuum persist (Tables A14–A17). They are, however, most consistent in the case of the popular core: Irish, English, mathematics, French, biology and geography are provided in almost 80 per cent of all schools irrespective of their size, gender composition, location or administrative character. The only exceptions are biology and geography, the former being available in just 79 per cent of all-male schools and the latter in 72 per cent of vocational schools.

When we analyse history, business organization and accounting (the next most popular trio) according to the same criteria, we find history and business organization in at least 60 per cent of all types of schools, while accounting is provided in at least 50 per cent of each (Table A14–A17).

If we take an 80 per cent absence-rate as a cut-off point for determining the marginality of subjects it is clear that there are six subjects which are consistently marginal in all types of schools, namely, Italian, Greek, Hebrew, economic history, agricultural economics and mechanics. The four remaining least popular subjects, however, are less consistent in their marginality. For example, applied mathematics is available in 40 per cent of both male schools and large schools compared to 5 per cent of female schools and 7 per cent of small schools. Agricultural science is available in 40 per cent of community and comprehensive schools, but in no more than 20 per cent of any other type. Spanish and Latin are also available in approximately 30 per cent of large schools and in over 20 per cent of schools in cities and large towns, but in only 7 per cent or less of small schools or schools in rural areas and villages. Gender differences between schools in these marginal subjects are indeed statistically significant for both applied maths and Italian; differences in administrative character lead to statistically significant differences in the provision of mechanics; size gives rise to statistically significant differences in applied maths, Spanish, Latin and economic history, while location is associated with statistically significant differences in Spanish and economic history.

In summary, therefore, it is evident from our data on knowledge provision at the senior cycle level that universalistic practices are evident in both the inclusion and exclusion of subjects. (A summary of these subjects according to classification is outlined in Table 4.) There are, in all, 12 subjects which are characterized either by almost total inclusion, i.e. present in 80 per cent of all types of schools or by almost total exclusion, i.e. absent from 80 per cent of all types of schools. These subjects represent, in the case of the highly inclusive ones, four classes of knowledge; native languages, modern languages, sciences and humanities; three classes are represented in the excluded category, modern and ancient languages, business studies and applied science. When we extend the high–inclusion end of the continuum to incorporate subjects present in at least 60 per cent of all types of schools, the business studies area, in the form of business organization, is also seen to be highly represented as indeed is history, a humanities subject.

Table 4.   Six classes of knowledge in the senior cycle

Class	No. of subjects	Title	Names of subjects
I	2	Native languages	Irish and English
II	7	Modern and ancient languages	French, German, Italian, Spanish, Latin, Greek, Hebrew
III	4*	Arts and humanities	History, Geography, Art, Music
IV	4	Practical/technological	Construction studies, Home economics (general), Technical drawing, engineering.
V	5	Business studies	Business organization, agricultural economics, accounting, economics, economic history
VI	9	Science/applied sciences	Physics, chemistry, biology, physics and chemistry, agric.-science, maths, applied maths, mechanics (now dropped), home economics (scientific and social)
	31		

*Five since 1985 when classical studies was introduced.

What is notable at senior level as with junior, therefore, is that five of the six major knowledge classes are fairly universally represented in the subject provisions of second-level schools. The exception at the Leaving Certificate level is the practical/technological knowledge system, the same as in the junior cycle. While there is high variability, therefore, in the provision of knowledge in different types of second-level schools, this variability is at its strongest between particular individual subjects. When we compare the provision patterns (and indeed exclusion patterns) of the major knowledge systems, variability is less conspicuous. It is only in the provision of the practical/technological knowledge class that major differences consistently emerge.

Our findings here lend support, therefore, to our earlier contention, that schools are consistently oriented to the development of the intellectual individual. Those knowledge systems with a large practical (non-intellectual) element are the only ones which are not consistently provided. Of course, there is high variability in the allocation of subjects within schools as Hannan *et al.* (1983) have shown. However, this does not discredit the claim that schools are simultaneously universalistic in other ways. Indeed it is precisely because schools are universalistic, particularly in their public side, that they can be highly particularistic in their more private spheres. Without visible, universalistic dimensions, such as a wide-ranging curriculum, a school's legitimacy would be easily threatened.

Curriculum Changes and Technical Knowledge

One of the arguments of this book is that schooling is not only oriented to the development of cognitive-intellectual individuals, but also that this intellectualism was increasingly directed towards the technical knowledge sphere—the word technical being used as a synonym for commercial, scientific and applied scientific or technological knowledge. To substantiate this claim, principals were queried about the changes made in the curricular provision of their schools since their appointments. Because the modal length of appointment was 6 years or less (57 per cent) and because almost 80 per cent were principals in their schools for 12 years or less, the changes documented refer principally to those occurring in the 1970s. Supplementary evidence was also collected on changes made in the 5 years prior to the principal's appointment; this was especially important for those schools in which principals were new.

Although there was an enormous growth in the number of students undertaking the Intermediate Certificate Examination since the introduction of free education in the mid–1960s,[9] this change was not reflected in subject provision at the junior level. The only notable change was in the discontinuation of drawing, domestic science, agricultural science and manual training in 1968 and the introduction of mechanical drawing, home economics, woodwork and metalwork in their place in 1969. Consequently, when we examine the forms of knowledge introduced at junior level, the range and degree of change is not as great as that at senior level. While 57 per cent (49) of the schools in our sample were involved in making 88 curriculum changes, almost half (46 per cent) of these changes merely involved extending the range of subjects in the arts, humanities and/or languages programmes. A further 17 per cent of the changes mentioned were in the non–academic sphere. Only 26 per cent of the changes involved the introduction of some science, business and/or practical subject. Ten schools (eight of which were vocational) claimed that they introduced 'a very wide range of changes' in their academic curriculum without giving any details.

When we analyse curriculum changes in the schools, taking account of their size, gender composition, location and administrative system, we find that the principal change in all types of schools had been the extension of subject options in the arts, humanities and/or languages. However, certain differences are notable. Firstly, it was vocational schools which were most involved with change; 74 per cent of them (n = 20) introduced changes compared to 48 per cent of secondary schools.[10] Secondly, the increased orientation towards the humanities and languages was considerably greater in girls' schools than in boys'. The strongest bias in the latter was towards the introduction of practical–type subjects. Girls' schools did show a tendency, however, to advance into the sciences which no boys' school did: this probably reflects the higher provision in the science area in boys' schools already.

With boys' schools incorporating the practical subjects, girls' schools increasing their science provision and vocational schools engaging in a wide range of academic changes, it is clear that there was a process of synchronization occurring in the knowledge provisions of second–level schools for the past 15 + years. Although this process does not mean that huge differences do not still exist, in some subjects especially, the *trend of change* would seem to be towards greater standardization in the provision of different types of knowledge.

When we analyse changes in curriculum provision at senior level we see a very different pattern to that which obtains in the junior cycle. Firstly, as can be seen from Table 5, a larger number of schools (64) were involved in change and almost twice as many changes occurred. Also, unlike the junior cycle, few of the changes were in the non–academic sphere (8.7 per cent); however, as with the junior cycle a large proportion of the academic changes

Table 5.   Type of knowledge introduced in the senior cycle since the principal was appointed

Subjects	No. of responses	% of responses	% of schools	No. of schools
Modern and ancient languages	13	7.6	20.3	64
Arts and humanities	19	11.0	29.7	64
Science and applied science	52	30.2	81.3	64
Business studies	22	12.8	34.4	64
Practical/technical	19	11.0	29.7	64
Other academic	32	18.6	50.0	64
Non-academic	15	8.7	23.4	64
Total responses	172	100.0		

(18.6 per cent) which occurred were not specified in detail. This limitation must be borne in mind in the following discussion.

The most significant way in which the senior cycle differed from the junior is in the clear trend toward a more technological, scientific and commercial-type curriculum. Only 18 per cent of the changes were in the humanities and languages, while 54 per cent were in the sciences, business or technological spheres. These latter changes reflect the expansion of technical knowledge which occurred in the 1970s as a result of changes in government policy; biology, economics, accounting, business organization, agricultural economics, economic history, technical drawing, construction studies, engineering, mechanics, home economics (scientific and social) were all only introduced on the Leaving Certificate Examination for the first time in 1971.

When we control separately for school size, gender, location and administrative type, we find that the increased orientation towards technical knowledge (our synonym for the sciences, applied sciences, business and practical subjects) exists in all types of schools. As with the junior cycle there are slight differences between different types of schools in their degree of emphasis. Firstly, boys' schools were by far the least likely to be involved in change of any kind. While 64 + per cent of all other types of schools were involved in change only 45 per cent of boys' schools were. Girls' schools and medium-sized schools (251–500 pupils) were indeed the ones most involved in changes, 86 per cent of each having introduced some changes. Girls' schools were also the ones to show the strongest trend toward the sciences. All of the eighteen girls' schools introduced a new science subject since the principal was appointed, one school introducing two new sciences. As in the junior cycle, however, girls' schools did not show any trend towards the more practical technological subjects unlike boys' and co-educational schools. All three types of schools were fairly similar in their introduction of business studies.

Large schools show a greater tendency to introduce technical subjects than small schools, the differences being greatest in practical and business subjects. Schools in cities and large towns were also more likely to introduce business subjects than those in rural areas or smaller towns. Differences between vocational and secondary schools *within* the technical sphere are in the business studies and practical areas, secondary schools being more likely to introduce the business subjects and vocational schools the practical. One must remember here however, that percentages for each type of school are based on different base numbers; while 85 per cent of vocational schools were involved in change only 68 per cent of secondary schools were.

Finally, regarding modern languages and humanities, it is clear that they were poorly represented in the expansion plans of all types of second-level schools. However, they were most strongly represented in girls' schools and least represented in boys' schools, small schools and vocational ones.

Despite the differences between types of schools, the overall pattern of change in the senior cycle was towards the incorporation of far greater amounts of technical knowledge in the formal curriculum. Unlike our evidence on change in the junior cycle, evidence from the senior cycle supports our claim that the intellectual bent of second-level schools is increasingly technical in focus. As the senior cycle is the one in which most change occurred over the last fifteen years, it is indeed a better barometer of change than the junior cycle.

Evidence on the type of subjects abandoned by schools (since the principal was appointed) adds further weight to our argument that schools are becoming increasingly technical. Our data on exclusion, however, is not as detailed as that on inclusion; it is not broken down by sector (junior/senior) and only two categories were used: 'technical knowledge' which refers to all the sciences, business and practical subjects, and 'humanities and languages' which includes all languages, arts and humanities subjects. Only 24 of the 86 (28 per cent) principals said that they dropped subjects. Of the subjects dropped from the curriculum the majority (61 per cent) were in the languages and humanities area. When we control for size, gender, location and administrative character of the school these patterns of exclusion persist.

Because a large proportion of school principals (57 per cent) were principals for six years or less it was decided to get information about changes made prior to the present principal's appointment. Although the number of principals who could provide information on what happened prior to their appointment was small, the information which they provided corroborates our thesis. (Principals who gave information here were generally people who had been teachers, managers or vice-principals in the school prior to their appointment as principals.)

Ten school principals identified 14 subjects introduced in the school prior to their appointment as principals. In all but one of the 14 cases, the subjects introduced were either sciences, business studies or technological subjects — the actual breakdown, respectively was 7, 1 and 5. The remaining school introduced a humanities subject.

A similar though reversed pattern was evidence in the dropping of subjects prior to the principal's appointment. Although only seven of the principals were able to identify subjects dropped from the curriculum prior to their appointment, in all cases they reported that languages were the subjects abandoned.

While our evidence on what happened prior to the principals' appointment is limited, it does help substantiate the claim that the school's productive sub-system is increasingly oriented towards the dissemination of technical knowledge and that this is occurring at the expense of languages and humanities.

Time Allocated to Different Knowledge Forms

To determine the relative importance of different knowledge forms within schools, principals were asked to provide information on the allocation of class periods to different types of subjects. Information was collected at both senior and junior level on subjects which were allocated most and least class periods per week. We will examine the junior cycle first.

From Table 6 we can see very definite patterns of emphasis in the distribution of time in Irish second-level schools. The importance of Irish, English and mathematics is clearly evident: only 23 per cent (16) of the 69 schools which distributed time differentially failed to mention one or more of these three subjects as receiving extra time each week. Almost one-fifth of the schools, 19 per cent, however, mention mathematics as the only subject to be allocated extra time. Mathematics, therefore, is singularly the most likely subject to be allocated extra class periods each week in the junior cycle.

When we examine time allocation between subjects in different types of schools the importance of Irish, English and mathematics persists. No statistically significant differences emerge. There is, however, some variability in the types of schools which allotted most time to mathematics. Smaller, rural, co-educational and vocational-type schools were all more likely to give extra time solely to mathematics. One must bear in mind here though that larger, urban, male, single-sex secondary, and community schools were more likely than the former group to allot extra time to Irish and/or English

Table 6.   Subjects with most class periods per week in the junior cycle

Subjects	Number of schools	Percentage
Irish + English + mathematics	27	31.4
*Irish or English + mathematics	7	8.1
*Irish and/or English	6	7.0
Mathematics	13	15.1
Practical subjects including home economics	5	5.8
It varies for each class	2	2.3
All equal except occasionally	9	10.5
Not applicable	14	16.3
Information incomplete	1	1.2
Don't know	2	2.3
Total	86	100.0

*In both of these cases, the principals stated that the emphasis on Irish and/or English varied from time to time.

plus mathematics. Consequently, one cannot say that big, urban, single-sex or community schools give less time to mathematics; rather, they give more time to Irish and English than the others. It seems, therefore, that when resources are limited, as they are likely to be in the smaller, vocational and rural schools, they are directed towards mathematics rather than other subjects.

The focus on Irish, English and mathematics in the junior cycle is understandable for a number of reasons: competence in mathematics and English especially is vital for the development of skills in a variety of other subjects; Irish, English and mathematics are prerequisites for the attainment of the Intermediate Certificate and later, for entry to many third-level institutions. The reason why mathematics is given more time on the timetable than other subjects would seem to arise from the growing importance of the sciences, business and technological subjects, all of which have a mathematical base. In the senior cycle, for example, 17 (57 per cent) of the 30 subjects are in the technical spheres. This represents a significant shift from the early 1960s when only 10 (42 per cent) of the 24 Leaving Certificate subjects were in this category. Furthermore, Clancy (1988: 15) has shown how the same trend is evident in third level, with 67 per cent of the new entrants being in the technical spheres.

The bias in timetable provision toward Irish, English and mathematics is strongly evident in the senior cycle as well. The proportion of schools giving equal weight to all three subjects is slightly lower than at junior level; however, the proportion giving most time to mathematics alone is higher, 26 per cent of the differentiating schools give most time solely to mathematics compared with 19 per cent in the junior cycle (Table 7). Although a larger

Table 7.   Subjects with most class periods per week in the senior cycle

Subjects	Number of schools	Percentage
Irish + English + mathematics	22	25.6
Irish, or sometimes Irish + mathematics	8	9.3
English, or sometimes English + mathematics	3	3.5
Other subject + mathematics	3	3.5
Mathematics	16	18.6
Other academic subject	1	1.2
Practical subject	7	8.1
Varies with each class	1	1.2
Not applicable	24	27.9
Don't know	1	1.2
Total	86	100.0*

*Total percentages are presented in rounded figures throughout the text.

proportion of schools do not make any differentiation in the time allocated to subjects in the senior cycle than in the junior, 28 per cent compared with 16 per cent, among those schools which do make differentiations, mathematics is more frequently mentioned in the senior cycle. It is identified as one of, or the only subject, to get extra periods per week, in 85 per cent of the schools in question. Complementing the time-bias toward mathematics primarily, and Irish and English to a lesser degree, is a reasonably strong emphasis on the practical subjects excluding home economics. That is to say, engineering, construction studies and technical drawing are the next most likely group to be given extra-time each week. (This was also true in the junior cycle although the practical group included home economics.)

Although no statistically significant differences are evident between different types of schools in the overall prioritization of particular subjects on senior cycle timetables, there are, nonetheless, some noticeable differences between schools in the time allocated to certain subjects. For example, although roughly equal proportions of secondary and vocational schools allocate time differentially (74 per cent compared with 66.7 per cent respectively), 27.8 per cent of the vocational schools in question allocate extra time to the practical subjects compared with 2.5 per cent of the secondary. On the other hand 32.5 per cent of secondary schools *only* allocate extra time to mathematics compared with 5.6 per cent of vocational schools. What this seems to indicate is a division within the technical knowledge system itself; the practical dimension of technical knowledge is emphasized mostly in those schools with a large working-class and small farm cohort, vocational schools (Breen, 1984: 31). Mathematics, a more academic technical knowledge form, is emphasized most in the more middle-class secondary schools. It must be noted here though that the other public schools in the study — the community and comprehensive — were different to the vocational schools in that two of the three involved in making time differentiations between subjects gave most time solely to mathematics and the other gave it to practical subjects.

Compared with the differences between vocational, secondary and community schools, differences arising from gender divisions, size or location are minimal. As was the case in the junior cycle, however, small schools were more likely to allocate extra time to mathematics than any other subject. To summarize, therefore, English, Irish and mathematics are the subjects most likely to get maximum time allocations in the junior cycle and also, but to a lesser extent, at senior level. Mathematics, however, is consistently the most likely subject to be designated extra class periods each week in all types of schools. This is especially true at Leaving Certificate level. Practical subjects were also likely to be allocated extra time, though this generally only happened in vocational schools or in community or comprehensive ones. Given the fact that secondary schools are less likely than others to offer practical subjects in the first place, this latter finding is not very surprising.

As pointed out above already, the timetable-bias towards Irish, English and mathematics is understandable (a) in terms of the key role these subjects play in attaining credentials at second level, and (b) because the subjects in question are generally prerequisites for gaining access to jobs and third-level education. The fact that mathematics is clearly the subject allocated most time in all types of schools at both levels, and that practical subjects are the only other subjects (apart from Irish, English and mathematics) allotted extra time — albeit primarily in vocational and community schools — adds further weight to our argument that the development of a technically competent individual is a priority value in second-level education. A brief perusal of the types of subjects allocated the *least* amount of time each week also supports this contention.

Fifty-seven per cent of the sample schools had one or more subjects which were allocated less time each week than others. The types of knowledge allocated least time in over 75 per cent of the relevant cases were the humanities and arts. Only in 10 per cent of cases was scientific, practical or commercial knowledge identified as that which is allocated least time. Neither school size, gender composition, location or type of administrative control had any effect on these patterns.

While some subjects are allocated extra time on the senior cycle timetable, very few schools actually discriminate between the remaining subjects in terms of time. Only 15 schools, or 17 per cent of the sample, claimed to have subjects which were allotted considerably less time than others at senior level. Of this 15, 10 mention a modern language, humanities or arts subject as one of the subjects, if not the only subject, to be given the least number of periods each week. Seven mention a technical subject as one of the subjects, if not the only subject, most likely to be allotted fewer class periods. A slightly larger proportion of schools mention the humanities, arts and modern languages as the only ones to be allocated least time (7 schools) compared with the proportion solely mentioning the technical (5). The bias towards the technical is evident, but not very strongly, therefore, when one compares subjects allocated least time in the senior cycle. However, as the numbers involved are very small it is difficult to make a judgement either way.

The Marginal Status of Activities and Knowledge Divorced from Credentials

In the preceding sections it has been shown firstly, that schools operate certain universalistic practices in their provision of different forms of knowledge. In particular it has been demonstrated that five of the six major knowledge forms are well represented in the provisions of all types of schools. The exception is the knowledge form which is least intellectual — practical/ technological knowledge. It was suggested, therefore, that schools were primarily oriented to the development of an intellectual individual. Secondly, we went on to show how schools were also universalistic in their increasing orientation towards technical knowledge. This was evident in the changes in the schools' knowledge provisions occurring over time, and in their allocation of time between subjects. Not only are schools oriented therefore to the development of the intellectual individual, they are increasingly concerned with developing her/his competence in the technical sphere. It is not only in the positive allocation of time to certain curriculum-specific subjects that the schools' biases become evident. The fact that schools allocate little time to certain knowledge forms which cannot be credentialized also provides us with information as to its priorities.

The most important factor to bear in mind in any discussion about time in school is that time is a scarce commodity. Department of Education regulations specify the length of the school year, the school week and the school day; consequently there is a remarkable similarity between all types of school in the time available to them. Almost all schools in our sample, for example, operated a five-day Monday to Friday week (97.7 per cent); the remaining two schools (2.3 per cent) had a half-day during the week and had school on Saturday mornings. Also, when one examines the number of class periods in a given school day, one finds remarkably little variability between schools. All schools have from 8 to 10 class periods each day. The standardization of the time available for teaching in the formal school day both reflects the extent of external control on schools and indicates the pressure on schools to ration time carefully. When we examine the amount of time allocated to non-examinable subjects we see the effects of rationing most clearly.

As Table 8 indicates, only religion, civics (in the junior cycle) and physical education (PE) are timetabled consistently in second-level schools. Schools are, of course, expected to make provision for physical education and civics at junior level, and for PE at senior level under departmental regulations (*Rules and Programme for Secondary Schools*, 1984/85: 11). No such stipulation is made in the case of religion. The fact that it is timetabled in all schools reflects the central role religion plays in Irish education (none of the schools was reported to be secular institutions; 60.5 per cent were Catholic, 38.4 per cent were multi-denominational and 1.2 per cent were Protestant). What seems to matter most in schools, therefore, after the attainment of skills in specified credentialized spheres, is the learning of the tenets of one's religion and the rules and regulations of the state (in civics). Almost all schools encourage the development of pupils' sporting skills as well, in PE. That many schools are involved in the pupils' development in a wide variety of ways *outside* the formal timetable is undoubtedly true and will become evident in the analysis of extra-curricular activities. However, the fact that so few of these are timetabled, and in so few schools, is proof that they have a marginal status in the school system. Although music is timetabled in a reasonable proportion of schools (in all 34 schools, 39.5 per cent have some

Table 8. Non-examination subjects *: proportion of schools including those on their timetable at junior and senior levels

Subjects	Junior		Senior	
	No.	%	No.	%
Religion **	86	100.0	84	97.7
Civics	86	100.0	not applicable	
Physical education (PE)	82	95.3	72	83.7
Music (dancing)	22	25.6	8	9.3
Music (choir/singing)	16	18.6	12	14.0
Drama/speech	11	12.8	4	4.7
Craft work	4	4.7	0	0.0
Leisure club	—	—	4	4.7
Typing	—	—	4	4.7
Social development	—	—	2	2.3
Current affairs	—	—	1	1.2

*The time allocated to pastoral care, remedial classes and career guidance is not documented here as these are strictly speaking not content-oriented, or 'subjects' in the quantitative sense.

**Religion refers essentially to religious instruction in Irish schools; it does not refer to religious studies as an academic subject.

type of music), all other subjects are absent from the timetable in almost 90 per cent or more of schools (Table 8). Furthermore, when we analyse the actual amount of time given to the various subjects at junior and senior level their low status is evident.

Table 9 lists the various non-examination subjects timetabled in schools and the number of periods allotted to each. It is clear from this that with the exception of religion, and to a small extent PE, most schools only allocate one or two periods at most to any given non-examination subjects. In terms of the distribution of time, therefore, within the formal school day, religion is the only knowledge form which is accorded fairly equal status with examination subjects. The almost entire focus of the pupils' school day therefore is on the pursuit of intellectual (increasingly technical) knowledge in preparation for competitive examinations.

To say this, of course, is not to deny that there are important differences between different types of schools in the allocation of time to the non-examination subjects, with the exception of civics which is compulsory. When we control separately for gender, size, location and administrative type, we find that music (in the form of singing) is much more likely to be provided in girls' schools than in co-educational schools or boys' schools at both junior and senior level—52.4 per cent of female schools provide it on the timetable at junior level and 47.6 per cent at senior. By contrast only 10.0 per cent of boys' schools and 6.7 per cent of co-educational schools timetable it at junior, while no boys' school and only 4.5 per cent of co-educational schools timetabled it at senior level. Differences here are statistically significant (P < 0.01). Forty per cent of boys' schools however, did have some music provision (other than singing) timetabled at junior level compared with one-third of the girls' schools and 15.6 per cent of the co-educational ones. At senior level there was a huge drop in the provision for music in all schools, but especially in the boys' and co-educational schools—only 5.3 per cent and 4.5 per cent of each respectively had music timetabled, while 24 per cent of girls' schools had. Gender differences at the senior level were statistically significant (P < 0.05). Girls' schools were also the most likely to provide time for drama/speech and typing although few did so; only 9.5 per cent timetabled drama/speech while 14.3 per cent timetabled typing.

School size does not seem to be a major factor contributing to differences in the timetabling of non-examination subjects. While small schools were the least likely to have singing in the junior cycle, they were more likely than medium-sized schools, for example, to give time to some other form of music. They were, however, the least likely to timetable either PE or craft work at junior level. Differences here were statistically significant at the P < 0.05 level. Location also seemed to influence the provision of time for PE at junior level, rural schools being least likely to give it time. This indeed

Table 9. Time allocation for non-examination subjects in both the junior and senior cycle: the proportion of schools offering the subject for different periods per week

Name of subject	Cycle	No. of periods per week on which the subject is timetabled (% distribution)					
		One or two periods	Three periods	Four–six periods	Varies for each year	Information incomplete	Not applicable
Religion	Junior	27.9	33.7	32.6	5.8	0.0	—
	Senior	24.4	37.2	29.1	3.5	3.5	2.3
Civics	Junior	97.7	0.0	0.0	1.2	1.2	—
	Senior	not offered in senior					
Physical education	Junior	75.6	8.1	0.0	11.6	0.0	4.7
	Senior	65.1	5.8	0.0	10.5	4.4	14.3
Music (and dance)	Junior	16.3	3.5	1.2	3.5	1.2	74.4
	Senior	7.0	0.0	2.3	0.0	0.0	90.7
Choir	Junior	15.1	1.2	0.0	1.2	0.0	81.4
	Senior	11.6	0.0	0.0	2.3	1.2	86.0
Drama and speech	Junior	9.3	0.0	0.0	3.5	0.0	87.2
	Senior	3.5	0.0	0.0	1.2	0.0	95.3
Craft	Junior	3.5	0.0	0.0	1.2	0.0	95.3
	Senior	not offered in senior					
Leisure club	Junior	not offered in junior					
	Senior	4.7	0.0	0.0	0.0	0.0	95.3
Typing	Junior	not offered in junior					
	Senior	0.0	1.2	0.0	1.2	2.3	95.3
Social development	Junior	not offered in junior					
	Senior	1.2	0.0	0.0	0.0	1.2	97.6
Current affairs	Junior	not offered in junior					
	Senior	1.2	0.0	0.0	0.0	0.0	98.8

Junior N = 86   Senior N = 84

was also the case with music (other than singing) at both junior and senior levels. However, one must bear in mind here that size of school and location are fairly closely correlated ($r = 0.47$). When we cross-tabulated school size by location we found 61.3 per cent of the small schools (i.e. those with 250 pupils) to be rural ones (cf. Tables A2–A9 for the cross-tabulation and correlation of all the main variables with each other. Table A9 is the one in which location and size are cross-tabulated). The fact that a large proportion of rural schools are small, therefore, would help explain why so little time is allotted for particular activities within them. Schools may not have the staff or facilities to allow for it.

Finally, and not surprisingly, the type of administrative structure within the school also seems to lead to considerable differences in the provision of time for non-examination subjects. At both junior and senior level secondary schools are much more likely than either vocational or community/comprehensive schools to give time to drama and singing (only secondary schools, in fact, did singing). This may well be explained by the Department of Education stipulation (p. 11 of the *Rules and Programme* 1984/85) that singing should be included in the timetable of secondary schools. No such stipulation exists for other schools. Music (other than singing), however, is timetabled in 40.2 per cent of the community schools at junior level and in all of them at senior level.

The differences which do exist between different types of schools are important in so far as they highlight the bias in girls' secondary schools towards music and drama and the tendency for vocational schools, on the other hand, not to make any provision for them. Size of school does not explain this either as there is only a weak correlation ($r = 0.25$) between school type and size (Table A4). Given the likely social class composition of vocational and secondary schools, it is clear that social class and gender are important determinants of the amount and range of non-examination knowledge made available in schools.

The importance of gender and social class again become evident when we analyse the allocation of time on the timetable to one particular non-examination subject, namely, religion. As can be seen from Tables 10 and 11 both gender and school type are important determinants of the time allotted to religion. Girls' schools are by far the most likely to give a high number of periods each week to religion: 71.4 per cent of girls' schools gave 4–6 periods to religion each week in the junior cycle and 76.2 per cent gave that number at senior level. The comparable figures for boys' schools were 40.1 per cent and 31.6 per cent, and for co-educational schools, 11.1 per cent and 7.3 per cent. Differences of a similar magnitude emerge when we analyse the allocation of class periods to religion in community/comprehensive, vocational and secondary schools. Vocational schools allocate

Table 10.   Gender differences in the timetabling of religion

Time Hours on timetable	Cycle	Gender type		
		All female	All male	Co-educational
1 or 2 periods	Junior	0.0	10.0	48.9
per week	Senior	0.0	10.5	46.3
3 periods	Junior	19.0	35.0	40.0
per week	Senior	14.3	57.9	43.9
4–6 periods	Junior	71.4	40.1	11.1
per week	Senior	76.2	31.6	7.3
Varies for	Junior	9.5	15.0	0.0
each year	Senior	9.5	0.0	2.4

Junior (N = 86)   Senior (N = 81)
Junior cycle P < 0.01   Senior cycle P < 0.01

Table 11.   Differences between various types of schools in the timetabling of religion

Time No. of periods per week	Cycle	Type of school		
		Vocational	Secondary	Community/ comprehensive
1 or 2 per week	Junior	70.4	7.4	20.0
	Senior	73.9	5.7	20.0
3 per week	Junior	22.2	35.2	80.0
	Senior	21.7	43.4	80.0
4–6 per week	Junior	3.7	50.0	0.0
	Senior	0.0	47.2	0.0
Varies for	Junior	3.7	7.4	0.0
each year	Senior	4.3	3.8	0.0

Junior cycle = P < 0.01   Senior cycle = P < 0.01

the least time to religion, while secondary schools allocate the most. Community and comprehensive hold an intermediate position. As can be seen from Table 11 differences here are statistically significant at the P < 0.01 level at both junior and senior levels.

Neither size nor location are very important determinants of the time allotted to religion with one exception. There is a slight tendency for larger schools to allocate more time to religion than smaller ones, especially at senior level. One must remember here though that 60 per cent of the medium-sized schools and 70 per cent of the very large ones are secondary (Table A4).

The size of the school, its gender, location or administrative type do not seem to bear any influence on the time allotted to PE, music, singing or other extracurricular activities. It was generally very little anyhow, one or two periods at most. What is noticeable in the timetabling in all types of schools is a slight tendency to withdraw time from the particular subjects as pupils get older and are competing for terminal examinations. Religion is the only exception to this.

When we queried principals on the services and time available for the 'personal needs' of the students we deliberately avoided using the term 'pastoral care'. To ask principals directly if they had a pastoral-care system in the school would have been leading, as it is widely believed that schools should have such a system at present. Instead we asked principals if there was any formally organized system in the school for attending to the personal needs of the pupils. Forty-four schools (51.2 per cent) claimed to have some kind of formal system. Of this 44, 39 (89 per cent) gave information on the time allotted to it. Even within these schools which allocated time to personal care programmes (N = 17) none gave them more than one or two periods each week on the timetable.

In fact if we examine the 17 cases in question, we find that in 11 of them the schools only gave one period each week to pastoral-care-type programmes. An almost equally common method of operating pastoral care programmes was through tutor contact with pupils within formal lesson periods. This, of course, did not involve any allocation of special time to pastoral care.

When we control separately for size, gender, location and administrative style in the school, two clear differences emerge. Boys' schools are much less likely than female or co-educational schools either to have a personal care programme or formally to allocate time each week to pastoral care. Only 6 boys' schools (30 per cent) gave details of a pastoral care programme compared with 11 (52 per cent) of girls' schools and 22 (49 per cent) of co-educational schools. Of these, only 16.7 per cent of boys' schools compared with 54.5 per cent of girls' and 45.5 per cent of co-educational schools actually allocated time to pastoral care on the weekly timetable. The second notable difference is between community/comprehensive schools and others. The former were the most likely to allocate some special time each week to pastoral care; 75 per cent of community/comprehensive schools allocated pastoral care 1 or 2 class periods each week compared to 30.8 per cent of vocational schools and 45.5 per cent of secondary schools.

In spite of the differences between various types of schools in their allocation of time to both non-examination subjects and pastoral care-type activities there is a remarkable similarity between them in the marginal status they accord to non-examination subjects. Religion, civics (at junior level) and, but to a lesser extent, PE are the only non-examination subjects consistently available in all types of schools. Religion, in fact, is the only one allocated time on a fairly equal basis with mainstream subjects. Provision for pastoral care occurs in less than half the schools sampled and less than half of these again actually allocate time to pastoral care on the timetable.

What this testifies to is the importance attached to the dissemination of intellectual — and, as shown above increasingly technical — knowledge.

Undoubtedly, there are differences in the degrees of emphasis on particular aspects of individual development in different types of schools. Girls' schools are consistently more likely than boys' to emphasize the religious, aesthetic and personal development of their pupils. Secondary schools are also more likely than vocational schools to emphasize these. Finally, community/comprehensive schools seem to be the most likely ones to stress personal development. However, the fact that schools lay strong emphasis on the religious or personal development of pupils does not mean that they devalue the intellectual. As will be seen when we examine the academic climate of the schools it is frequently the schools which are most academically competitive which also lay strongest emphasis on personal and religious development.

Notes

1 The Leaving Certificate is the major terminal examination taken at the end of second-level education (age 17–18 years). The Intermediate is undertaken mid-way (after three years) through second level, while the Group Certificate is undertaken generally after two years in second level. The newly formed (1987) National Council for Curriculum and Assessment (Information Bulletin, Jan. 1988) has announced that the Intermediate Certificate and the Day Vocational (Group) Certificate are to be replaced by a new Junior Certificate from 1989 onwards. The subjects on the Junior Certificate comprise of an amalgam of those in the two previous Certificates with some syllabus changes.

2 Physical Education and Singing must also be allotted time in the Junior Cycle timetable of secondary schools.

3 See Ch. 1, note 2 for a description of the different types of schools in the Republic of Ireland.

4 The 20 recognized Intermediate Certificate Examination subjects are Irish, English, Mathematics, History and Geography (one subject), French, German, Italian, Spanish, Hebrew, Latin, Greek, Science, Home Economics, Music and Musicianship, Classical Studies, Art, Woodwork, Metalwork, Mechanical Drawing and Commerce.

5 The Leaving Certificate subjects are Irish, English, Agricultural Science, Agricultural Economics, Mathematics, Applied Mathematics, French, German, Art, Music, Hebrew, Latin, Italian, Spanish, Greek, History, Classical Studies, Geography, Accounting, Economics, Economic History, Business Organization, Physics, Chemistry, Biology, Construction Studies, Engineering, Technical Drawing, Home Economics (General), Home Economics (Scientific and Social) and Physics and Chemistry.

6 Since this book went to print, new syllabi have been introduced in seven junior cycle subjects and plans are afoot to change most of the others by 1991. Arising from the new syllabi, the Intermediate and Group Certificate Examinations are

to be replaced by the Junior Certificate Examination in 1992. While the content of the syllabi has been modified considerably in some subjects, control is still highly centralized and the forms of knowledge offered are broadly similar to what they were previously.

7 The present quota for secondary schools 'is one teacher for every 20 "recognized" pupils' (Council of Managers of Catholic Secondary Schools (1984) *A Handbook for Managers of Secondary Schools*, Dublin, p. 7 (Private Circulation only).) As of Autumn 1988 vocational, community and comprehensive schools will have a 20 : 1 ratio also.

8 The distribution of the sample in terms of the main independent variables is presented on Table A1 of the Appendix. The interrelationships between the independent variables is presented also in Tables A2–A9. Given the limits of space in a book such as this, it is not possible to present all the detailed tables we have available. Findings are often summarized in the text and a select and representative range of related tables are available in the Appendix.

9 Up to the mid-1960s students attending secondary schools had to pay fees.

10 The fact that vocational schools experienced most change is not surprising as after the *Investment in Education Report* was published in 1966 vocational schools were encouraged to offer a full range of second-level courses. Given their weakness in the arts and sciences in the mid-1960s, it is not surprising to find them introducing a lot of changes.

Chapter 3

The Relational Context of Learning: The Universality of Competitive Individualism and Hierarchical Control

From our analysis of the types of knowledge distributed in schools and the time allocated to each we have seen how the development of the technically competent individual is gaining increasing pre-eminence. This process is taking place, however, in a very specific relational context. Not only are students primed to be competent in the scientific, technological and commercial spheres, they are also primed to compete with others in the process. The final rewards of schooling—high grade credentials—are contingent on outcompeting others. It is in the process of evaluation that the structural conditions for competitive individualism are laid.

Developing the Competitive Individual

The Process of Evaluation

To establish the level of competitiveness, we examined the schools' involvement in both public examinations and internal assessment. The pattern of involvement in state public examinations is highly predictable reflecting both the high level of state control on schools and the requirements of third-level colleges and employers. All schools do the Intermediate Certificate, while all but two (small, rural, vocational schools which were in the process of amalgamating with other schools) did the Leaving Certificate. On the other hand, only just over half do the Group Certificate, an indication of the low status currently accorded to that credential on the job market. Less than one-third do the Matriculation as students who go on to third-level education usually matriculate for university entrance through their Leaving

Certificate. Apart from those students who leave school without sitting any examinations (in 1982, 92,000 persons (25.5 per cent) out of a total of 361,000 in the youth labour force—i.e. 15–24 years—had left school without a qualification, Sexton *et al.*, 1983), therefore, all students are involved in preparation for some kind of examination in which they are assessed as individuals. Even if students never sit an examination, almost all are nonetheless prepared for them.

It should be noted here that the class and gender composition of the school both have a bearing on the type of knowledge in which pupils are publicly assessed. All community, and 96.3 per cent of vocational schools in our sample did the Group Certificate, while only 24.1 per cent of secondary schools did. Forty-five per cent of boys' schools also prepared pupils for the Group Certificate examination while only 4.8 per cent of girls' did. Thus, we see the existence of particularistic and universalistic practices side by side.

Internal Examinations and Reports

To assess the level of competitive individualism in schools by examining participation in public examinations alone, would be to underestimate the extent of it in school life. Most schools operate a complex system of continually grading pupils vis-à-vis their classmates, both in curricular and extracurricular activities, and it is to the analysis of these processes that we now turn. The most effective method for obtaining data on the type and frequency of in-school assessment would be to ask the teachers. Owing to the limited resources available to us, however, we had to rely on the principals as informants. Our data, therefore, is not as detailed as we would like it to be. Accepting this limitation, we can see from Tables 12 and 13 that both non-examination and examination classes in all schools have at least one formal assessment in the school year. Indeed, over 80 per cent of schools held two end-of-term examinations for students doing public examinations within the year. A small proportion of schools (9.4 per cent) conducted other assessments as well, such as end-of-term profiles or reports. The pattern of assessment for the non-examination classes is very similar; all schools held house examinations or assessments at least once a year, the majority of schools (59.3 per cent) indeed holding them twice a year and approximately one-third having them three times per year. Non-examination classes have slightly more in-house assessments than examination classes.

When we compare different types of schools, we find little variability between them in the frequency of holding in-house examinations for public examination classes (Tables A18–A21). There were slight differences, however, in the area of end-of-term reports: while 11.1 per cent and 9.5

Table 12.   Frequency of internal examinations for the examination classes (i.e. taking public examinations)

Frequency	No. of responses	% of schools operating each type	No. of schools
1. Exam. twice a year	70	82.4	85
2. Exam. once a year	17	20.0	85
3. End of term reports	8	9.4	85
Total number of responses	95*		

*The reason the number of responses (95) exceeds the number of schools (85) both here and in Table 13 is because the categories involved are not mutually exclusive. Although categories 1 and 2 would appear to be (and also categories 2, 3 and 4 in Table 13) a small number of schools–no more than 2 or 3 in each case–operated both systems. That is to say they had two examinations for Intermediate classes, but only one for Leaving Certificate or they alternated between the two systems from year to year and hence were counted twice.

Table 13.   Frequency of internal examinations for non-examination classes (i.e. not taking public examinations)

Frequency	No. of responses	% of schools	No. of schools
1. Monthly reports	12	14.0	86
2. Examinations three times per year	27	31.4	86
3. Examinations twice per year	51	59.3	86
4. Examinations once per year	10	11.6	86
5. Other assessments	4	4.7	86
Total number of responses	104		

per cent of co-educational and female schools respectively gave them, only 5.3 per cent of male schools did. Medium-sized schools and schools in cities or very large towns were also much more likely to give them than either very small or very large schools or schools in smaller towns and rural areas. No vocational schools mentioned giving end-of-term reports, while 20 per cent of community/comprehensive schools and 13.2 per cent of secondary schools did.

When we compare schools in their patterns of assessing non-examination pupils, differences are noticeable again but only at extreme ends of the scale. That is to say, the vast majority of all types of schools (approximately 80 per cent) hold in-house examinations for non-examination classes two or three times per year. There are however, some differences between the various types of schools in the giving of monthly assessments/reports and in the tendency to hold only one in-house examination per year. While 19 per cent of girls' schools and 20 per cent of boys' schools had monthly assessments only 8.9 per cent of co-educational schools had. Similarly, while 20 per cent of very large schools and 14.3 per cent of medium-sized schools had them, only 9.7 per cent of small schools did. Location also seemed to be involved (although one must bear in mind the correlations between location and size, and between location and gender; rural schools also tend to be small co-educational ones, Tables A3, A7) with almost 30 per cent of schools in cities and large towns having monthly assessments compared with 3.3 per cent of those in medium-sized towns and 10.3 per cent of those in villages and rural areas. It was, however, schools in medium-sized towns which gave examinations most frequently. Secondary and community schools also seem much more likely to have monthly assessments for non-examination classes than vocational schools: no vocational schools reported having monthly assessments compared with 20 per cent of both secondary and community schools.

What is evident from the foregoing discussion on the frequency of assessment, therefore, is the fact that approximately 80 per cent of all types of schools hold in-house examinations *at least* twice yearly for both those classes doing public examinations and those not doing them. Small numbers of schools (8 in the case of examination classes and 14 in the case of non-examination classes) also give other assessments as well, usually end-of-term reports in the case of examination classes, and monthly assessments in the case of non-examination classes. It is in these latter areas that differences between schools emerge. Both male and female single-sex schools (90 per cent of which were secondary) were more likely to give these extra assessments than co-educational schools (56 per cent of which were vocational). While medium-sized schools were most likely to give them to examination classes than either large or small schools, *both* large and medium-sized schools were more likely to give them to non-examination classes than small schools. Finally, schools in cities or large towns and community and secondary schools were more likely to give extra assessments than either schools in smaller towns and rural areas or vocational schools.

Continuous Assessment

In our discussion on school assessment procedures so far we have seen how pupils compete against each other in public examinations and again (usually twice a year or more) in the internal examinations of the school. These events, however, do not exhaust the opportunities for competitiveness. As can be seen from Table 14, 84 per cent of schools also expect, or compel, their teachers to give class tests/assessments on a fairly regular basis. Only in 14 schools, 16.3 per cent of the total, was there no requirement for continuous assessment. Because the majority of principals said that continuous assessment

Table 14. Types of in-term assessment used in schools (excluding formal examinations)

Type of assessment	Number	%
Continuous assessment (class tests) expected but not compulsory	53	61.6
Continuous assessment is compulsory for all classes	16	18.6
Continuous assessment is compulsory for some classes only	3	3.5
There are no in-term tests	14	16.3
Total	86	100.0

was expected, but was at the discretion of teachers (61.6 per cent), we have no way of knowing how much variability there is in this cohort, either between schools or between teachers in a given school. What we do know from these figures, however, is that continuous assessment was part of school policy in a clear majority of cases. In almost one-fifth of schools it was compulsory for all classes.

When we analysed the continuous assessment practices of schools according to size, gender composition, location and administrative type, no statistically significant differences emerged. We did find, however, that larger schools and those in towns and cities were slightly more likely to have compulsory (as opposed to voluntary) continuous assessment for some or all of their pupils than either small schools or rural ones. One must remember though that 29.6 per cent of schools in cities and large towns had no continuous assessment compared with only 13.8 per cent of rural schools. Also, 20 per cent of very large schools had none compared with 16.1 per cent of very small ones.

While fairly equal proportions of both male and female schools tended to have continuous assessments (above the norm of two in-house examinations) in the school year, it is clear from Table 15 that girls' schools are considerably more likely than boys' to have compulsory continuous assessment for some or all pupils — 28.6 per cent compared with 15 per cent. Boys' schools on the other hand are more likely than girls' to have no continuous assessment at all — 20 per cent of boys' schools having none and 9.5 per cent of girls'. Girls' schools are also more likely to have compulsory continuous assessment than co-educational schools — 28.6 per cent of girls' schools have it compared with 22.2 per cent of co-educational schools.

When examining frequency of internal assessment, secondary schools and community schools were found to be fairly similar in their practices, both having more monthly assessments and end-of-term reports than vocational schools. While it is obvious from Table 16 that

Table 15.   *Gender differences in the character of in-term school assessment*

Gender	Type of assessment				
	Continuous assessment: class tests expected but not compulsory	*Continuous assessment for all pupils (compulsory)*	*Continuous assessment for some pupils only (compulsory)*	*No in-term assessment*	*N*
Female	61.9	23.8	4.8	9.5	21
Male	65.0	10.0	5.0	20.0	20
Co-educational	60.0	20.0	2.2	17.8	45
Total number of schools with each arrangement	61.6	18.6	3.5	16.3	86

$P = $ N.S.

Table 16.   *Differences between secondary, vocational and community/ comprehensive schools in in-term school assessments*

Type	Type of assessment				
	Continuous assessment: class tests expected but not compulsory	*Continuous assessment for all pupils (compulsory)*	*Continuous assessment for some pupils only (compulsory)*	*No continuous assessment*	*N*
Vocational	70.4	3.7	3.7	22.2	27
Secondary	61.1	24.1	1.9	13.0	54
Community/ comprehensive	20.0	40.0	20.0	20.0	5
Total number of schools with each arrangement	61.6	18.6	3.5	16.3	86

$P < 0.05$

community/comprehensive and secondary schools are a lot more likely than vocational schools to have compulsory continuous assessment and slightly less likely than them to have none, it is also clear that community and comprehensive schools are more likely to have compulsory continuous assessment than secondary schools. Unlike differences arising from size, location or school gender, differences here are statistically significant. It would seem, therefore, that while fairly equal proportions of vocational, secondary and community schools operate a system of continuous assessment — secondary schools being in fact the most likely to have it — they vary a lot in the extent to which it is compulsorily imposed. Community and comprehensive schools are at one end of the continuum with three of the five schools in the sample having compulsory continuous assessment for at least some pupils, while vocational schools are at the other end with only 7.4 per cent making it compulsory. Secondary schools hold an intermediary position with 26 per cent having compulsory continuous assessment for at least some pupils. Next to community schools, girls' schools (which are exclusively secondary schools) are the most likely to have compulsory continuous assessment.

While there is evidence from our data on internal examinations and continuous assessments, therefore, that all-female secondary schools and community schools are the most likely to facilitate competitive individualism — because of the greater frequency and compulsoriness of their assessment procedures than in other schools — it must be borne in mind that differences are notable in only one area, that of compulsory continuous assessment. In terms of both in-house examinations and continuous assessment, 80 per cent of all types of schools — big and small, rural and urban, vocational and secondary, single-sex and co-educational — have continuous assessment for all pupils and internal examinations at least twice a year for both non-examination and examination classes. There are two exceptions: 29.6 per cent of schools in cities and very large towns have no continuous assessment and 40 per cent of community and comprehensive schools only give one internal examination each year to the examination classes. As community/comprehensive schools are the most likely to give end-of-term reports on examination classes, this obviously counterbalances the impact of having only one in-house examination during the year.

The final question which principals were asked relating to examinations was whether or not they displayed test or examination results in any public place in the school. Displaying test results would obviously intensify the level of competition in the school. Only eight schools, 9.3 per cent, however, publicized test/examination results in any way (other than giving them to parents). The most likely schools to do it were female secondary schools with 19 per cent (N = 4) of them displaying results. No male schools or community schools displayed results, while two vocational schools and two co-educational secondary schools did. Although the numbers involved here are very small we find girls' secondary schools once again appearing as the ones with the slightly stronger competitive climate.

Prize-giving for School Work and Extracurricular Activities

Another feature of school life indicating the level of individual competitiveness within it is the extent of prize-giving. By awarding prizes for academic or extracurricular successes, the school both reinforces the importance of the particular activity involved, and encourages pupils to compete with each other even more strongly to gain the designated prize. As is evident from Table 17 the awarding of prizes for extracurricular activities is very common in Irish second-level schools; 86 per cent of schools give some prizes in this area. Prizes for success in school work, however, were far less common. Only 37 (43 per cent) schools gave prizes for curriculum-related work.

No significant differences emerged between the various types of schools in the area of extracurricular prize-giving. Girls' schools, large schools, those in cities or large towns and vocational schools were, however, slightly more likely than others to award extracurricular prizes. This is the one occasion when vocational schools appear to have a *slightly* more competitive climate than either the secondary or community schools (Table A22). The competitive context here, of course, is not academic.

When we compared schools in terms of the prizes awarded for curriculum work, we found that girls' schools were again slightly more likely than others to give prizes for school work: 52.4 per cent of them gave prizes, compared with 40 per cent of boys' schools and 40 per cent of co-educational schools. Differences between community/comprehensive schools and secondary and vocational schools were not significant either, yet community/comprehensive schools were more likely to give prizes for school work than the other two; 80 per cent of community schools reported awarding prizes compared with 40.7 per cent of each of the others. Large schools and those in cities or large towns were also significantly ($P < 0.01$) more likely to give prizes for school work than either smaller schools or those in villages or rural areas (Table A23).

Differences between schools in the awarding of prizes for school work, therefore, are similar in a number of ways to those which emerged when we examined continuous assessment and internal examination procedures. Big schools and those in cities are more frequently to the fore in competitiveness than small schools or those in rural areas. Girls' schools generally exceed boys' or co-educational schools also in this dimension. While community and secondary schools both exhibit greater emphasis on assessment than vocational schools, community schools tend to lay greater stress on competitive assessment at times than secondary schools.

Table 17. The proportion of schools giving prizes/rewards for school work and extracurricular activities

Activity	N	%
School (curriculum) work	37	43.0
Extracurricular activities	74	86.0

N = 86

Principals were also asked here about the holding of prize-giving ceremonies, be they for the awarding of prizes for examination-related or extracurricular accomplishments. Just over half of them, 53.5 per cent (N = 46) did have prize-giving ceremonies, usually once a year. Only five schools had them more frequently than that. Once again differences emerged between the various types of schools. Differences were in the expected direction with regard to size, gender and school location. Girls' schools were significantly (P < 0.01) more likely to have prize-giving ceremonies than boys' schools (76 per cent of girls' schools had them compared with 30 per cent of boys'). They were also a good deal more likely to have them than co-educational schools, 53 per cent of which held prize-giving ceremonies. Small schools were also the least likely to have them as were schools in rural areas. Differences here were not statistically significant, however. The one somewhat unusual finding was that vocational schools were the most likely to have prize-giving ceremonies — although the differences between themselves and community schools were very small, 63 per cent compared with 60 per cent — and secondary schools were least likely to have them (48 per cent). As it is clear from the findings on gender that it is the male secondary schools which were least likely to hold prize-giving ceremonies, this lack of emphasis on prize-giving depresses the total score for the secondary sector.

Our findings on prize-giving show that prize-giving for extra-curricular activities is a very pervasive practice in Irish second-level schools. It occurs in at least 75 per cent of all kinds of schools. Prize-giving for curricular-related work is less frequent; it occurs in less than half (43 per cent) of the schools and there is quite a lot of variability between the various types of schools in whether prizes are awarded or not. Finally, the same holds true for prize-giving ceremonies themselves. They are held in just over half the schools, but the gender (especially), size, location and administrative style of the schools, all seem to have some bearing on whether or not these ceremonies are held.

When prizes are awarded in schools, especially in the extra-curricular areas, they are not necessarily individual rewards. Consequently, principals were asked to give some information on the types of activities and people (i.e. individuals or groups) who were awarded prizes in their schools. The intention here was to see if schools tried to counterbalance the clearly individualistic character of competition in formal curriculum studies with a more collectivistic-type competition in their awarding of prizes. As we can see from Table 18 this was clearly not the case in the awarding of prizes for academic work. The schools' prize-giving system actually reinforced the individualistic competitiveness of the formal examination system.

Out of a total of 93 prizes given in the 37 schools which awarded prizes

Table 18. *The type of persons and activities which are awarded prizes in the formal curriculum-related sphere*

Person and activity rewarded	No. of prizes given	% of all prizes given	N
Individual awards for success in internal or public examinations	38	40.9	37
Individual awards for success in one particular subject only	31	33.3	37
Individual awards for positive work attitudes (e.g. improvement in work, diligence etc.)	16	17.2	37
Group award for project work	8	8.6	37
Total	93	100.0	

for school work, only 8 (8.6 per cent) were for group projects. All the rest were individual awards mostly for success in some kind of examination. It is interesting to note here too that in 7 of the 8 cases in which group work was awarded, it happened in secondary schools (3 female, 2 male, and 2 co-educational). The only other school to give a group award was a vocational one.

Seventy-four (86 per cent) schools gave some kind of prize for extracurricular accomplishments. Those schools were then asked to specify whether prizes were awarded to individuals or groups. Table 19 gives a breakdown of the practices. Details were not obtained on every single prize given, hence there are a lot more prizes awarded than the 114 which appear on the table. Schools were merely asked to signify whether they gave prizes

Table 19. *The awarding of prizes for extracurricular activities*

	No. of responses	% of responses	% of schools awarding each	No. of schools
Only individual prizes awarded for non-sporting activities	43	37.7	58.1	74
Only individual prizes awarded in sport	7	6.1	9.4	74
Both individual and team prizes awarded in sport	54	47.4	73.0	74
Only group/team prizes awarded for both sport and non-sporting activities	10	8.8	13.5	74
Total	114	100.0		

for sport or for non-sporting activities and secondly whether these prizes were for individuals or groups.

What is evident from Table 19 is the greater tendency to reward collective accomplishments in the extracurricular field (of sport especially) compared with the curricular one. In almost half the cases (54, 47.8 per cent) team effort was rewarded in sport and in a further 8.8 per cent of cases, team effort was rewarded in both sport and non-sporting activity. Because the schools which give prizes for team success in sport also give prizes to individuals, overall, individual success seems to be highly rewarded in the extracurricular sphere as well as in the curricular.[1] In only 10 (8.8 per cent) of the 114 cases are team prizes the only ones given in the school. In fact, outside of sport, most prizes awarded are given to individuals.

When we examine the pattern of extracurricular prize-giving in different types of schools the patterns identified in the overall group persist with certain variations. Most importantly perhaps, one finds *individual* success to be the type which is most persistently rewarded. As it is in the non-sporting areas (drama, music, art, debating and general behaviour for example) that individual prize-giving is most exclusively concentrated, it is interesting to compare various types of schools on this practice. Bearing in mind that larger proportions of female schools give extracurricular prizes than boys' or co-educational schools in the first place, we found that 90 per cent of girls' schools give individual prizes in the non-sport areas compared with 33.3 per cent of boys' schools and 51.3 per cent of co-educational schools. Medium-sized schools and those in cities and large towns are also more likely to give them than either very small, very large schools, or those in towns and villages. Finally, one finds that community and secondary schools are a lot more likely to give individual prizes in the non-sport areas than vocational schools, the figures being 75 per cent of community/comprehensive schools and 67.4 per cent of secondary schools with individual prize-giving, compared with 37.5 per cent of vocational schools.

Although only seven schools gave prizes for sport solely to individuals, it is interesting to note that all were secondary schools, three being boys' schools, three being co-educational and only one being a girls' school. Thus, it seems that boys' schools are slightly more likely than girls to give individual rewards in sport, while girls' schools are a lot more likely than boys to give rewards (mainly individual) for non-sporting successes.

One might expect schools which reward individual success not to place such a high value on collective accomplishments. Such does not seem to be the case; rather we found those schools which were most likely to give individual rewards to be the ones which were also most likely to give group rewards. For example, 20 per cent of girls' schools gave team prizes only, compared with 13.3 per cent of boys' schools, and 10.3 per cent of those which were co-educational; 25 per cent of community/comprehensive schools gave group prizes compared with 13.0 per cent of secondary and 12.5 per cent of vocational schools.

What our data on prize-giving suggests, therefore, is that whenever prize-giving occurs — and prizes are awarded in almost 80 per cent of all types of schools for extracurricular activities and in slightly less than half the schools for curriculum-related achievements — it tends to reinforce rather than counterbalance the competitive individualism of the formal school system. Almost all the prizes (91.4 per cent) awarded for curriculum-related work are given to individuals (Table 18). While 56 per cent (64) of the prize-giving systems in the extracurricular area involve the rewarding of the group effort a far higher proportion of them, 91.2 per cent (104), involve giving rewards to individuals (Table 19). Outside of sport almost all the extracurricular rewards given are to individuals rather than groups.

Class Allocation and Selection at Entry

The Pervasiveness of Meritocratic Individualism

In our discussion so far it has emerged that differences exist between schools in the level of competitive individualism evident in their internal evaluation and reward systems. It was noted how girls' secondary schools tended at all times to be the most competitive. Community and comprehensive schools were also found at times to be more competitive than secondary schools as a whole — especially in terms of the giving of end-of-term reports on examination classes, having compulsory continuous assessment and in the awarding of prizes for school work. Our focus so far, therefore, has been primarily on the degree of competitiveness in one area of the school's productive sub-system — the evaluation of student competence in the acquisition of formal curriculum knowledge. We have shown also, of course, how evaluation is not just confined to the formal productive sub-system, it also exists in the extracurricular area. In so far as extracurricular activities are defined as servicing the formal productive system, they are part of the schools' maintenance and procedural system. In so far as they are defined as a knowledge system in their own right, they form an ancillary productive sub-system in the school. Whichever way we define them, however, it is clear that competition between individuals is reinforced by the methods of awarding prizes in this area within schools.

To confine our discussion on competitiveness to the process of evaluation would be to misrepresent the extent of it in second-level schools. There are two stages prior to evaluation at which pupils generally compete — at entry to second-level schools and when classes are being streamed or banded within schools. *Within-class* competition for credentials therefore is preceded by *between-class* competition and *between-school* competition. Hence, the level of competition which we see in the evaluation system is itself a function of both the level of competition at school entry and the level of competition when pupils are being allocated to classes. If schools can select pupils on the basis of academic competence and can then allocate them hierarchically into different classes, the need for a pressurized evaluation system would seem less than if they have either non-selective entrants or mixed classes. We will proceed from here, therefore, to examine the process of competition at both the entry phase and the class allocation phase in second-level schools.

Ability Grouping:[2] Competition for Favourable Places

One of the major findings of Hannan *et al.*'s study (1983: 146, 317) is that the level at which one is offered a subject in second-level schools, or indeed whether one is offered certain subjects at all, depends on the group to which one is allocated. Consequently, if students wish to have access to higher level courses they must also gain access to high streams or bands within which this type of knowledge is distributed. The extent to which students are currently competing with each other for favourable places in this distribution process becomes evident from our data on class-grouping (Table 20).

Over three-quarters of schools in our sample divided pupils into streams or bands for some, if not all, subjects. When one excludes the seven (8.1 per cent) schools which were too small to group pupils, one finds that 83.5 per cent of all those engaged in grouping actually practise streaming or banding. Only 5.1 per cent of schools which are in a position to group pupils practise mixed ability grouping exclusively. Setting is also a very common

Table 20. Proportion of schools using various methods for grouping pupils in classes

	N	%
Entirely streaming	23	26.7
Streaming or banding combined with setting	20	23.3
Streaming combined with mixed classes and setting	23	26.7
Entirely setting	2	2.3
Setting and mixed classes	7	8.1
Entirely mixed classes	4	4.7
Not applicable (only one class in each year)	7	8.1
Total	86	100.0

practice although usually in combination with streaming or banding. Setting is most common at Leaving Certificate level as almost all subjects have higher and lower level papers. Students may opt for the higher course in one and the lower course in another, therefore rigid streaming is not practicable. Two other factors facilitating setting are the wider subject options at senior level and the smaller numbers due to drop-out at the Intermediate Certificate.

When we compare the grouping practices in different types of schools the persistence of streaming or banding is still in evidence. What is interesting, however, is the fact that the types of school which were less likely than others to be competitive in their evaluation systems are now found to be the most competitive. That is to say, boys' schools are a lot more likely than girls' schools especially, and than co-educational schools as well, to have all classes streamed. Secondly, vocational schools are also far more likely to have streaming in all classes than either secondary or community schools. From Table 21 we can see the differences between male schools and female schools very clearly. Almost half of the male schools (47.4 per cent) operate a straight system of streaming compared to only 15 per cent of girls' schools. Indeed streaming or banding of some form exists in 94.8 per cent of boys' second-level schools compared with 70 per cent of girls' schools. Differences also emerge between vocational and secondary schools (Table 22). Almost all (95.6 per cent) vocational schools operate some system of streaming or banding compared with 76.5 per cent of secondary schools. At the same time, 47.8 per cent of vocational schools stream all classes while only 21.6 per cent of secondary and 20 per cent of community schools do. It is important to note here, however, that while community and comprehensive schools are a good deal less likely than vocational schools to operate a system of streaming exclusively, streaming or banding of some form existed in all five community/comprehensive schools in the sample.

Table 21.   Gender differences in ability grouping

| Gender | Entirely streaming | Methods of grouping | | Entirely setting | Setting + mixed classes | Entirely mixed classes | N |
		Streaming or banding and setting	Streaming + mixed classes + setting				
Female	15.0	25.0	30.0	5.0	15.0	10.0	20
Male	47.4	26.3	21.1	—	5.3	—	19
Co-Ed.	27.5	25.0	32.5	2.5	7.5	5.0	40
Total no. of schools with each arrangement	23	20	23	2	7	4	79

P = N.S.

Table 22. Differences between vocational, secondary and community/comprehensive schools in ability grouping

| Type | Methods of grouping | | | | | | |
	Entirely streaming	Streaming or banding and setting	Streaming + mixed classes + setting	Entirely setting	Setting + mixed classes	Entirely mixed classes	N
Vocational	47.8	30.4	17.4	4.3	—	—	23
Secondary	21.6	21.6	33.3	2.0	13.7	7.8	51
Community/ comprehensive	20.0	40.0	40.0	—	—	—	5
Total no. of schools with each arrangement	23	20	23	2	7	4	79

P = N.S.

Our data on ability grouping suggests two patterns therefore. Firstly, streaming or banding is the most common method for grouping pupils in all types of Irish second-level schools. Seventy per cent of all types of schools stream or band pupils for some, if not all, classes. Secondly, there seems to be a tendency for those schools — namely vocational and all-male ones — which have lower levels of competition than others at the evaluation phase (i.e. in terms of continuous assessment, in-house examinations and prize-giving) to have the highest levels at the class allocation or ability grouping phase. Community schools, however, seem to have fairly high levels of competition at both the evaluation and allocation phases. Girls' schools occupy a position which is opposite in many ways to boys' schools. While they were the schools most likely to have a strongly competitive evaluation system, they are the least likely to have streaming or banding. Hence, it seems that when competition is low at the class allocation phase, as it is in girls' schools, it will be fairly high at the evaluation phase. The variability between schools therefore is not just in terms of whether or not competition exists within them; rather, they vary in the degree to which they emphasize competition at different stages.

When competition occurs at the evaluation stage it is a more pervasive feature of school life than when it occurs at the class allocation stage because evaluation is a much more constant feature of schooling. Continuous assessment, regular in-house examinations and prize-giving expose all types of pupils to competitive norms. Once pupils are streamed or banded however, it is likely the competitive ethos will be strong only in the top streams or bands (Hargreaves, 1967; Lacey, 1970; Ball, 1981). Furthermore, when principals in our study were asked if pupils tended to stay in the one class group throughout their school career, 62 per cent of them claimed that they did. Evidence from both Northern Ireland and England also suggests that there is little movement between classes once they are streamed (Lunn, 1970; McKernan, 1981). This supports our claim that, once streamed, students tend to be exposed to the same type of normative climate for a considerable part of their school career as they stay in the one class.

Selection by Schools: Competition at School Entry[3]

Work by Clancy (1982) and Raftery and Hout (1985), on the Irish educational system, suggests that pupils attending different types of second-level schools vary considerably both in their length of stay within the educational system and in their probability of entering higher education. Whether differences in outcomes between school types (most notably between vocational and secondary schools) is a function of school intake or school quality is, of course, a subject of recurrent controversy both in Ireland and abroad. This debate is not, however, our immediate concern here. What is our concern is the fact that secondary schools, especially, seem to be perceived as being the more educationally advantageous. This is evident from the fact that almost half the secondary schools in our sample, 46.3 per cent, had more than one application for each place. Vocational schools were rarely in the position that applicants exceed places (11.1 per cent), although overapplication was also experienced by two of the five community/comprehensive schools in the sample. Because community and vocational schools are public they cannot freely select pupils like secondary schools can. Therefore, competition at the school entry phase is very different from that at either the evaluation or class-allocation stage. Not all schools are free to select pupils at will, unlike allocation or evaluation practices. In all, only 24 (28 per cent) of our sample schools engaged in regular selection and all but two of these were secondary schools. However, because secondary schools are still the largest sector of second-level schools — approximately 66 per cent of all second-level schools are secondary and these contain about 60 per cent of all pupils — and because they are all technically free to select at entry, the level of competition for places at certain second-level schools cannot be underestimated.

Our finding on selection practices and competition at school entry confirms our hypothesis about the inevitability of competition and its rotational character. Secondary schools are clearly the most likely schools to operate a competitive system at entry, and vocational schools were the least likely to do so. This pattern is reversed at the class-allocation stage. Vocational schools are the most likely to stream pupils — to order pupils hierarchically on the basis of competitive performance on some academic-type test — while secondary and community schools operate a less stratified system, being more likely to combine streaming or banding with setting or mixed groups for at least some classes. In-school evaluation, on the other hand, is marginally higher in community schools than in secondary, and considerably greater in both of these than in vocational schools.

The rotational character of competitive-individualism is also evident when we compare male and female schools. In the preceding sections we noted how girls' schools were noticeably more likely than boys' schools to have persistent internal evaluation, and how boys' schools on the other hand were a lot more likely than girls' to have all classes streamed. At the entry phase the pattern is again reversed with girls' schools being a lot more likely than boys' to have competition at entry: 62 per cent of girls' schools select regularly while only 30 per cent of male schools and 11 per cent of co-educational schools do. Differences are statistically significant at the $P < 0.01$ levels. Although the proportion of co-educational schools selecting is even smaller than that of boys' schools, what must be borne in mind here is that 66.7 per cent of co-educational schools are public schools (i.e. community, comprehensive or vocational) and hence can only select in very limited circumstances. On the other hand, all of the female schools are secondary and 90 per cent of boys' schools are.

One of the most pervasive features of school life at second level, therefore, is competition between individuals. It occurs at entry to the system when pupils compete with each other for favourable school places; at the time of class allocation when competition for the benefits of high stream/band places is keenest; and finally, in varying degrees, throughout one's school career when prizes (for both extracurricular and curricular activities), grades and ultimately credentials, are distributed to the successful. Before proceeding from here it is important perhaps, to make some comments on the selection and distributive mechanisms which operate at the entry and allocation phase respectively as these provide us with more detailed understanding of the nature of competition.

Procedures for Grouping and Selection

Given the fact that 83.5 per cent of all 79 schools involved in grouping pupils practise streaming or banding with at least some classes, and since these practices are by definition ways of grouping pupils according to perceived academic ability, it is no great surprise to find schools using academic tests or records more frequently than any other method to group pupils (Table 23). Of the 79 schools involved in grouping pupils, 68 (86.1 per cent) used either an academic test or an assessment of the pupils' primary school performance (indeed, quite a few used both) to group the pupils. Even when

Table 23.   Criteria used to allocate pupils to class groups in first year

Criterion	No. of responses	Proportion of all schools using each	Proportion of schools involved in grouping using each	No. of schools involved in grouping
		%	%	
Entrance test	25	29.1	31.6	79
Tests within the 1st year	26	30.2	33.0	79
Standardized achievement tests	28	32.6	35.4	79
IQ Tests	13	15.1	16.5	79
Aptitude tests	2	2.3	2.5	79
Primary school reports	21	24.4	26.6	79
Subject choices	17	19.8	21.5	79
Consult with primary teachers	4	4.7	5.1	79
Consult with parents and child	10	11.7	13.4	79
Alphabetical/random grouping	9	10.5	11.4	79
Total number of methods used	155			

7 schools (8.1%) did not group pupils as they had only one class in each year.

schools used techniques such as consultation with parents or random grouping, these never operated alone. For example, all four schools which consulted primary teachers on how children should be grouped used a standardized test as well. Six of the nine schools which claimed to use random methods to group pupils did so only after subject choices had determined the wider group to which they belonged in the first place. Four of the ten which consulted parents also used a standardized test. The persistent use of academic-type tests and assessments to group pupils, therefore, highlights once again the primacy of academic skills in determining one's status location in the school's hierarchy. Neither school size, gender composition, location or administrative system had any impact on this. While some schools are likely to use one test more than another (for example, both male and female schools are significantly ($P < 0.05$) more likely to use IQ tests than co-educational schools, and community schools are significantly ($P < 0.01$) more likely to use standardized tests than others), these differences are offset by the fact that both co-educational and secondary schools are the most likely to use tests within the school year, while vocational schools are the most likely to use entrance tests to stream.

Contrary to the procedures for class allocation, selection practices at entry do not give primacy to the intellectual. A list of selection procedures operating in the 24 selecting schools is presented in Table 24. Of the 84 procedures used for selection only 9 involve the use of some academic-type test or record. Because 2 of the schools which used an entrance test also used primary school records to select pupils, only 7 of the 24 schools (29 per cent) were involved in the use of academic-type tests at all. What is most striking about selection practices is the extent to which nepotistic-type practices are used. Being a child of a past pupil is used as a selective mechanism just as frequently as is proximity to the school. In all, we found that half the schools engaged in selection used either or both 'child of past pupil' or 'other family connections' as criteria by which to select pupils. Seventeen schools (71 per cent of those selecting) used either 'order of application' or 'proximity to school' as the mode of selection. While it is obvious from these figures that schools do not just use one method of selection, and that the more objective criteria are used more frequenty than the nepotistic-type, many would dispute the objectivity of such criteria as 'order of application' or 'proximity to school'. The former gives priority to pupils whose parents

Table 24.   Criteria used to select pupils at entry

Criterion	No. of procedures	Proportion of all schools using each %	Proportion of those schools which select using each %	No. of schools
Entrance test set by school	5	5.9	20.9	24
Primary school record	4	4.7	16.7	24
Proximity to school	10	11.6	41.7	24
Sibling in the school already*	(14)	(16.3)	(58.3)	24
Past pupils' children	10	11.6	41.7	24
Family connections with school (unspecified)	6	7.0	25.0	24
Prior attendance at the school's own junior school	9	10.5	37.5	24
Order of application	12	14.0	50.0	24
Interview with family/parent to see if they agree with school's aims	6	7.0	25.0	24
Child's own wish	1	1.2	4.2	24
Random selection	1	1.2	4.2	24
Miscellaneous methods	6	7.0	25.0	24
Total procedures	84	100.0		

*This is not a selection procedure, of course, for first entrants.

are educationally wise enough to apply early, while the latter ensures that in class-segregated urbanized areas the school will have a socially selective cohort of entrants.

To analyse the selection practices of schools is a major task in its own right. It is not our immediate concern here. What we wished to establish, and what is clear from Table 24, is that the pupils' academic competence is not a very important criterion in determining their entry to selective second-level schools. It is important to note, however, that academic competence is far more important among the selective boys' schools than among the girls'. Although only 6 (30 per cent) of the boys' schools select compared with 13 (42 per cent) of the girls', none of the selecting girls' schools used an entrance test to select pupils, while two of the selecting boys' schools did. The same proportion of boys' schools also used primary records to select, compared with only 7.7 per cent of girls' schools. The five selective co-educational schools were indeed the most likely of all to use entrance tests with 60 per cent of them using tests. What these figures suggest is that those schools which are most likely to select at entry (girls' secondary schools) are the ones which are least likely to select on the basis of academic tests, while those which are least likely to select (boys' and co-educational schools) are the most likely to use academic-type tests.

The rotational character of individual competition is again evident here therefore. The type of schools which are most competitive at entry are the least likely ones to use stringent academic tests within their selection system. The obverse is true for the least selective schools: these are the most likely to use a competitive examination as a mode of selection.

Conclusions on Competitive Individualism

What the evidence on evaluation, class allocation and selection suggests, therefore, is that competitive individualism is an endemic part of life in second-level schools. The structural organization of school life requires one to compete persistently against others whether one desires to do so or not. Even if one elects (if choice is the appropriate term here at all) not to compete at the entry stage, one will most likely have to compete at the class-allocation stage. Furthermore, if after allocation, one happens to be in one of the few mixed ability classes or in lower streams or bands within streamed schools, one cannot opt out from competition either. Evaluation, and its inevitable correlate, grading, are persistent features of all schools, but most especially of those which do not organize pupils hierarchically at entry.

To argue for the universalistic character of competition is not to deny that it takes particularistic forms. Eight (9 per cent) of the schools in our sample, for example, were private secondary fee-paying schools. By definition all these schools exclude all those pupils whose parents cannot afford to pay fees, although there are occasional exceptions to this. Competition for entry to these schools is, therefore, qualitatively of a different order to that which exists when order of application' or an entrance-test score is the criterion. It also has very definite implications for competition at the class-allocation phase. Because the children of higher income groups are the only ones in a position to seek and attain entry to these schools and because these children (for a variety of cultural and financial reasons) are likely to have fewer basic problems of literacy and numeracy than others, there is less emphasis on rigid streaming. For example, when we compare the class-allocation practices of secondary schools in the free scheme with those of fee-paying schools we find that none of the fee-paying schools operates a straight streaming system, while 24 per cent of the non-fee paying (free scheme) secondary schools do. At the other extreme, half of the fee-paying schools which group pupils (N = 3) had no streaming or banding, while only one-fifth of the free scheme schools (N = 9) were operating that arrangement (Table A24). As with girls' secondary schools, however, the lack of competition for class places was more than offset by the emphasis on competition through continuous assessment and internal examinations. We found that fee-paying secondary schools placed greater emphasis on the latter than either secondary schools in the free-scheme or public schools (i.e. community, comprehensive and vocational schools (Tables A25–8)).

In the way that private fee-paying schools rotate competition they are no different to other schools. In so far as this rotation occurs with a highly socially selective cohort they are worlds apart from *all* non–selective second-level schools.

Hierarchical Control

In Lukes' analysis of individualism he defines autonomy as one of its essential components. The idea of 'autonomy or self-direction' implies that 'an individual's thought and action is his own, and [is] not determined by agencies or causes outside of his control' (1973: 52). Closely allied to this is the notion of privacy, which Lukes also claims to be a key dimension of individualism. To have privacy is to have 'a private existence within a public world, an area within which the individual should be left alone by others and able to do and think whatever he chooses' (ibid., 59). In so far as attendance at school is compulsory (by law) until the age of fifteen, the principle of autonomy is clearly violated in the junior cycle of second-level schools. Much of the pupil's thought and action are determined by agencies outside of his/her control. The degree of external control on the school organization (as discussed at the beginning of Ch. 2) sets the initial limits to pupil autonomy. The length of time spent in school, the type of subjects learned, the distribution of time between subjects are all specified by government regulation. Hence, centralized and external control of the organization means lack of autonomy for pupils. Furthermore, because schools are involved in social selection and allocation, hierarchical control is, in some ways, inevitable. As Livingstone observes:

> Somewhat as the social relations of capitalist production have become characterized by extensive supervisory hierarchies and impersonal rules in the attempt to control wage labourers and better extract their labour, the school system has taken on a similar social organization in order to control and select students and to accomplish its own social division of labour (1983: 100).

In spite of this, however, schools do have autonomy in a number of their organizational procedures. For example, the way in which pupils are grouped in classes, the organization of extracurricular activities and the disciplinary system of the school are all matters in which the schools can exercise great discretion. We will proceed, therefore, to analyse the level of pupil involvement in these areas.

Class Allocation and Subject Choices

In Table 23 above we identified the various practices for grouping pupils into classes. In only 10 schools (11.7 per cent of all schools) were pupils consulted. In fact, there were only 6 schools (7 per cent) in which the pupils' wishes were considered independent of their parents. Although it might seem from Table 23 that a reasonable cohort of pupils had autonomy in determining their group placement, in so far as the pupils' subject choices were considered in determining their group placement in almost one-fifth of schools, it must be borne in mind that in 47 per cent of these same schools, restrictions were imposed on pupils' subject choices. Consequently, there were only nine schools in which unrestricted subject choice was a determinant (though never the sole one) of group position. The fact that the principal restriction imposed on subject choice at junior level was the pupils' academic ability (as determined by some or all of the test or assessment procedures identified in Table 23) shows even further how limited pupils' choices are. Of the 81 restrictions identified in the 48 schools which imposed limits on pupils' subject choices, 55.6 per cent were pertaining to the pupils' academic ability. Restrictions arising from administrative considerations (not having large enough numbers in a subject to form a class or the availability of teachers in a given year) were the next most frequently mentioned, with 11.1 per cent of schools claiming these as reasons to restrict pupils' choices. Academic ability (as determined by Intermediate Certificate results) was also the major factor restricting one's subject choice at senior level, although the staff's opinion (no doubt also informed by pupils' perceived academic ability) was also of considerable importance at this stage.

Restrictions on subject choices are not as pervasive as those imposed on class grouping. Only just over half the schools claimed to impose restrictions on subject choices at junior (54.7 per cent) and at senior (56.6 per cent) level. This contrasts with a figure of 86.1 per cent of schools using academic ability to stream or band pupils. Having choice of subjects is, however, of less consequence than choice of stream or band for at least two reasons. Firstly, both examination and third level entry requirements (as identified in the opening part of Ch. 2) predetermine the central core of pupils' options in the first place. Secondly, the subject choices one has are greatly circumscribed in a streamed or banded situation. As Hannan and Boyle (1987: 75) have shown, being located in low streams limits one's chances of gaining access to high-status knowledge (i.e. higher level courses). This, combined with school policies in deploying resources when classes are streamed (cf. Hargreaves, 1967, for example), greatly reduces one's chances of gaining access to the type and level of credential required for access to high-status occupations. Although 40 per cent of schools do allow pupils autonomy in subject choice, therefore — within the limits imposed by the Department of Education and third-level colleges — this autonomy seems rather insignificant when one realizes that it is preceded in 63.6 per cent of cases in the junior cycle and in 76.4 per cent of cases at senior level by some form of streaming or banding.

Pupils' lack of autonomy with regard to group position is complemented by their lack of choice in other matters pertaining to the school's productive sub-system. For example, when asked about persons consulted regarding the introduction of new subjects into the curriculum, only two schools reported seeking pupil opinion. In no school did pupils have a say in the appointment of new teachers, or in the timetabling of teachers. Other matters of general school policy, such as whether or not it should be single sex or how big it should be, were also clearly outside the zone of student influence. Even on the sensitive issue of displaying examination results publicly within the school, none of the eight schools (9.3 per cent) which engaged in it said that pupils had any choice in the matter.

Although the focus of our study was not on privacy *per se*, one practice within the school day which gives us some idea of levels of privacy is the use of free class periods. Given the public pressures on teachers to prepare pupils for examinations within the timetable period, and indeed the school organization's requirement that order be maintained (Metz, 1978), there seems to be little scope for privacy within class time. The pupil's psychic energy is meant to be directed toward the lesson material under the teacher's direction, while her/his physical bearing is expected to bear witness to her/his psychic concentration; no 'gazing out the window', 'lounging over the desks', etc. Consequently, within the formal teaching day the pupil has little private space, either physically or mentally. With the exception of lunch breaks there is no officially private time in school, and even this is not totally private. Between–class time (which is officially non–existent on timetables) does allow one some scope for privacy. It is, however, of very limited duration. Because free periods are the only officially classified as free times for pupils, it is interesting to see to what extent they are 'free'.

Almost three-quarters of the schools had free periods for at least some of its pupils, while 25.6 per cent had no free periods at all during the school day. Female schools were significantly ($P < 0.05$) more likely to have free classes than either male or co-educational schools. All community and comprehensive schools had free periods compared to 83.3 per cent of secondary schools and 51.9 per cent of vocational schools. Differences were significant at the $P < 0.01$ level. Neither school size or location has any significant effect on the existence of free classes.

Differences between school types in the provision of free classes, however, are less important as indicators of privacy than they might first appear. In all but one of the 64 schools with free periods, pupils are expected to work/study during their free classes. We see therefore that although pupils can pursue private interests, the parameters of these interests are tightly circumscribed. The fact that one is expected to study in a designated place during one's free time means that the differences between schools with or without free periods are not very important in terms of pupil privacy. Furthermore, it should be noted that free periods are mostly the prerogative of senior students.

The Ancillary Curriculum: Extracurricular Activities and Pupil Autonomy

One aspect of school life which is not subject to tight external control is its extracurricular programme. Consequently, schools have considerable scope to develop in this area, and to involve pupils in the process. Principals were asked two questions pertaining to pupils' involvement in the extracurricular programmes. Firstly, whether pupils played any role in *introducing* activities into the school, and secondly, whether they played any role in *organizing* them once initiated.

Pupils were only involved in the initiation of new activities into the

school in 13 (15.2 per cent) cases. There were only three schools in which $\times$ 2
pupils were the most likely group to introduce new activities. Helping to
organize extracurricular activities clearly does not symbolize as high a level
of autonomy as does initiation and it is in this area that pupils are most likely
to be involved. We found that pupils helped in organizing extracurricular
activities in 38 per cent of schools. The opportunities for pupils to take
initiative or administrative responsibility in the extracurricular area are limited
therefore in Irish schools. Only a minority permit even the more limited
forms of involvement.

No significant differences emerge when we compare different types of
schools in their level of pupil involvement in the initiation of extracurricular
activities (Tables A29–A32). However, there are statistically significant
differences between schools in terms of pupils' involvement at the
organizational level (Tables A29–A32). Girls' schools are a lot more likely
to have pupils involved than either boys' or co-educational schools. Equally,
larger schools are considerably more likely to have pupils involved than small
ones, as indeed are schools in cities. No significant differences exist between
vocational, secondary and community schools, although secondary schools
are slightly more likely than the others to have pupils' involved in the
organization of events. Pupils in girls' schools, in schools in cities, and in
large schools would seem, therefore, to be the most involved in the
organization of extracurricular events. There is no evidence, however, that
these schools are radically different to others at the initiation stage.

Religious Socialisation and Autonomy

In Irish second-level schools, socialization into one's appropriate
denominational culture is a major feature of school life. As we saw in the
section on the distribution of time between subjects, religion is the only non-
examination subject which is allocated similar periods of time to the
examination subjects. As there are no governmental rules specifying how
and when it should be taught, religious education is strictly speaking not
part of the formal curriculum. It seems appropriate, therefore, to include
discussion on religious education under the broad term of ancillary
curriculum.

In all the schools in which we interviewed, circumstantial evidence
suggests that pupils were expected to attend the timetabled religious classes
appropriate to their specified denomination. Although no specific question
was asked regarding compulsory attendance at religion classes *per se*, it was
evident from a variety of questions pertaining to religion and timetabling
that pupils were expected to attend religious classes in the same way as they
were expected to attend all other classes. We found, for example, that there

were 22 classes in which pupils had free periods because they were 'exempt from a given subject'. In none of these cases was religion identified as a subject from which pupils were exempt. (Irish was indeed the most commonly mentioned one.) Principals did indicate that pupils were exempted from religious classes if there was no person available to provide classes in their religion, or if their parents expressly wished them to be exempted — in which cases they went to study. These pupils were, however, the exception rather than the rule.

Unlike our indirect evidence on compulsory attendance at religious classes, we have direct evidence regarding pupils' attendance at religious services. The findings are presented in Table 25. Eighty-four of the 86 schools had religious services organized during the school year. In all, 114 types of services were identified, the majority (69 or 60.5 per cent) being held on a regular basis. Although there were more regular than irregular services in schools, most pupils had a choice about attending the former. Compulsory attendance at regular services for all pupils was required in only 19 (16.7 per cent) incidences. It must be pointed out, however, that in the 47 classes in which services were regular and voluntary (usually masses organized for individual classes) many principals did stress that while attendance was voluntary in principle, pupils rarely if ever asked to be exempted from attending them.

Unlike regular services, attendance at infrequent services, such as annual school masses, was compulsory in a majority of cases (25 of the 43 or 58.1 per cent) in which they existed. The norm with regard to attendance at religious services therefore seems to be that most pupils have a choice about attending regular schools services — at least in principle — while most do not have a choice about attending the more formal infrequent services. In 68.1 per cent of the cases in which regular services existed, all pupils had a choice,

Table 25. *Choice granted to pupils regarding attendance at religious services*

Level of choice and frequency of service	No. of responses	% of responses	No. of schools
Regular service (at least once per month): compulsory attendance for all	19	16.7	84
Regular services: compulsory for some only, e.g. boarders	3	2.6	84
Regular services: voluntary for all	47	41.2	84
Infrequent services: compulsory for all (once per term or less)	25	21.9	84
Infrequent services: voluntary for all	18	15.8	84
Services for Catholics only: no information given on level of choice	2	1.8	84
	114	100.0	

while only 41.9 per cent had a choice about infrequent services. It would seem, therefore, that pupils have a reasonable level of autonomy with regard to one aspect of their religious socialization. While they must attend instruction on the tenets of their religion in classes the majority are not forced to attend regularly at those services in which beliefs are given ritualistic expression.

Not all types of schools are the same, however, in the level of autonomy granted in religious services. For example, although boys' schools are the most likely to have regular services, they are slightly less likely than either girls' or co-educational schools to make attendance at these services compulsory. Also, although services tend to be more irregular in co-educational and girls' schools than in boys', attendance at these services is much more likely to be compulsory in the former: while only 10.5 per cent of boys' schools required compulsory attendance at the infrequent services listed, 38 per cent of girls' schools and 34 per cent of co-educational schools required it. Lack of frequency in services provision, therefore, in girls' and co-educational schools seems to be compensated for by making the services which are provided compulsory.

Vocational schools were by far the least likely type of school to have regular religious services. They were also a good deal less likely than either secondary or community schools to make attendance at regular services compulsory: attendance at regular religious services was compulsory in only 8 per cent of vocational schools compared with 30 per cent of secondary and 20 per cent of community and comprehensive schools. Vocational schools were also the most likely to have irregular religious services and to make attendance at these compulsory. However, the differences between vocational and secondary schools in the extent to which infrequent services were compulsory, was not very great.

Overall, therefore, vocational schools seem to be the type which allow pupils most autonomy in attending religious services. Secondary schools allow least autonomy, while community and comprehensive schools occupy an intermediate position. While all-male schools also allow pupils slightly more autonomy than girls' or co-educational schools in choosing to attend services, it must be remembered that this lack of compulsoriness is offset by the high level of provision of regular services in boys' schools.

Pupil Autonomy and the Maintenance Sub-System

The question of discipline

One of the aspects of school life in which schools are relatively autonomous is in the organization of their disciplinary system. They are free to involve pupils in the disciplinary system of the school if they so wish. Consequently, we decided to obtain information from principals on the disciplinary procedures in their schools; to see if pupils were involved in either their construction or maintenance.

Only one school claimed to involve pupils (viz. senior prefects) in the construction of their disciplinary procedures. Rules and sanctions were normally worked out by the staff and/or the principal. It is obvious, therefore, that pupils do not have autonomy in the construction of rules and sanctions which apply to themselves in 99 per cent of second-level schools. Pupils were involved, however, in the maintenance of order via the prefectship system. Fifty-four schools (62.8 per cent) had prefects and the majority of the 54 (57.4 per cent) had prefects for each class. There was, however, a good deal of variability between different types of schools in the area of prefectships. Ninety per cent of girls' schools had prefects compared with only 55 per cent of boys' and 53 per cent of co-educational schools; 82 per cent of schools in cities and large towns had them compared with 57 per cent of those in medium-sized towns and 52 per cent of those in towns and villages with ≤ 1500 people. Finally, 74 per cent of secondary schools had them compared with 44.4 per cent of vocational schools and 40 per cent of community and comprehensive schools. Differences in all three cases are statistically significant (Tables A29–A32). It would seem, therefore, that pupils in girls' schools, those in cities and large towns, and those in secondary schools, are the most likely to exercise control in the maintenance of the schools' disciplinary system. Their autonomy is in interpreting the rules, however, not in defining them. Furthermore, when we analyse the character of the tasks undertaken by prefects in schools we see how limited pupils' control actually is. As Table 26 shows, only 35.7 per cent of the tasks in which prefects engage involve exercising control or authority. Helping in the administration of activities and acting as a liaison between staff and pupils are their primary tasks. Indeed, these findings concur with the reasons given by principals for having prefects in the first place. Only 25 per cent of the reasons given stated that the prefectship system was designed to teach pupils a sense of responsibility. The main reasons for having prefects were to help

Table 26. Tasks undertaken by prefects

Tasks	No. of responses	% of responses	% of schools	No. of schools
Assist in the control system	35	35.7	64.8	54
Help in the organization and administration of the school	36	36.7	66.7	54
Act in a mediating capacity	27	27.6	50.0	54
Total responses	98	100.0		

in the administration of school events and to maintain good relations between staff and pupils. Girls' schools and secondary schools were also the most likely to have pupils involved in the control system just as they were the most likely to have prefects in the first place. Schools in cities or large towns were no more likely than those elsewhere, however, to designate control tasks to their prefects.

Pupil autonomy in the control system is also measured by the degree of pupil choice in the election of prefects. If pupils are not free to select the representatives they desire, then clearly they have less power to influence control procedures than might appear from merely counting the (albeit high) proportion of schools with prefects. Of the 54 schools with prefects in our sample, only just over half, 53.7 per cent, actually allowed pupils a totally free choice in the selection of prefects. In 20.4 per cent of schools prefects were chosen entirely by staff, while both staff and students were involved in their selection in the remaining 25.9 per cent of schools. It is interesting to note too that although girls' schools were more likely than boys' or co-educational schools to have prefects and to involve them in the control system, they were the least likely to allow pupils freedom in choosing them. The same kind of situation obtains in secondary schools compared with the vocational sector; while the former were the most likely to have prefects and to give them control, they were a good deal less likely than the vocational sector to allow students a totally free choice. Finally, no community school allowed pupils a free choice in selecting prefects. Differences arising from both gender composition or administrative type are not statistically significant, however.

Mode of dress

The mode of dress required of pupils in school is not specified by any state regulation. Schools are free, therefore, to allow pupils considerable autonomy in this area if they choose to give it. Most Irish second-level schools do not allow pupils much autonomy in their dress however, as 68.6 per cent (n = 59) of them require pupils to wear a uniform.

Moreover, a majority (74.6 per cent) of those requiring a uniform expect all pupils to wear it at all times. The fifteen schools which have a uniform but do not insist on it being worn by all pupils show interesting gender differences. Nine of the fifteen did not expect boys to wear the uniform. It must be noted that this practice was being changed in three of the schools — uniforms were being made compulsory for boys too the year after the study was completed. Senior pupils were the other major exception to the uniform rules, 20 per cent of those exempted were senior pupils.

Significant gender differences were evident in three major matters of dress: all of the girls' schools required pupils to wear uniforms but only 50 per cent of boys' schools and 62.2 per cent of co-educational schools demanded it; 100 per cent of girls' schools required all pupils to wear their uniform at all times, while only 70 per cent of male schools and 57.1 per cent of co-educational schools required it; finally, 90.5 per cent of girls' schools had a variety of other rules on dress (apart from those re uniform) while these existed in only 55 per cent of male and 48.9 per cent of co-educational schools (Table A29). Finally, 66.7 per cent of girls' schools claimed to be very strict in their enforcement of rules on uniform, while only 30 per cent of boys' and 39.3 per cent of co-educational schools were.

It may not be surprising to find gender differences in levels of autonomy permitted in mode of dress. However, what it does show is that those pupils who are most likely to exercise choice in dress (girls, at least in our society) are those least likely to be granted autonomy to do so within schools. Evidence from cities and large towns also support this claim as schools in these areas were a good deal less likely than those in rural areas or villages to be granted autonomy in dress. (Differences arising from school location are statistically significant, however, in only one case.) As with girls, pupils in cities would be more exposed to a variety of modes of dress than those in rural areas. They would, therefore, be the most likely to exercise choice. Schools, however, do not permit it.

Significant differences in pupils' autonomy in the area of dress were also found between secondary, vocational and community schools: 83.3 per cent of secondary schools had uniforms compared with only 40.7 per cent of vocational schools and 60 per cent of community and comprehensives. Secondary schools were also the most likely to have a variety of rules pertaining to dress, other than uniform. However, all the community schools which had uniforms made it compulsory for all pupils, while this happened in fewer secondary schools (93.3 per cent) and in far fewer vocational schools (36.4 per cent).

While differences between vocational and secondary schools, especially, are very real in terms of pupils' right to free expression in dress, two important factors must be borne in mind. Hannan *et al.* (1983) have pointed out that vocational schools 'cater mainly for pupils from working class or small farm origins' (p. 89); furthermore, 60.7 per cent of those attending vocational schools in the year this study was carried out were male (cf. Department of Education, *Statistical Report*, 1981/82: 102). The dominant group in vocational schools, therefore, are working-class boys or those from small farms. These are not the most likely group in our society to want to express their individuality through dress. Consequently, the relative autonomy of dress in vocational schools may merely reflect the tendency, identified above already, to grant most choice in dress to pupils who are the least likely to want to exercise it.

Conclusions Regarding Autonomy and Control

The relational context within which Irish pupils are socialized in second-level schools is profoundly hierarchical. Pupils have little control over either what they do in school, when they do it or how they do it. In neither the school's productive sub-system or its maintenance sub-system are pupils granted much autonomy.

With regard to the schools' productive sub-system (viz. the organization of the formal curriculum and its presentation) we have seen how pupils are consulted in only 12 per cent of schools about the group or stream to which they wish to belong. While pupils are given a choice about certain subjects in over 40 per cent of schools at both senior and junior level, the majority of schools still impose (almost always academic) restrictions. Furthermore, the choice open to pupils within the 40 per cent with unrestricted choices is delimited in the first place by the stream or band to which the pupil has been allocated. In addition, at both junior and senior level, external controls — in the form of government regulation and third-level requirements — operate to constrain real choices in all schools.

Neither do pupils have any autonomy in determining school policies which might affect their formal learning. Only two schools consulted pupils about the adoption or exclusion of subjects from the timetable, while no schools allowed pupils involvement in the appointment of teachers or in their allocation to classes. Even in the 9.3 per cent of schools which publicly displayed test and/or examination results, pupils were not consulted on the matter. Likewise, when pupils are nominally given free periods we find that they have little option as to how they use their time. Even senior pupils must work/study in a designated place.

In the realm of what we termed the ancillary curriculum — the non-examination knowledge systems — we also found little evidence of pupil autonomy. Only 15.2 per cent of schools actually involved pupils in the initiation of extracurricular activities into the school. While 38.4 per cent allowed pupils to assist in the organization of activities, this clearly involves very little exercise of power. There was no evidence either that pupils had much choice about attending formal religion classes. Religion was never mentioned as a subject from which pupils were exempted. There was choice, however, regarding attendance at religious services, especially if these were held regularly. Some interesting differences between various types of schools also emerged in this area. While boys' schools were the most likely to have regular services, they were the least likely to have compulsory services. Girls' schools had fewer services, but more compulsory ones than boys'. Vocational schools were the only type of schools where pupils clearly had more autonomy than those elsewhere regarding attendance at religious services.

Finally, we also examined pupil autonomy in forming and implementing the rules and regulations of the school, and in determining their own mode of dress. Here we found that while 63 per cent of schools involved pupils in the implementation of rules — via the prefectship system — only one school involved pupils in formulating school policy on discipline. Furthermore, in practice, prefects were primarily involved in assisting in the administration of the school, not in exercising power. Pupils' lack of autonomy in determining the rules which influenced their own lives is also shown by the fact that the schools which were most likely to have prefects *and* to give them authority (girls' schools and secondary schools) were the least likely to allow pupils a free choice in choosing prefects. Even when a student council or student union existed in the school, as was the case in 22.1 per cent and 3.5 per cent of schools respectively, there was little evidence that these exercised any more power than prefects. In all but one case, the functions of the council or union were stated to be either those of administration or mediation.

There was little evidence either that pupils exercised choice in their mode of dress as 69 per cent of schools required pupils to wear a uniform. Although boys' schools and vocational schools were significantly more likely to have autonomy in this area than girls' schools, it must be borne in mind that pupils in the former type of school are quite likely not to want to exercise choice in dress to a great extent. The cultural mores of our society do not encourage boys to express their individuality through dress to the same extent that they encourage it among girls.

Even when pupils are granted autonomy in schools, therefore, it is usually a circumscribed autonomy. While prefects in girls' schools are the most likely to be involved in the exercise of control, pupils in these schools have the least freedom of choice in selecting prefects; while boys have considerable autonomy in their mode of dress compared with girls, school authorities know that peer-group mores among boys are such that they act as an external control on their exercise of choice in dress. Even when principals were reporting on pupil choice regarding attendance at religious services — in particular class masses — a number pointed out that, while pupils were free in principle to attend or not, in practice it was 'unthinkable' that they would not attend. The school did not have to require attendance as the cultural mores make it unnecessary.

Unlike our data on competitive individualism, we find few areas of school life in which schools differ widely in the autonomy granted to pupils.

One such area is religious practice. Here we find that pupils in vocational schools are a good deal more likely than those in secondary (especially) and community schools to be allowed the freedom to exercise choice. Vocational schools were also significantly more likely than other schools to allow pupils freedom of choice in dress as indeed were boys' schools compared with girls' schools.

Notes

1 There is, however, a problem of comparability here. By definition teams are less numerous in schools than individuals; therefore, it is questionable whether one can compare the proportion of prizes for teams with those for individuals. The crudeness of the measure must be borne in mind when interpreting findings here. The same question arises in Table 18.
2 The phrase 'ability-grouping' is normally used to describe the process of allocating pupils to streams or tracks. There is an implicit essentialist suggestion in this term that some pupils have 'ability' while others have not. We do not subscribe to this thesis (Lynch, 1987b). All pupils have some kind of ability. It may not, however, be an ability or competence which is highly appreciated in schools in our culture at this time in history (cf. Gardner, 1983 for a discussion of this issue).
3 Since the data for this study were collected in 1982, there has been a steady decline in the birth rate. This will no doubt affect selection practices in time: with declining numbers, many schools will not be in a position to select at entry.

Chapter 4

Conclusions from Research Data: With Special Reference to Some Particularistic Features of Schooling

Particularism in the Production and Relational Life of Schools

In Chapters 2 and 3 we have identified three universalistic orientations within the second-level educational system: the bias towards the technical development of the individual within the productive sub-system; the competitive individualism which characterizes relations between pupils in both their formal curriculum and ancillary curriculum learning; and the lack of individual autonomy permitted to pupils within both the productive and maintenance sub-systems of school life. However, as noted in Chapter 1, the hidden curriculum of the school is not solely universalistic in character. The universalistic aspects of school life interface with the particularistic, to reproduce the existing pattern of educational relations. In this chapter then, we shall show how particularism is as much a feature of the school's productive and maintenance sub-systems as is universalism.

Like Hannan *et al.* (1983) our data shows that vocational and community/comprehensive schools are the only ones with a comprehensive range of practical subjects (see Tables 2 and 4 above and Tables A12, A13). On the other hand, vocational schools are far less likely than either secondary or community schools to offer chemistry or physics at Leaving Certificate level (Table A15). What these findings show is the social-class specificity of knowledge dissemination within the technical knowledge sphere itself. The schools with the highest working-class and small farming cohorts (vocational schools) make comprehensive provision for disseminating knowledge and skills which are appropriate for workers at the lower end of the technical spectrum (via woodwork, construction skills, metalwork, for example) while comprehensive provision is not made for these in the more middle-class secondary sector. Indeed it should be noted that there are important differences within the secondary sector itself reflecting the further class divisions within this sector.

While 47.8 per cent of secondary schools in the free scheme (i.e. non-fee-paying) offered woodwork in the junior cycle, none of the fee-paying secondary schools did. Similarly with mechanical drawing: 46 per cent of free-scheme secondary schools offered it but only one of the eight fee-paying schools did. From Table 27 one can see that the same patterns emerge at the Leaving Certificate for technical drawing and construction studies, although engineering has a similar status in both types of schools: 43.5 per cent of the 'free' secondary schools offered technical drawing, while no fee-paying school did; 13 per cent of free-scheme schools offered construction studies and no fee-paying schools did; approximately 13 per cent of both types of school offered engineering. When we compare free-scheme secondary schools with the fee-paying ones in terms of provision of the more academic-type (and ultimately more marketable in terms of higher education) technical subjects such as physics, applied maths, biology and chemistry, we see a different pattern emerging. Although the free-scheme schools are equal to the fee-paying schools in the provision of biology, and indeed a larger proportion of them offer chemistry — 84.8 per cent compared with 75 per cent — they are far less likely to offer physics or applied maths: 50 per cent of the fee-paying schools offered applied maths and 87.5 per cent offered physics. The corresponding figures for the free-scheme schools were 15.2 per cent and 58.7 per cent.

Fee-paying secondary schools, therefore, are very strongly oriented in their curricular provisions to the academic–intellectual end of the technical knowledge spectrum.[1] The same is not true of free-scheme secondary schools. A large cohort within them, mostly male schools indeed, make considerable provision for the more practical technical subjects, while they do not seem to have quite the same extensive range of pure and applied sciences.

Gender is also a factor influencing the character of the technical knowledge disseminated. As is well-known, girls' schools make little or no provision for practical subjects with the exception of home economics (Hannan *et al.*, 1983). Although we found that provision in girls' schools for junior cycle science and for senior cycle biology and chemistry was roughly comparable to that in boys' schools, boys' schools did have a wider range of science subjects. In particular, boys' schools were significantly ($P < 0.01$ level) more likely to offer physics and applied maths than girls' schools. Provision for *business-type* technical subjects was also superior in boys' schools in the senior cycle though the differences here are not very pronounced. A larger proportion of girls' schools, indeed, offered business

Table 27. Differences between public free-scheme secondary and fee-paying secondary schools in senior cycle subject provision

Subjects	Public N = 32 %	Free-scheme Secondary N = 46 %	Fee-paying Secondary N = 8 %	Statistical significance
Irish	100.0	100.0	100.0	N.S.
English	100.0	100.0	100.0	N.S.
Mathematics	100.0	100.0	100.0	N.S.
French	86.7	100.0	100.0	P≤0.05
Biology	96.7	89.1	87.5	N.S.
Geography	76.7	100.0	100.0	P≤0.01
History	66.7	100.0	100.0	P≤0.01
Business organization	76.7	76.1	50.0	N.S.
Accounting	66.7	76.1	50.0	N.S.
Art	60.0	65.2	87.5	N.S.
Chemistry	30.0	84.8	75.0	P≤0.01
Home economics (scientific and social)	63.3	58.7	62.5	N.S.
Technical drawing	100.0	43.5	0.0	P≤0.01
Physics	50.0	58.7	87.5	N.S.
Economics	40.0	50.0	50.0	N.S.
Engineering	80.0	13.0	12.5	P≤0.01
Home economics (general)	30.0	41.3	37.5	N.S.
Construction studies	80.0	13.0	0.0	P≤0.01
Music	13.3	37.0	87.5	P≤0.01
German	10.0	41.3	50.0	P≤,01
Physics and chemistry	16.7	21.7	12.5	N.S.
Applied maths	6.7	15.2	50.0	P≤0.01
Aggricultural science	23.3	8.7	12.5	N.S.
Spanish	10.0	15.2	25.0	N.S.
Latin	3.3	15.2	25.0	N.S.
Economic history	3.3	13.0	0.0	N.S.
Italian	0.0	6.5	12.5	N.S.
Mechanics	3.3	0.0	0.0	N.S.
Greek	0.0	0.0	12.5	P≤0.01
Agricultural economics	0.0	0.0	0.0	N.S.
Hebrew	0.0	0.0	0.0	N.S.

organization. Overall, therefore, our data suggests that girls' schools are not as technically directed as boys' schools. However, it must be remembered that our data on curriculum change since principals were appointed does suggest that girls' schools are rapidly moving in the technical direction too — especially towards the scientific sphere. Evidence on the take-up rate in Leaving Certificate higher mathematics, physics, chemistry and biology in 1984/85 shows also that over the last eight years girls have increased their participation in the sciences and allied areas at an enormous rate: for example, while only 1,030 girls took higher mathematics at the Leaving Certificate in 1977, in 1985 7,594 did (Lynch, 1987a: 1–2).

Although the technical-intellectual development of the individual is gaining pre-eminence at second level, the form which it takes varies greatly with the class and gender of the pupil. It also varies with so-called 'ability'. Vocational schools are not only predominantly working-class in intake, they also have a disproportionate number of pupils with 'educational disabilities' (Hannan *et al.*, 1983: 89). As the vocational schools are strongest in their bias towards the practical end of the technical continuum this means that the educationally disabled are also directed towards this type of technical knowledge.

Within a given school, being labelled as 'low ability' or 'weak' also has serious implications for one's experience of schooling. We found, for example, that 83.5 per cent of all schools with more than one class in each year use some form of ability grouping, and that there is little movement between streams. Thus, the pupil who is labelled as being of 'low ability' in first year is very likely to be in a low stream for the rest of his/her second-level schooling. The 'low ability' label also means that one is allocated different types of teachers and receives different types of knowledge, than if one is classed as being of high ability. In terms of understanding the particularistic character of second-level schools, therefore, ability would seem to be an important factor to bear in mind. Recent work in Ireland by Hannan and Boyle (1987) also lends support to this hypothesis.

Moving away from the formal curriculum, we sought to examine the relative importance of non-examination subjects within the school day. Our information on the allocation of time to non-examination subjects highlights the preoccupation of schools with credentials. The only subject or activity which was allocated time on a roughly equal basis with other subjects was religion. Although girls' schools were more oriented to the aesthetic and personal development of their pupils than boys'—and community and comprehensive schools were the most likely of all to give time to pastoral care—in neither girls' nor community schools were aesthetic or personal activities ever given more than two class periods per week.

The particularistic character of pupils' experience, however, does emerge here. The more one moves from the central state-controlled part of school life—and indeed the central Church-controlled part, in the case of Catholic schools—the more particularistic schools become. Religious-controlled secondary schools, for example, allocate more time to religion than those schools in which religious are only one of the controlling groups, namely community schools, while vocational schools allocate the least time to religion classes (Table 11). Equally, the teaching of drama, certain forms of music or the development of pastoral care programmes are not controlled by either state regulation or law. In these areas we find considerable variability between school types, boys' schools being those with the least provision (cf. pp. 61, 65). Boys' schools are also considerably less likely to allocate a large number of periods each week to religion than are girls' schools (Table 10). Single-sex schools, therefore, seem to be facilitating the development of a greater religious, aesthetic and personal awareness among girls than among boys. Secondary schools also facilitate aesthetic and religious development more than the vocational or community schools, with the latter allocating most time to personal development. There was no evidence here, however, of major differences within the secondary sector. Fee-paying schools were no more likely than free-scheme schools to give time to non-examination subjects. Indeed, they tended to give slightly less time to religion classes in particular.

Chapter 3 was devoted to elaborating the relational context within which individual self-development occurs. Here we identified two universalistic trends: relations between peers in schools are structurally defined as competitive, each individual's success being contingent on the relative lack of success of another; relations between pupils and adults (school staff) are essentially hierarchical, pupils being permitted very little autonomy in most schools. Although there is little evidence of particularistic practices with respect to autonomy — the exception being vocational schools which permit higher levels of autonomy in religious practices and in dress than all other types of schools — the form of individual competition does vary considerably between school types.

One of the most pronounced features of the second-level system, apart from the pervasiveness of individual competition, is the rotational character of the latter. That is to say, those schools which are most likely to select at entry are the least likely to stream pupils rigidly, while the schools which stream rigidly are the least likely to have a wide-ranging system of internal assessments and prize-giving for academic attainments. For example, while girls' schools were considerably more likely than boys' to select at entry, boys' schools were more likely to stream pupils rigidly than girls'. However, girls' schools compensated for their lack of rigid streaming by having a wide-ranging system of internal competitions and assessments throughout the school year. The same situation obtained for secondary schools compared with vocational schools. The former were most selective at entry, but less rigidly streamed than vocational schools. Again we find secondary schools as a group, however, operating a more extensive system of academic competitions and gradings throughout the school year than vocational schools. While schools vary therefore in the time and form which competition takes within them, competitiveness is a pervasive feature of all schools.

Having established the level of individual competitiveness in the productive sub-system of schools — the formal curriculum — we then sought to establish if this competitiveness was counterbalanced in the sphere of extra-curricular activities. Were competitions held and prizes awarded in extracurricular activities in the same way as in the academic sphere?

Firstly, it is clear that competition is widespread in the extracurricular area too as 86 per cent of schools awarded prizes for attainments in the extracurricular area. Although it is clear from Tables 18 and 19 that group effort is much more likely to be rewarded in extracurricular activities than in the formal curriculum, the collective (team) prizes that were awarded were predominantly in sport. Indeed, one finds that individual prizes in sport are as frequent as team prizes, while prizes for drama, music, debating, general behaviour etc. are almost entirely individual awards. Consequently, while prizes awarded in sport do counterbalance the individualistic competition of formal scholastic learning, to some degree, in other ways they reinforce it. Indeed the character of the prizes given in non-sporting areas almost entirely reinforces it. It is interesting to observe too that there is no evidence that schools which are most individually competitive in the formal work of school are any less individually competitive in the extracurricular sphere. In fact, while girls' schools are the most likely to give all types of extra-curricular prizes, they also allocate most to individuals, especially for non-sporting activities. Also, community and secondary schools tend to award a lot more individual prizes for non-sporting activities than vocational schools.

Ability as a Determinant of Particularistic Experience

Neither functionalists nor neo-Marxists have given much attention to the question of 'ability' in their analysis of the hidden curriculum. Gender, race and social class are the major variables used by neo-Marxists to explain particularistic experiences in school. While the interface between social class, race and ability — especially as measured by IQ-type tests — is undoubtedly a complex one (Gould, 1981), one cannot justifiably subsume the question of ability under class or race labels. Ability is an attribute used independently of social class, gender and race to distribute pupils into groups in schools. Qualitatively, the concept of ability also differs fundamentally from gender, class or race. At this present time in history, grouping pupils on the basis of ability has scientific legitimacy. There is an enormous industry based on the testing of ability (Kamin, 1974). Furthermore, test constructors claim to have devised objective criteria for measuring ability. Although there were times in past and recent history when social class, gender or even race were readily accepted as criteria on which to base differential (and often unequal) education, grouping on the basis of such criteria never had quite the same scientific credibility that ability grouping has.

Consequently, to challenge the efficacy of streaming or banding by ability is a very complex process. It requires one to have detailed scientific knowledge of the procedures for measuring ability. The challenge cannot be just a matter of collectively voicing the righteous indignation of an oppressed group. One must also demonstrate empirically how arbitrary our understanding of ability is within the educational system,[2] and how spurious, and indeed class-related, tests of ability usually are. I have already argued such a case with respect to a test widely used in Ireland, the Drumcondra Verbal Reasoning Test (Lynch, 1985).

Although our data demonstrating the particularistic effects of ability is not as detailed as we would like it to be — it would require ethnographic evidence of what happens within classes particularly, evidence which could not be obtained in a large-scale study such as this — the data which we do have strongly supports the particularistic thesis. Eighty-six per cent of the 79 schools which streamed or banded at least some of its pupils grouped pupils on the basis of academic ability. Standardized tests were singly the most frequently used method for grouping (Table 23). Furthermore, we found that pupils' choice of subject was more likely to be restricted, at both junior and senior level, by their perceived (by staff) or measured, intellectual ability than by any other criteria. Although there were slight differences between various types of schools in the degree of emphasis on ability, the pattern was the same throughout.

Finally, principals were asked if pupils' ability informed their timetabling practices. In other words, when teachers were being timetabled in the school, did principals try to match teachers to particular streams or bands? A total of 28 schools (32.5 per cent) reported allocating teachers according to their 'suitability to different types of pupils'. When principals were probed about what this meant in practice, it was clear that in a majority of cases (23) it meant allocating the more competent teachers (as seen by the principal) to examination classes (especially the Leaving Certificate classes) or to the top streams or both. Four principals stated that certain teachers did not want to teach the lower streams or were too impatient with them; therefore these teachers were given higher streams. In one school, the principal recruited teachers for the lower streams each year by asking teachers to volunteer for the work. The procedure of suiting teachers to classes (a decision which was made in 23 of the 28 cases by the principal) is summed up well in the response of one principal. 'Bad teachers are put where they'll do least damage.' Allocating poorer teachers to the low streams was clearly not perceived as damaging in the way that allocating them to top streams (or 'honours classes' as they were usually called) was.

Because only one-third of the schools allocate teachers to classes with explicit ability considerations in mind, we cannot claim that this is a widespread practice. However, we must also exercise care in interpreting these findings. The remainder of the principals claimed to be primarily concerned with either the good of the pupils or fairness to teachers when timetabling. These responses give us little explicit information on actual practice. They may well conceal real biases in timetabling. Admitting to allocating teachers to classes according to the ability of each is not, after all, a highly lauded educational ideal! It is a difficult question on which to get accurate information at interview. More detailed information would be required, therefore, before we could draw definite conclusions as to the extent of teacher–pupil matching in school timetabling. What we do know, however, is that the ability of pupils is a conscious variable in the minds of one-third of the school principals in our sample when teachers and pupils are being timetabled. Ability must be considered therefore if one wishes to comprehend the particularism of school life.

Gender, Social Class and Extracurricular Life

When we examined formal curriculum provision in Chapter 2 we found that external constraints (in the form of either government regulation or third-level entry requirements) ensured fairly universalistic pátterns in knowledge provision in different types of schools. Although variability does occur, it is most conspicuous between subjects rather than between forms of knowledge. To get a more complete picture of knowledge dissemination in schools we also investigated extracurricular provision and curricular provision in non-examination subjects. As the latter issue was examined in Chapter 2 it is now time to turn our attention to extracurricular activities *per se*.

Outlined in Table 28 are the 50 most popular extracurricular activities in schools. Not surprisingly sport forms the largest single cohort, although there is variability between schools in the popularity of each sport. In all, 24 (48 per cent) of the 50 activities are sports; 8 are field games, 9 are court games, while 7 are other outdoor games of various kinds. Five of the 50 activities could be defined as 'arts', although some of the other 14 indoor activities might also be classified in this way, namely film, photography and poetry. Finally, there were three formal religious societies found in schools — Pioneers, Legion of Mary and St Vincent de Paul[3] — and two quasi-religious ones, namely activities for charity and social action groups. Social action groups referred to the giving of practical assistance to 'needy' groups.

There are some activities in which only one school is involved; this was true of a variety of activities not listed here: archery, fencing, karate, touch football, wildlife club, stamp-collecting and dress design, were each only mentioned once. It was decided, however, only to include a sample of these least popular activities in the table.

Table 28. Percentage of schools with particular extracurricular activities

Name of activity	% of school with each
Court games	
Basketball	88.4
Netball	17.4
Volleyball	59.3
Badminton/squash	24.4
Tennis	64.0
Table-tennis	38.4
Gymnastics	58.1
Handball	16.3
Boxing	3.5
Arts	
Arts and crafts	43.0
Dancing	7.0
Musical activities	68.6
Drama	62.8
Debating/public speaking	80.2
Other indoor interests — mostly non-sport	
Needlework/cooking	4.7
School magazine	50.0
Board games	47.7
Question time/quizzes	9.3
Radio/CB club	4.7
Record club	1.2
Science/astronomy club	4.7
Business game club	1.2
Computer society	16.3
Other indoor–mostly non sport	
Historical society	2.3
Irish club	9.3
Poetry club	1.2
Film society	10.5
Photography	11.6
Field games	
Camogie	30.2
Hockey	23.3
Hurling	45.3
Gaelic football	65.1
Soccer	53.5
Rugby	15.1
Cricket	5.8
Golf	3.5

Table 28 (contd.)

Name of activity	% of school with each
Other outdoor	
Athletics	80.2
Adventure sports	37.2
Swimming	46.5
Horse riding	4.7
Cycling	11.6
Fishing	5.8
Gardening/horticulture	3.5
Car club	1.2
Travel/skiing	2.3
Religious related	
Pioneer Total Abstinence Association (PTAA)	52.3
Legion of Mary	12.8
St Vincent de Paul	15.1
Activities for charity	20.9
Social action group	9.3

The first point to note from Table 28 is the lack of universality in extracurricular provision. There are only 3 of the 50 listed activities which are found in over 80 per cent of schools—basketball, debating/public speaking and athletics. In fact, there are only 11 (22 per cent) activities which are available in 50 + per cent of schools. Of these 11, 7 are sports—volleyball, tennis, gymnastics, soccer, gaelic football, basketball and athletics; 3 are arts—music, drama and debating; and 1 is religious—Pioneer Total Abstinence Association.

The particularistic character of extracurricular activities becomes more clear when we compare different types of schools (Tables A33–6). There are 16 activities in which there are statistically significant differences arising from gender, 15 arise from size, while community, secondary and vocational schools differ significantly in 9 areas. There are, indeed, 11 areas in which fee-paying secondary, free-scheme secondary and public schools differ significantly.

The most noticeable differences arising from gender are in the arts sphere. Four of the five arts activities listed in Table 28 are significantly more likely to be found in girls' schools than in boys' (especially), or co-educational schools; dancing is the exception. However, film societies are more frequent in boys' schools, while photography clubs are equally proportioned between male and female schools. The Pioneer Total Abstinence Association is also significantly more likely to be found in girls' schools than in boys' or co-educational schools, as indeed are Irish clubs, needlework or cookery societies, and quiz clubs. The bias in girls' schools towards the arts and other home-related activities shows, therefore, how the extracurricular life of the school reinforces traditional gender stereotypes. It is interesting to note too that three of the five religious activities are found in higher proportions of girls' schools than elsewhere. Both this finding, and that on the arts, corroborates the evidence of Chapter 2. There, it was established that girls' schools allocate most time to religion, and that they are considerably more likely than boys' schools to have music or drama on the timetable (as non-examination subjects that is). Significant sex differences in certain field games were also established. Some of these are not particularly surprising as sports such as hurling and rugby are exclusively male sports, while camogie is an exclusively female one.

While external controls constrain schools in their formal curriculum provision no such constraints exist in the extracurricular field. Consequently, we find even greater variability between schools in the extracurricular area than in the formal curriculum sphere. This is again evident when we compare small schools with larger ones. In almost all activities listed in Table A34 there is a tendency for the small schools to have the least provision. The arts area is again the one which is most likely to be omitted from the extracurricular programme of small schools; statistically significant differences between smaller and larger schools are evident in arts and crafts, film, music and debating. Differences between small, medium and large schools are also statistically significant in certain sporting areas, particularly in indoor activities. Clearly, small schools do not have the resources and facilities to offer the range of activities which large schools can afford.

The particularistic character of extracurricular provision is also evident from Tables A35 and A36. From Table A35 we note that there are 9 activities in which there are statistically significant differences between vocational, secondary and community/comprehensive schools — hockey, hurling, gaelic football, soccer, boxing, music, computer societies, pioneer societies and social action groups. In these, as in 18 (36 per cent) other activities, there is clear evidence that community/comprehensive schools have the most extensive extracurricular provision. (Because of the small number of community/comprehensive schools in our sample, however, we must be careful in interpreting findings.) Although 14 of the activities in which community/comprehensive schools have best provision are sporting, they are also to the fore in the arts sphere and in four of the five religious activities listed.

By contrast with this, vocational schools only exceed other schools in their provision of a narrow range of sports. All but one of the seven activities in which they have the highest provision are sports — hurling, gaelic football, camogie, handball, volleyball, fishing and record clubs. There are 15 activities in which secondary schools have the highest extracurricular provision. These cover a wide range of interests ranging from poetry, photography, cricket, horse-riding and golf to debating, the St Vincent de Paul and school quizzes.

The capital costs involved in some of the activities in which secondary schools have highest provision—photography and horse-riding, for example—reflect the income and class differences between children in these schools and those in vocational schools, especially.

The class-related character of extracurricular provision becomes even more evident when we compare public, free-scheme secondary and fee-paying secondary schools. From Table A36 we see that rugby, horse-riding, hockey and cricket are clearly most popular among the upper and upper middle classes, as it is in the fee-paying schools that provision in these activities is greatest. Camogie, hurling and gaelic football are strongest in the public schools, although they are also very popular in free-scheme secondary schools. Native gaelic games are more central therefore to the sports programmes of the lower middle classes and working classes in second-level schools than they are to those of the upper classes.

Provision in the five arts areas listed is also superior in the fee-paying schools. Differences are statistically significant in three of the five areas. Finally, it is interesting to note that while traditional religious groups such as the PTAA and the St Vincent de Paul Society are most popular in the free-scheme secondary schools, activities involving raising money for charity or social action are significantly more likely to be found in the fee-paying schools.

Facilities for Extracurricular Activities

The variability between different types of schools in the extracurricular sphere becomes even clearer when we examine the facilities available to schools to pursue them. In Table 29 we outline school facilities in eleven areas: playing fields, hard courts, gymnasiums, chapels or prayer rooms, library facilities, lecture halls, general purpose halls, dark rooms, swimming pools and special recreating rooms, such as senior common rooms.

With regard to the availability of facilities in the first five listed above (playing fields, courts, gyms, chapels and libraries), we find statistically significant differences between male, female and co–educational schools, and between secondary, vocational and community/comprehensive schools in each one. Indeed, school size is also associated with significant differences in the availability of playing fields and chapels.

With regard to the availability of playing fields, vocational schools have the poorest provision of any school type, 18.5 per cent of them have no playing fields, while a further 40.7 per cent rely on renting one. This means that only 41 per cent have playing fields (one or two only) of their own

Table 29. Proportion of schools with certain extracurricular facilities

Type of facility	Percentage of schools with different numbers of each						
	One %	Two %	Three %	Four or Five %	Six or more %	Rented %	None %
Playing fields*	31.4	15.1	4.7	3.5	9.3	23.3	11.6
Hard courts	24.4	20.9	7.0	10.5	8.1	7.0	22.1
Gyms	51.2	2.3	—	—	—	7.0	39.5
Chapel/prayer room	44.2	5.8	—	—	—	7.0	43.0
Library	73.3	1.2	—	—	Use a classroom 2.3	1.2	22.1
General purpose hall (with stage)	24.4	—	—	—	—	—	75.6
Lecture hall	7.0	—	—	—	—	—	93.0
Dark room	3.5	—	—	—	—	—	96.5
Swimming pool	4.7	1.2	—	—	—	—	94.1
Recreation (common) room for seniors	4.7	—	—	—	—	—	95.3
	3.5	—	—	—	—	—	96.5

N = 86
*Information on one school is missing.

compared with 74 per cent of secondary and 100 per cent of community/comprehensive schools (A38). While small schools (≤ 250) also have poor facilities, we find that 45.2 per cent of them have fields of their own with 9.7 per cent having 3–5 fields. None of the boys' schools was without playing fields, although 14.3 per cent of girls' schools, and 15.9 per cent of co-educational schools, were. Indeed, 30 per cent of the boys' schools had six or more playing fields (Table A37). However, one must remember here that male schools tended to be larger than female or co-educational ones; 50 per cent of them had 501 + pupils compared with 19 per cent of girls' schools and 13.3 per cent of co-educational schools.

Size, however, is clearly not the sole determinant in the provision of facilities as 45 per cent of boys' schools had no hard courts compared with 9.5 per cent of girls' and 17.8 per cent of co-educational schools. Indeed 30 per cent of large schools had no courts compared with 22.6 per cent of small ones. Vocational schools are once again the type of school with the least court facilities. One-third of them had no hard courts compared with 18.5 per cent of secondary schools. All community schools had courts of their own (Table A39).

Gym facilities are also best in community schools, although the differences between these and secondary schools are small compared with the differences between the two of these and vocational schools; only 22 per cent of vocational schools had gym facilities of their own compared with 66.7 per cent of secondary and 80 per cent of community schools. Size also clearly has a bearing on gym facilities as 54.8 per cent of small schools had no gyms of their own compared to 40 per cent of medium-sized and 15 per cent of large schools. Gym facilities are better, however, in girls' than in boys' schools, although the latter tend to be bigger.

It is not surprising to find vocational schools having fewer facilities for prayer than either secondary schools or community schools, given their more secular tradition. What is interesting to note, though, is that community schools are the most likely type of school to have a chapel or prayer room of their own. Facilities for religious practice are well provided for in the developing (and primarily state-funded) sector of second-level education. Interestingly, boys' schools are a good deal more likely than girls' schools to have no chapel or prayer room: 30 per cent of male schools have no chapel compared with 14.3 per cent of girls' schools. This finding is commensurate with our other findings on religious practice and teaching in male and female schools. Co-educational schools (55.6 per cent of which are vocational) have the poorest facilities for prayer or religious services.

Library facilities also vary considerably with school type. Vocational schools once again had the poorest facilities: 52 per cent had no library, while all community schools, and approximately 90 per cent of secondary schools had one. Although very small schools were the least likely to have a library the differences between them and medium-sized schools in library provision are not significant. Girls' schools also had slightly better library facilities than boys' and much better facilities than co-educational schools.

Differences between schools in the availability of halls, dark rooms, swimming pools, craft rooms or common (recreation) rooms were not as pronounced as those in the five areas discussed above. This is due largely, however, to the fact that these facilities exist in very small proportions of schools as a whole. While 24.4 per cent have a general purpose hall, only 7 per cent have a lecture hall; 3.5 per cent have a dark room; 3.5 per cent have a craft room, and 4.7 per cent each have a swimming pool and common room. Significant differences arise in only two areas. Community schools are significantly ($P < 0.01$) more likely than *either* vocational or secondary schools to have a lecture hall and dark rooms were only found in schools with ≥ 501 pupils. Despite the lack of significant differences, however, the trends are not that different to those discussed above, except with regard to gender. While girls' schools surpass boys' in their gym, hard court, library and prayer facilities, boys' schools are more likely than girls' (or co-educational schools) to have a lecture hall, dark room, swimming pool or common room. Girls are more likely to have facilities for crafts or general purpose halls.

Craft is the only area in which vocational schools have better facilities than secondary or community/comprehensive schools.

What our data on extracurricular facilities suggests, therefore, is that size of school and its administrative character — that is, whether it is secondary, vocational or community — are extremely important determinants of the range of facilities it possesses. Larger schools and community schools are likely to have better facilities than smaller schools, vocational schools or secondary schools as a whole. Undoubtedly a major reason why community schools surpass secondary and vocational in provision is due to their size. No community school had ≤250 pupils, while 35.2 per cent of secondary schools and 44.4 per cent of vocational schools had. Also, 60 per cent (three of the five) of community schools had ≥501 pupils, while 25.9 per cent of secondary, and 11.1 per cent of vocational schools were in this category.

However, size is not the sole determinant of facilities. Although 50 per cent of male schools were large (≥501 pupils) compared with 19 per cent of female schools, the latter had slightly better facilities in 6 of the 11 areas examined. Furthermore, when we compare fee-paying schools with public schools and with free-scheme secondary schools, it is also clear that size is not the only determinant of facilities. Half the fee-paying schools in our sample had ≤250 pupils compared with 32.6 per cent of free-scheme secondary schools and 37.5 per cent of public schools. Also, only one fee-paying school (12.5 per cent) had ≥501 pupils compared with 18.8 per cent of public schools and 28.3 per cent of free-scheme schools. Yet, we find that fee-paying schools have better facilities than either free-scheme secondary, or public schools in 7 of the 11 areas examined above. They all have playing fields, although 11.1 per cent of free-scheme schools and 15.6 per cent of public schools have none. Indeed, all but one of the eight fee-paying schools have three or more playing fields (A40). All fee-paying schools also have gymnasia, while 56.3 per cent of public and 34.8 per cent of free-scheme schools have none. None of the fee-paying schools are without libraries, although 43.8 per cent of the public and 10.9 per cent of the free-scheme schools are (Table A42). Fee-paying schools are also more likely than other schools to have a swimming pool, chapel, lecture hall or common room. Indeed their hard-court facilities are also extensive, although they are slightly more likely than free-scheme secondary schools to be without a hard court (A41). It is clear, therefore, that the social-class composition of the school has considerable bearing on the provision of extracurricular facilities. Schools with the largest cohort of pupils from higher income groups (fee-paying secondary schools) have, overall, the best facilities (A43). Size also determines the range of facilities available, while gender has a direct influence on the *type* of facilities available in schools.

Conclusion

What our data on extracurricular activities and facilities clearly demonstrate is the highly particularistic character of provision in these areas in second-level schools. Unlike formal curriculum provision which is subjected to both direct government regulations and indirect controls from higher education institutions, extracurricular provision is at the school's discretion. Being outside the sphere of public accountability, the extracurricular life of schools reproduces class and gender traditions in a variety of cultural spheres. The arts and religious activities are prioritized in girls' schools in a way which does not occur in boys'. Thus, gender stereotypes are reinforced, with boys being relatively deprived in the aesthetic and religious spheres. Field games, with their concomitant emphasis on physical skill, dexterity and strength, still form the core of extracurricular life in boys' schools. Gaelic football, soccer, athletics and hurling are the four most popular activities in boys' schools.

The reproductive role of extracurricular activities in terms of social class are most evident when we compare fee-paying secondary, free-scheme secondary and public schools. Hurling, gaelic football, camogie and boxing are primarily available in schools with large lower-middle-class and working-class cohorts. By contrast with this rugby, hockey, horse-riding and cricket are mainly available in the upper-middle-class fee-paying schools. Extracurricular provision in the arts is also much superior in fee-paying schools than in either free-scheme or public schools.

While our data on ability grouping is limited compared with that on extracurricular life, what evidence we have suggests that ability is an important variable explaining the particularism of school life. While pupils' gender and class are important determinants of school experience so also is ability. Indeed, because ability grouping is legitimated by 'scientific' evidence, unlike grouping by class, race and gender, it is a more difficult practice to challenge. Furthermore, it is a practice which is less visible to the public eye, taking place as it does within the internal arrangements of the school.

To highlight areas of particularistic practice (extracurricular life) and bases for particularistic treatment (ability) which have not been seriously considered in hidden curriculum thought to date is not to deny our basic universalistic thesis. In the relational sphere, competitive individualism and lack of autonomy characterize both the productive and maintenance sub-systems of school life. When knowledge is being disseminated within the formal productive sub-system itself the bias seems to be increasingly towards the technical development of the individual.

Notes

1 This is not to say that the arts are neglected. As can be seen from Table 27, music, art and modern languages are consistently more likely to be provided in fee-paying secondary schools than in free-scheme secondary schools.

2 Gardner's recent work, *Frames of Mind: The Theory of Multiple Intelligences*, 1983, goes a long way toward highlighting the paucity of current conceptions of ability and intelligence.

3 The Pioneer Total Abstinence Association promotes total abstinence from alcohol. The Legion of Mary is a society for the promotion of the Catholic faith and the St Vincent de Paul Society is mainly concerned with charitable work.

Chapter 5

Reproduction in Education: The Role of Cultural Factors, Social Classes and Educational Mediators

Introduction

Through the analysis of the process of knowledge dissemination (Ch. 2) and the relational context of learning (Ch. 3) it has been shown that schools are simultaneously universalistic and particularistic in their reproduction of educational individualism. A summary of the simultaneous universalistic and particularistic aspects of the process of schooling is represented in Figure 1. What is being suggested here is that schools operate according to contradictory sets of dynamics at the same time.

As Dale observes, there are both *practical* and *organic* limits to government control over education within a given society; the practical limits arise from the scale of the educational operation while the organic limits are rooted in the unique histories of the educational system (1982: 139). What this means, in effect, is that the mode of production within a capitalist (or indeed a socialist) state does not determine the form that educational state apparatuses will take (ibid., 140). Although capitalist interests can and do play a central role in influencing educational policies (the shift in Irish second-level education over the last twenty years away from the humanities towards technical knowledge is indeed proof of this), their influence is a mediated and negotiated one. In other words educational systems are not the clones of the capitalist state, they are characterized by 'operational autonomy' (Archer, 1982: 8). It is this that explains the contradictory processes within them.

As noted above, the character of a given educational system is dictated in no small part by those organic limits arising from the unique historical and cultural traditions of a particular society. There are a number of cultural

Figure 1: *Particularism and universalism in the process of schooling*

	(Four major sub-systems)			
	Central productive sub-system (formal curriculum)	*The ancillary productive sub-system (extracurricular activities)*	*The maintenance and procedural sub-system (procedures organising learning and maintaining order)*	*External relations sub-system (procedures pertaining to external relations)*
Universalistic features	The core curriculum; technical bias; equally qualified teachers	Religion Civics PE	Competitive individualism; Lack of individual autonomy	State control leads to rules, also 3rd level + employer demands
Particularistic features	The technical is defined differently for class groups: manual-technical, intellectual-technical. 'Ability' determines level of technical knowledge. Gender biases in curriculum provision	Outside the above 3, activities are frequently class and gender specific	Form of competitiveness varies with school, class composition and gender; so does autonomy, e.g. in religion	schools vary in level of control by Church and State

and historical factors, for example, which make the educational system in the Republic of Ireland different from that in other capitalist states. In particular, there are a number of factors which make education a key determinant of power and wealth and which thereby define the parameters of contestation, resistance and counter-resistance.

Organic Limits Arising from the Unique Historical and Cultural Context of Irish Education

At one level, the Republic of Ireland displays many of the features of a so-called advanced capitalist society: 'Average Irish incomes rank 27th among the 126 countries with populations in excess of one million recorded by the World Bank. . .levels of literacy, nutrition and health are high, as is life expectancy. The incidence of disease and of child and infant mortality is low' (Crotty, 1986: 1). Furthermore, educational retention rates are among the highest in the EEC: in 1983/84, 69 per cent of all those between 4 and 24 years of age were in full-time education (Department of Education, 1983/84: 3).

Like most of its Western European neighbours, Ireland also operates an extensive welfare state machinery of which education forms a part. Furthermore, in terms of its administrative structure, Irish education has much in common with other highly centralized systems, such as that of France: all major policy changes in education are dependent on central government for approval. In many respects therefore, Irish education operates within a socio-economic and administrative structure which is not that dissimilar from other Western European countries. However, to understand the dynamics of social reproduction in Irish education, one must also examine those cultural and historical features of Irish social life which distinguish it from other capitalist states in Europe and which have a major impact on educational policies.

By far the most distinguishing feature of Irish society is that it is a post-colonial state of relatively recent origin.[1] The economic infrastructure of the country displays a number of the features of post-colonial underdevelopment. Ireland is, for example, a major debtor country: per head of population, Ireland has a larger foreign debt than a number of the major debtor 'Third-World' countries (Crotty, 1986: 7). High standards of living have only been maintained at the expense of massive emigration: net emigration between 1911 and 1961 was 45 per cent of the number of births registered (ibid., 2).

Several hundred years of colonization by a capitalist power also left

Ireland bereft of profits for capital accumulation (Crotty, 1986: 47–48). This pre-empted the development of both an indigenous industrial sector and the powerful bourgeoisie that went with it. Post-independence Ireland therefore, is very similar to other recently independent post-colonial states in both its economic and social infrastructure. Just as a number of the post-colonial states of the Middle East and Asia did not generate the development of powerful polar classes of proleterians and bourgeoisie (Ahmad, 1985: 43–65), neither did Ireland. Rather, what emerged in the new 'Free State' were powerful intermediate classes or middle classes. The independence movement was inspired and led by middle-class people drawing support from all classes (Chubb, 1982: 264). In subsequent years, politics has been dominated at both local and national levels by the same middle classes (ibid., 91–111, 189–90). It is the offspring of the middle classes — in particular of the lower middle classes — who have tended to be the mainstay of the civil service (ibid., 265). The strategic location of the middle classes within the state machinery puts them in a powerful position therefore to influence state policies — including educational policies — especially in a highly centralized system.

The significance of colonization for education today is that Ireland never developed a large indigenous industrial base. (A high proportion of the profits from Irish grass farming were transferred to London in the eighteenth and nineteenth centuries where they were used to finance British industrial growth which, in turn, destroyed Irish manufacturing (Crotty, 1986: 47–8).) Consequently, cultural capital — particularly credentialized cultural capital — is a far more important determinant of status and power than is the case in core capitalist states with considerable indigenous industrial wealth. This has been especially noticeable in Ireland in the last twenty years as employment opportunities declined rapidly in the agricultural sector particularly, resulting in a massive increase in the employee labour force (and of course, in unemployment and emigration): in 1985, for example, 75 per cent of those at work were employees compared with 54 per cent in 1951 (Eurostat, 1987: 107; and Whelan and Whelan, 1984: 21).[2] Thus, in the absence of industrial opportunities, educational credentials have become the major determinants of wealth, status and power. A recent survey of school-leavers shows how important educational credentials continue to be in determining one's employment opportunities. In May/June 1987, 50 per cent of those who left school one year earlier with no qualifications were still unemployed compared with 24 per cent of those with an Intermediate and/or Group Certificate and 12 per cent of those with a Leaving Certificate (Department of Labour, 1987: Table 2, p. 12). The higher one's educational credentials, therefore, the better one's chances of being employed, even though the job one gets may not require the specific skills that the credential certifies.

It is not only the post-colonial context which must be taken into account, however, if one is to understand how social reproduction occurs in Irish education. One must also take congnizance of the power and influence exercised by the Churches, particularly by the Catholic Church. The Catholic Church exercises a degree of control in Irish education which is probably unprecedented in late twentieth-century industrial Europe. Although time and space do not allow us to elaborate on the origins of the unique Church–State partnership (cf. Coolahan, 1981 for discussion of this point), it has tremendous significance for policy-making. At present, 96 per cent of children in primary education attend denominational schools (mostly Catholic ones). In the second-level sector, almost 90 per cent of secondary schools — containing approximately 69 per cent of all second-level students — are owned and controlled by Catholic religious communities (Clancy, 1986: 121–3). While the state, via the Department of Education and the Minister, exercises control over curricula at primary and second level, the Catholic Church exercises administrative control over a majority of schools and therefore has a major say in both the appointing of teachers and in the day-to-day running of schools. State policy-making in Irish education, therefore, is not only influenced by the colonial heritage of the country, it is also influenced by the unique character of the Church–State partnership which had been a feature of public education since its initiation in the early nineteenth century.

A third culturally specific factor which must be considered when examining the role of education in Irish society is the position of teachers and their unions. The teacher unions in Ireland are extremely well organized and powerful in comparison with those in the United States or Britain, for example. All primary teachers are in the one union (the Irish National Teachers' Organisation, INTO) which was founded in 1868.[3] While there are two teacher unions at second level, the Association of Secondary Teachers of Ireland (ASTI) and the Teachers' Union of Ireland (TUI), these are also well-organized and all three unions have worked together in recent years when teacher interests have been threatened. For example, the three teacher unions collaborated in the spring and early summer of 1986 in protest at the government's refusal to pay them a 10 per cent salary increase. A number of concessions were won as a result of the strikes. Also, in the spring of 1988, the INTO organized a series of public marches involving teachers, religious, parents and pupils to protest at a government decision to increase the teacher–pupil ratio. The protests were successful in achieving their aim: the Minister for Education was forced to withdraw the directive ordering an increase in the teacher–pupil ratio.

The power of teacher unions is not solely a function of their long traditions or organizational abilities however. It also reflects the centrality of education as a political issue within a society in which educational credentials are major determinants of life chances.

What we are suggesting here is that to understand reproduction in education one must take account of the unique historical and cultural contexts within which it occurs. This means taking account not only of unique historical processes—such as post-colonialism in the case of Ireland—but also examining the role of the culturally specific mediators of educational services. That is to say, in all public educational systems there are an array of groups and personnel who manage and administer the educational services on a day-to-day basis, what we call educational mediators. The character, power and interests of these mediators will vary inevitably from one society to another. Whatever their location or identity, however, educational mediators play a key role in determining the balance between universalism and particularism within a given system.

Before analysing the role played by mediators in education, it is necessary to comment further on the balance of powers in the educational sphere.

Post-Colonialism, Social Classes and Education

As stated above, post-colonial Ireland was characterized by the absence of a large indigenous industrial sector and the related correlates of a polarized bourgeoisie and proletariat. The middle classes had been in the forefront of the fight for independence and they retained their leadership position in the new state (Chubb, 1982). Their project was greatly assisted by strong anti-colonial feelings which were fostered and developed by the middle classes themselves.[4] Class differences were minimized and nationalist values promoted; indeed, primary schools became one of the major sites for the promotion of nationalist values (Coolahan, 1981: 38–45). The promotion of nationalism is, as Ahmad (1985) observes, a common practice among the middle or intermediate classes especially in post-colonial contexts. He identifies similar developments in a number of post-colonial countries in West Asia. The category of the nation is attractive for the intermediate classes, he claims 'because of its predilection to suppress the class question and to pose the question of liberation on the level of "the people" or even on the level of the (classless) state' (1985: 62).

Middle-class hegemony in the new state would not have been possible, however, without a wide political base. This was supplied by a (relatively) newly established proprietorial peasantry in the early years, and, in more recent times, by a well-educated white-collar work force. As the work of Whelan and Whelan (1984) shows, the proportion of white-collar workers in the labour force has been increasing steadily over the last thirty years. The middle classes have little access to productive property however. To maintain income differentials between themselves, manual workers and the unemployed, they rely on the might of their educational credentials, on what Bourdieu calls 'institutionalised cultural capital' (Bourdieu, 1986: 243).

While the middle classes are heavily reliant on education to maintain their class differentials, the bourgeoisie (both the national and international), are a small but important interest group in Irish education. The massive re-orientation of both second and third–level education towards technical (i.e. commercial, scientific and technological) knowledge over the last twenty years is indeed proof of both their influence on, and interest in, education (Lynch, 1982; Clancy, in press). Their power over state managers does not rest in their numerical strength, but rather in their ability to convince the government of their importance for material accumulation in the country. The fact that both national and international capital relies heavily on state subsidization to engage in accumulation in the first place is a major contra-diction of the Irish capitalist economy and may in time, as Peillon (1982: 161) suggests, lead to a reordering of relationships between the bourgeoisie and the state.

Although the middle classes and bourgeoisie may play the key role in determining the educational agenda, what happens in schools has tremendous significance for all classes and strata in Irish society in the absence of other distributable forms of wealth.[5] For the children of the working class and the unemployed, attaining educational credentials is also the primary access route to labour force participation. As is evident from the recent Labour Force Survey (Department of Labour, 1987: 12), to enter the labour market at any level requires credentials.

While education is a political issue for all classes therefore, it matters most to those who gain most from it presently, namely, the middle classes. They have learned the educational formula by rote, it is in their interest that it does not change. As a power group, the middle classes are well positioned to have their interests defined as *the* public interest in education. In particular, they are in a position to hold the elected state managers to political account as they are a large group in political terms, highly educated[6] and strategically located within the state machinery itself (Chubb, 1982: op. cit.).

Just as the role of particular social classes within education varies somewhat with the unique cultural context of a given society, so does the role of the state. What is true of powerful capitalist economies like that of Germany, for example, does not necessarily hold in small dependent economies like Ireland.

The Role of the State in Education

Broadly speaking we tend to concur with Offe (1984: 119–29) that the state's role in education within a capitalist welfare state society is to universalize the commodity form of value, albeit in a decommodified manner. On the one hand, the state must ensure that the conditions necessary for capital accumulation are reproduced through schools; on the other hand, the political survival of elected state managers is contingent on ensuring that the democratic demands of civil society are accommodated within the school system. To comprehend fully the dynamics of the state's role in education, however, we need to elaborate a little on Offe's model.

In societies where the possession and control of cultural capital is a major determinant of privilege, creating the conditions for capital acumulation does not simply refer to creating the conditions for the accumulation of material (i.e. financial, industrial or commercial) capital. It may also refer to creating the conditions necessary for *cultural capital accumulation*. In a society such as Ireland, for example, in which 'institutionalised cultural capital' (Bourdieu, 1986: op. cit) constitutes a major form of wealth, much of the resources and energy of the state machinery is deployed in ensuring that the conditions necessary for cultural capital accumulation are reproduced. Reproducing the conditions necessary for cultural capital accumulation is especially significant for those propertyless middle-class workers whose status and income differentials are largely contingent on their educational credentials. One cannot draw a clear dichotomy therefore between the promotion of democratic rights and the promotion of accumulation. In so far as the middle classes constitute a large proportion of the electorate, a majority in a given society may well be in favour of promoting accumulation — in particular of promoting cultural accumulation — as their class futures depend on it.

While the middle classes and bourgeoisie may have a major interest in education, education is a highly contested domain nonetheless. The centrality of education as a route to privilege in a small dependent economy like Ireland's determines this. For the purposes of legitimacy, universalism is required in some areas at least. What our data suggests is that *universalism* does exist in some of the basic *provision* areas of education — in curriculum content, organization (Ch. 2) and evaluation (Ch. 3) especially. Also, in terms of their hierarchical systems of control and competitive ethos, Irish second-level schools are remarkably similar (Ch. 3).

The state's involvement in education, therefore, is by no means simply reproductive of inequality. There is more straightforward reproduction of class and gender inequalities in those sub-systems which are outside state control (extracurricular activities, for example, see Ch. 4) than there is in those which are within it (the formal curriculum). Also, it is state control which ensures that the credential attained in one school is equivalent to that obtained in another. It is, in fact, precisely because state regulations in education are either non-existent or insufficient that mediating bodies can adopt administrative strategies which ensure the reproduction of inequality in their own interests. For example, there is no government regulation preventing secondary schools engaging in selection practices. Consequently, secondary schools can choose the most educationally amenable students for their schools (Ch. 3). These students enhance the school's 'results' image and guarantee its survival and expansion. Such uncontrolled selection procedures also reproduce class inequalities by inhibiting those who are least familiar with the school's educational culture and its trappings (predominantly working-class parents with little formal education) from attending the selective sector. The same happens in the area of class grouping. Here regulations are confined to stipulations regarding teacher–pupil ratios; there is no control on grouping by gender or so-called ability. Thus, teachers' pedagogic interests and principals' administrative interests can take precedence over the interests of girls or the interests of the academically weak pupils.

State managers[7] therefore, have a universalizing effect on the educational system in so far as their own power and status interests are contingent on eliminating those gross, and highly visible forms of inequality, which might destabilize the political system and thereby put their own privilege and power in jeopardy. However, the universalizing interventions of the state create sameness in only some aspects of eductional life and thereby facilitate particularistic interests. The problem can be understood when one analyses the dynamics of the knowledge dissemination system in schools.

The State and the Provision and Consumption of Educational Services

When knowledge and skills are being disseminated through schools two sets of relations operate: actors have educational services made available to them (knowledge is given by teachers, in standardized forms of curricula; it is given under Department of Education rules, certified etc.) and they engage in the consumption of these services (they listen, acquire books, attend classes, spend time, do homework) for the purpose of attaining credentials for sale in the labour market. To date the state's role has been confined largely, however, to managing only one set of these relations—the *provision* of universal services. Here a problem arises, of course, as students can only acquire marketable credentials in proportion to their ability to exercise their *consumption* rights on what is provided. The universalization of provision does not ensure the universalization of consumption ability. Yet consumption ability is an intrinsic element in the process of acquiring knowledge and skills for the labour market.

What the existing organization of schools presupposes, therefore, is that, in consumption terms, the world consists of equally powerful individual actors. Such, of course, is not the case in a hierarchically ordered capitalist system, where labour and capital, and indeed different forms of both, have differential access to resources enabling them to consume. By largely intervening only in provision relations, the state fails to recognize the central dynamic of education — that provision and consumption are not coterminous. In essence state intervention does not go far enough. One must then ask, why?

The answer to this rests partly in the thesis that state managers are unwilling to extend intervention in ways which might prejudice their own power. Should state managers intervene in educational consumption processes to ensure significantly higher consumption rates among subordinate groups they would inevitably lose the support of two politically powerful and mobilized groups who are the prime beneficiaries of education at present, the bourgeoisie and the middle classes. Let us say, for example, that the Department of Education were to intervene to ensure that working-class pupils developed linguistic and educational skills comparable to those of the middle class prior to participating in public examinations and that time and energy were to be devoted to this task in school. That is to say, the state would intervene to supplement the consumption capacities of working-class pupils. Such a development would mean, of course, that resources and time would have to be deployed differently within the school organization. Resources available for the development of a technically competent elite would be reduced. The interests of capitalists, therefore, in acquiring an elite of technical knowledge producers for the further expansion of capital, could be seriously threatened.[8]

State intervention to improve the consumption capacities of working-class pupils would also threaten the 'inheritance' interests of those middle-income groups who rely on cultural property to transmit privilege to their children. To terminate or upset the allegiance of such groups would be, of course, to undermine the primary political support systems of state managers themselves: the employee middle class and the self-employed (especially those who do not own sufficient capital to finance the livelihood of more than one child) are jointly the largest class groups within the state (Whelan and Whelan, 1984: 21). They are also currently the most successful consumers of educational services (Clancy, 1988; Breen, 1984). Any change in consumption relations would immediately jeopardize their 'inheritance' interests.

The balance between particularism and universalism in education is not explicable solely in terms of class interests however. Intervening between the state, social classes and the schools are an array of educational mediators which play a key role in the educational process.

The Mediators of Educational Services

The mediators of educational services are basically those groups who manage, oversee and administer the services at local level. The principal mediators in Irish second-level education are the teachers, the churches, the vocational education committees, individual school managements and parents' organizations. (The character of the mediators would, no doubt, vary from one level of education to another and from country to country.) The character of state policies in education, therefore, is not only contingent on the ability of particular classes to engage in the political manipulation of elected state managers; it is also dependent on the co-operation and compliance of those who administer the services on a daily basis, namely the mediators. By drawing a distinction here between social classes and educational mediators, we are not implying that the mediators are somehow outside the class system — as they are not — however, as mediators of the services they can often have power and status interests in education which may not necessarily be related to their structural location in the class system.

We will proceed now to analyse the role of the three most powerful educational mediators in the reproduction process at second level. In particular we will show how mediators are strategically located to operate as agents of counter-resistance in schools. While there is no doubt that resistances do develop in the manner that Willis, Anyon and others have observed, it is also the case that these resistances are counter-resisted by certain groups whose educational power and/or privilege is threatened.

Teacher unions as mediators

Teacher unions are among the most powerful mediators of educational services in Ireland (Joyce, 1985). There are two major teacher unions at second level, the Association of Secondary Teachers, Ireland (ASTI) whose members are primarily in secondary schools, and the Teachers Union of Ireland (TUI) whose members are primarily in vocational, community and comprehensive schools.[9] While the ASTI has no formal arrangement whereby it can influence state managers directly (i.e. by having regular meetings with the Department of Education staff), meetings are arranged when requested. The TUI, however, has a standing arrangement with the Department of Education to hold monthly meetings on matters of mutual concern. At the primary level, the Irish National Teachers' Organisation (INTO), the union representing almost all primary teachers, has regular meetings also with senior Education Department civil servants. Not only are the teacher unions consulted by state managers in formulating policy in general, they are also well represented in any committees or review bodies set up to develop policies in particular areas (cf. the membership list of the Curriculum and Examinations Board (CEB) and its committees, 1984, or the membership list of the Primary School Review Body, 1987). The formal consultative role granted to teacher unions by state managers shows the extent to which teacher representatives occupy a powerful position in developing policy. With such involvement, teachers' support or interest in facilitating or fostering resistances in the manner suggested by Giroux (1983c) seems highly unlikely. In terms of *power* the teachers as a corporate body have too much to lose.

As a professional, occupational group, teachers also have a specific *class* interest in countering resistances and recycling them, when possible, into educational products. Teachers are very much part of the propertyless middle classes whose power and influence is contingent on maintaining traditional hierarchical distinctions between mental and manual labour. If intellectual labour were no longer defined as 'superior' to manual labour, then the whole basis of teachers' differentials, which distances them from manual workers, would not be legitimated. There is no reason, therefore, why teachers would try to utilize pupil resistances to generate a crisis in education which might result in a redefinition of what is valuable knowledge. Even at a pragmatic level, if teachers were to do so, it would very likely threaten the organizational order on which their own authority is vested in the first place. Furthermore, teachers are not very likely to be granted sufficient autonomy by school administrators to manipulate resistances for revolutionary purposes as the Tyndale case in Britain has shown.

We are not suggesting here that teachers are always indifferent to the specific inequities that are reproduced in education or indeed that they necessarily oppose change. However, one must distinguish between the minority or secondary interests of the teaching body and the primary or majority interests of *teachers as a corporate entity*. Certain remedial modifications are sought regularly by the teacher unions — extra remedial teachers, more flexible curricula, greater support for the transition year or pre-employment programmes etc. — but not radical changes which would challenge the existing consumption patterns of educational services. As John Coolahan's (1984) analysis of the largest union for second-level teachers shows, concerted political action has been largely confined to industrial action over pay differentials from the foundation of the ASTI in 1909 up to the present day. The most recent industrial action of teachers in the spring and summer of

1986 was also primarily concerned with maintaining differentials between teachers and other manual and non-manual workers.

In a certain sense, therefore, teachers' counter-resistance often takes the form of compliant indifference rather than overt action. However, second-level teacher unions, in particular the ASTI, have actively counter-resisted when changes proposed were likely to erode their own status. In the late 1930s, for example, the ASTI opposed the use of set texts as they feared it would facilitate unqualified teachers and thereby lower the status of secondary teachers as a whole (Coolahan, 1984: 166). For the same reason, the ASTI opposed affiliation with the Trades Union Congress and the INTO in the 1940s and opposed joint Conciliation and Arbitration with other teacher unions in the late 1960s and early 1970s (ibid., 281–308). While the ASTI welcomed 'free education' in the late 1960s, it was less than enthusiastic about the rationalization which might be required to implement it (ibid., 257–63). Within the last year (1987/88) the ASTI also spoke out in favour of the state subsidization of private fee-paying secondary schools although these schools are known to perpetuate privilege. The TUI (whose members are primarily in the public schools) opposed it.

Finally, whether teachers will it or not, their mediation of state policies in schools adds its own weight to the legitimacy of the prevailing system. Teachers are certified and registered by public organizations (colleges of education, universities, Registration Council etc.) before they can teach in schools. Such certification creates public faith in the neutrality of their position vis-à-vis different kinds of pupils. Their 'professional' image helps legitimate the school organization as an impartial distributor of knowledge and expertise. Teachers' counter-resistances therefore take both explicit and deliberate, and implicit and non-deliberate, forms. First, teachers' own class and power interests are bound up with recycling resistance into organizationally non-threatening forms. This is a conscious and deliberate exercise. Second, teachers' own credentialized status implicitly legitimates the educational system with its semblance of impartiality and 'professionalism'.

The Churches as Mediators

Although there are a number of churches which exercise control over educational services in Ireland, the Roman Catholic Church is by far the most powerful and influential one. (We shall confine our discussion here therefore to the Catholic Church.)

The Church–State relationship in Irish schools represents a form of trade-off. In return for its capital investment in schools and its silent collaboration in the promotion of capitalist culture, state managers grant the Church the right to propagate its own dogmas and rituals in all schools. For example, the state lays down no regulations regarding religious education (except that religion should be taught), even in the state-controlled sectors. All churches are granted complete autonomy over religious socialization in their respective schools. Having negotiated a zone of influence for itself within the present school sector, therefore, neither the Catholic Church nor the other churches have any immediate power interests in radically altering a system of education which grants them unprecedented power and influence by international standards. Without its current rate of access to schools, the ideological impact of the Church in Irish society would be greatly reduced (Peillon, 1982; Inglis, 1987).

Just as teachers are part of the professional middle classes of society so too are the religious personnel—something which is often forgotten in social analysis. The corporate location of religious in the middle classes has meant that they have more often acted in line with the interests of that particular class than in promoting the interests of the unemployed or the working class in education. The Church has in fact been an agent of counter-resistance in a number of ways.

From the foundation of the state (1922) up to the 1960s it was evident that there were glaring class inequalities in access to second- and third-level education. While individual religious orders and personnel showed care and concern for this situation, as a corporate entity the Catholic Church was not greatly concerned. The setting up of vocational schools in the 1930s— aimed primarily at providing technical education for working-class pupils— elicited little interest from the churches. They merely sought and received an assurance from the state that 'general education' would not take place in these schools (Coolahan, 1981: 97). The schools were to be strictly practical and vocational in emphasis—thereby providing no threat to the Church-controlled secondary and national sectors. Consequently, for over thirty years, those small farm and working-class children, who were the principal participants in vocational schools, were deprived of access to the academic and intellectual subjects which their middle-class contemporaries availed of in the largely Church-controlled secondary school sector.

The *Council of Education Report* (Department of Education, 1960) is further proof of the corporate indifference of certain church members to the plight of working class and small farmers' children, and of counter-resistance to social equity. The Council was largely composed of religious personnel. In discussing the 'nature and aim of secondary education', the Council proclaimed that their primary concern was that schools should 'prepare pupils to be God-fearing and responsible citizens' (1960: 88). The intellectual development of the few was seen as the other major concern of secondary education. The notion of free education for all was rejected as 'untenable' and 'utopian', the argument being that 'only a minority of pupils would be capable of profiting by secondary (grammar school) education' (1960: 252). When free secondary education did come about in 1967 it was at the initiative of the state managers not the churches. In more recent times, the corporate interest of the Catholic Church in facilitating the perpetuation of class privilege is evident from the fact that the majority of fee-paying secondary schools which exist in the country are either run directly by religious personnel, or are under the patronage of some religious body. While the majority of Catholic schools are non-feepaying — and indeed one can see a tension within the Church between those who do not support the principle of elite schools and those who do — both recent historical and contemporary evidence suggests that the Catholic Church, as a corporate entity, has served the educational interests of the middle classes and the bourgeoisie more effectively than those of the working classes.

The Church's involvement in education in Ireland may also be seen to reproduce inequality in a more indirect manner. As Clancy (1983: 15–17) has observed, the status of religious in Irish society is high. By virtue of their high moral status, the churches bring an aura of moral legitimacy to bear on the educational process thereby immunizing it from attack. In addition, unlike lay teachers, religious teachers have no conspicuous class interests of their own. This is not to say, of course, that they cannot be located structurally in class terms, as I have pointed out above. However, their religious status supersedes their corporate class identity in the public eye. This further contributes to the image of impartiality that religion brings to bear on the educational site. In a word, through the dominance of religion in education, the Church's own legitimating armoury is transferred to the educational scene. It becomes unthinkable that the Church (as arbiter of moral goodness in society) would be a prime mover in a system of education which is daily involved in the reproduction of inequalities. It is, therefore, a combination of the Church's power interests in education and the impact of their legitimating armoury which pre-empts contradictions between Church interests and those of state managers from leading to major conflict in education. While resistances may develop in schools — in the form of pupil alienation or withdrawal — the Church, as educational mediator, has little to gain, and indeed much to lose, by cultivating this alienation to the point of political action or overt educational rebellion. In any such event, state managers could, and indeed have in limited ways in the past, ceased to underwrite the Church's agenda in schools. Given the corporate power interests of the Church in education, therefore, it is more likely to be an agent of counter-resistance than a facilitator of resistance in schools. The Church's own political survival is contingent on recycling resistances into viable educational commodities just as much as that of teachers is.

The Vocational Education Committees (VECs) as Mediators

By virtue of their composition[10] the VECs are a highly politicized and powerful mediating force in second-level education. While the VECs are, in some ways, a part of the state machinery — in the local rather than the national sense — their interests are by no means synonymous with it: the conflict in 1986 between the VECs and the Minister of Education over the failure of the latter to promote VEC-controlled schools is indeed proof of this.[11] Neither are their interests synonymous with those of teachers, although the latter form a significant group within the VEC. The fact that teachers in vocational schools are in a separate trade union (the TUI), for example, shows how vocational teachers differ in their sectional interests from teachers in the secondary sector. The VECs, and their staff, therefore, are distinctive administrative and organizational entities with their own survival problems within the educational site. Indeed, because vocational schools exemplify some of the more negative particularistic aspects of education (low retention rates, high levels of streaming, sexist curricular provision etc., Hannan *et al.,* 1983; Hannan and Boyle, 1987), they have little to gain by encouraging resistance in their schools. Given the fact that they are in daily competition with the more prestigious secondary sector, an over-elaboration of the contradictions of schooling could bring about the demise of the VEC sector itself.

The class composition of members of the vocational education committees would also suggest that they are more likely to be agents of counter-resistance than facilitators of resistance in education. The VECs are largely controlled by representatives of local authorities. Local authorities, in turn, are dominated by middle-class personnel (Chubb, 1982: 91). The success of the middle classes in benefiting from the educational status quo has already been noted above. Given this, it is highly unlikely that representatives of that class would want to alter radically the patterns of educational outcome reproduced in schools, whether they are vocational or not.

Finally, just as the religious bring an aura of moral righteousness to bear on the educational site which may reproduce inequalities by camouflaging the real outcomes of schooling, the seeming democratic representativeness of the VECs serve the same function. Being composed of elected personnel, the VEC seems to be a highly representative body serving the educational interests of a wide array of class groups. The VECs bring an aura of democratic representativeness to bear on the educational site which immunizes the educational system from attack. After all, if local elected representatives do not find the educational system wanting or iniquitous then why should radical change be necessary?

Parents as Mediators

Parental groups — be they in the form of parental representatives on boards of management, parent councils in secondary schools or nationally representative bodies of parents — play an increasingly important role in the mediation of educational services. While they do not exert direct power and influence over timetabling and curricula like the teachers or religious do, they play an important monitoring role: they oversee the organizational functioning of the schools. Given that parent representatives are generally elected by others to committees and councils, one would expect that the democratic process would ensure that all class interests would be proportionately represented on them. While there has been no research conducted in Ireland on the composition of parent councils or of parent representatives on boards of management, both recent[12] and past research in Britain (McGeeney, 1969: 105) shows that upper socio-economic groups are likely to dominate parent committees and governing bodies. (Although I did not collect statistical data on this question during my interviews with principals, the dominance of parent councils and committees by middle-class parents was a matter they frequently commented upon when discussing the relationship between parents and schools.)

If our assumption regarding middle-class dominance of parent councils is correct — and circumstantial evidence suggests that it is — then there is little reason for parents' councils to upset the consumption patterns being reproduced in schools. The children of the middle classes and bourgeoisie are after all the prime beneficiaries of the system as we noted above already.

The control dynamics of mediating organizations, such as parent councils, therefore, may also help explain why the contradictions of schooling do not generate major changes. It is contrary to the interests of the controlling groups within them. Indeed the seemingly democratic representativeness of parents' councils actually adds legitimacy to the process. If democratically elected parents' councils are there to monitor what is happening in schools and they do not find schools wanting, then it seems that schools must be operating according to principles which are fair and just.

Concluding Remarks

Hitherto we have identified two factors which would support the claim that the mediators of educational services are potentially forces of counter-resistance in education. First, we saw how the class/power/status interest of mediating groups are closely bound up with the educational status quo. Second, we showed how the legitimating armoury of the mediating groups

Figure 2: *Significant educational mediators: their interests, legitimating armouries and potential conflict paths*

	The churches	The VECs	The teachers	Parents' councils
1. Interests:	Maintaining power over consciences	Jobs and career maintenance	Maintaining status differentials and authority	Controlling role of middle-class parents
2. Legitimating armoury:	Moral authority	Democratic representativeness	Professional autonomy	Democratic representativeness
3. Potential conflict paths in the matrix of power groups	*Contestants* * (Examples): Church versus VEC Church versus teachers Parents versus teachers		*Possible power issue* School expansion or survival (this takes the form of inter-school competition for pupils) Administrative control within schools: career interests of *both* at stake Teachers' autonomy claim conflicts with parents' accountability claim	

*Any one or more of the mediating groups can, of course, form alliances with others to pursue specific interests at a given time.

135

themselves serves the ideological purpose of bolstering existing patterns of educational provision and consumption. A third factor which may explain why mediators are frequently agents of counter-resistance is power conflicts between the mediating groups themselves (cf. Fig. 2). What is being suggested here is that conflict between any, some or all of those groups mediating educational services itself acts as a stabilizing force within the educational system. Should one group resist the reproduction of existing patterns of educational consumption, it runs the risk of losing power to its competitor. Should the Churches decide, for example, not to foster the technical skills and competitive individualism which parents now expect from schools, the state could easily withdraw funds and expand vocational and lay control instead.

The conflict possible within the matrix of mediators is not confined, of course, to those which we have outlined in Figure 2. Any one or more of the groups can form alliances to oppose another group should a particular power interest be threatened. The case of the dismissal of Ms Eileen Flynn in Co. Wexford is an example of how Church and parent groups formed an alliance against a teacher in the interests of preserving a particular code of sexual behaviour among teachers.[13] Thereby, the Church's administrative control and the parents' accountability demands were ratified.

Territorial conflicts between educational mediators therefore forestall the possibility that anyone will exploit the contradictions of schooling to the point where they threaten their power base. Should the mediators be in a position, however, where they have little to lose in power, status or income terms by exploiting the contradictions of schooling they may well become active agents of resistance. Such is not the case in Ireland, however, for the various cultural and historical reasons we have outlined above.

While one cannot deny that the mechanisms of social and cultural reproduction are frequently ineffective and are often faced 'with elements of opposition' (Giroux, 1983c: 100), it is necessary to highlight the conditions under which resistances are likely to be effective and those in which they are not. Using evidence from Ireland, we would suggest that the possibilities for resistances leading to radical educational change are greatly reduced: (a) when credentialized knowledge plays a key role in both producing and distributing privileges as is the case in many post-colonial states; (b) when large and politically mobilized groups (such as the propertyless middle classes in Ireland) are already highly successful in utilizing the educational system to perpetuate their own class power and when no alternative route for the reproduction of their class power is readily open to them; (c) when groups mediating educational services have a major stake in the educational status quo—either independent of, or due to their class affiliations. The strategic location of mediating groups at the centre of the educational enterprise is, we suggest, an important factor in explaining how resistances get recycled into educational products. Having access to both classrooms and centres of administration, mediating groups can identify resistances at an early stage and redirect them (by means of pressure on state managers if necessary) into marketable educational products should they think it desirable.[14]

Notes

1 Only in 1922 was the Irish Free State established; only in 1949 did the 26 counties of the original Free State become a Republic. The remaining 6 countries of Ireland comprise Northern Ireland, and are still under British colonial rule.

2 One of the factors which must be borne in mind when examining the role of education in Irish society is that Ireland did not experience the rapid expansion of the white-collar public (modern) sectors, which characterizes many post-colonial states in the immediate post-independence period, until nearly 30 years after independence. Protectionist policies fuelled by an intense nationalism pre-empted it. Thus, education did not become *the* major determinant of status and power until the early 1960s when the public-service sector expanded rapidly to direct the industrial expansion heralded by the accession of Sean Lemass to power in the late 1950s. The expansion of the 1960s was similar to other such developments in a variety of less 'developed' countries. It was greatly aided by international borrowing (Crotty, 1986).

3 Ireland has had a national primary education system since 1831 and a long tradition for centuries prior to that of hedge schools. No doubt this facilitated early teacher organization.

4 It is interesting to note that the two major political parties in the Republic of Ireland, Fianna Fail and Fine Gael, are divided on nationalist grounds, not on a left-right dichotomy as is common in most Western European states. The Fianna Fail party claims strongest allegiance to nationalist ideals and has been in power for a great proportion of the period since independence.

5 It is fair to say that agricultural land is a major source of wealth in Ireland which is by no means distributed in an equitable manner (Commins, 1986). However, given the tradition of a patriarchal stem family system in Irish farming combined with capitalist values, land is not regarded as a distributable source of wealth.

6 As Clancy (1988: 30) and Breen (1984: 32) have shown, both the upper and lower non-manual groups are currently among the most successful consumers of educational services in Ireland. They are therefore well educated and well able to articulate their interests when the need arises.

7 When referring to state managers here, we are speaking primarily of the elected state managers, namely politicians, and in particular the Minister of Education. Under Irish law, the Minister is accountable to the Dail (Parliament) and the public for all decisions of her/his Department (Joyce, 1985: 17). The Minister is the principal state decision-maker. This is not to deny however, the very influential role played by appointed state managers (principally senior civil servants) as advisers to the Ministers). As Chubb observes, senior civil servants are among the 'proximate policy-makers of the State' (1982: 171–99).

8 Otto Newman suggests that innovation is vital for the functioning of industrial capitalism (*The Challenge of Corporatism (1981),* London, Macmillan, p. 60). Innovation requires education.

9 See Ch. 1 note 2 for a description of the different types of schools in the Republic of Ireland.

10 Of the 809 second-level schools in the Republic of Ireland in 1984/85, 30 per cent (242) were vocational schools controlled and managed by the 38 county-based Vocational Education Committees. The original remit of the vocational schools was to provide technical and continuation education at the post-primary level. Since 1966 the vocational schools are also free to offer any or all of the academic subjects traditionally confined to secondary schools, and virtually all have availed of this opportunity. Each VEC comprises of 14 members, a maximum of 8 and a minimum of 5 of whom must be elected members of the local rating authority. The remainder of the committee is composed of representatives of specific interest groups including trade unions, employers and groups with specific educational interests (Coolahan, 1981: 96).

11 In the spring of 1986, the national organization representing all the VECs threatened to cease co-operating in the development of new community schools unless the Minister of Education made a more concerted effort to promote and develop vocational schools.

12 A recent study by Michael Golby and Stephen Brigley (Exeter University, School of Education) of parent governors in secondary schools in Devon, England shows that parent governors are primarily middle-class. (Reported in the *Observer,* Sunday, 18 Sept. 1988, pp. 7, 49).

13 This is a reference to a recent (1982–5) controversy in which a teacher lost her post in a second-level school. The parents and religious authorities of the school collaborated in order to obtain her dismissal.

14 With the development of free education in the late 1960s and the raising of the school-leaving age to 15 in 1972, large numbers of working class and small farmers' children entered second-level schools which they had not done traditionally. As the curriculum was not altered sufficiently to accommodate their wide-ranging interests and capabilities, pressure from teachers and practitioners grew throughout the 1970s to introduce some changes to forestall rebellion. (One could call it counter-resisting resistances.) The response was the development of alternative educational programmes outside the mainstream system: Pre-Employment Courses (PECs) flourished in schools with large working-class cohorts as did Vocational Preparation and Training Programmes (VPTPs) (cf. Crooks and McKernan (1984) *The Challenge of Change,* Dublin, Institute of Public Administration; and Williams, K. and McNamara, G. (1985) *The Vocational Preparation Course,* Dublin, Cumann na Meánmhúinteoirí, Éire, for an account of these).

Both PECs and VPTPs represent, in my view, successful attempts at counter-resistance by teachers, vocational education committees and other mediators. They are a means of recycling working-class resistances into viable educational products which, in turn, reproduce their class position as the courses are not given the status or credit of the mainstream examinations. By syphoning off resistances into alternative programmes, schools are left free to facilitate the successful consumption of educational services by the bourgeoisie and the middle classes.

Chapter 6

The Rise of Technical Knowledge and Competitive Individualism in Schools: A Comment

Introduction

The two most prominent features of Irish second-level education to emerge from this study are its increasingly technical orientation (at the formal curriculum level) and the competitive individualism evident in the daily organization of school life. Schools are also strongly hierarchical institutions in which pupils are given little autonomy. While it is evident that schools generally are becoming technical in orientation (and it must be remembered that what Gardner (1983) calls logical-mathematical and linguistic intelligences are still the primary ones emphasized in the technical subjects, not manual skills, see Ch. 2) and competitive at the individual level, this is not to deny that the form which both technical knowledge and competition takes varies considerably with the class and/or gender composition of the school (Chs 2–4). Neither is it to suggest that Irish schools are somehow unique in their individualism.[1] Educationalists as diverse as Bidwell (1980), Hargreaves (1980), White (1980) and Apple (1982) have all commented upon the individualistic ethos of contemporary education in other countries. What makes the individualism of Irish schools interesting is that it seems to contradict the educational ideals of Catholic teaching in certain ways. And the Catholic Church controls a majority of second-level schools.

The narrow emphasis of the curriculum on the development of a limited range of academic skills (be these in the technical sphere or not) would seem to contradict the Church's ideal that education should contribute to the development of all aspects of the individual (Vatican Council, 1965: 637–51). Equally, the highly competitive ethos of schools would seem to be anathema to the Christian (collectivistic) ideals of love and care for others. Indeed the state also endorses the notion of 'educating the whole person' as an educational ideal (Curriculum and Examinations Board, 1984: 12–14). The contradiction

139

between rhetoric and practice is evident therefore in both Church and State. Exploring the meaning and significance of these contradictions is a major research task in its own right and could not be addressed comprehensively here. What we intend to do in this final chapter, however, is to comment on the rise of particular forms of individualism in Irish education. We will also examine its social and educational implications.

The Rise of Technical Knowledge

Up to the mid-1960s, the Irish second-level curriculum was a prime example of a classical-liberal system. The arts and humanities dominated the curriculum while commercial, scientific and technological subjects were few in number and were only available in a limited range of schools. Third-level education was also heavily oriented to the classics and arts. Indeed, secondary education was regarded as a preparation for university entrance; that is, for entry to a system in which the arts and classics were dominant (cf. Coolahan, 1981, for a detailed historical account of the Irish educational system).

Preceded by years of massive emigration, unemployment and economic stagnation, the early 1960s witnessed a number of major economic and educational changes: export-oriented industrialization became a priority value; protectionist trade policies were abandoned and education was defined in human capital terms. Education was regarded as an investment like any other form of capital investment. The influence of human capital theory and technological functionalism, so prevalent in Europe and North America at the time (Karabel and Halsey, 1977), were clearly in evidence therefore. They were particularly in evidence in the OECD backed *Investment in Education Report* (Department of Education, 1966) which strongly endorsed the expansion of the technical sector.[2] Economic salvation was equated with technological, commercial and scientific expansion.

The expansion of technical knowledge that followed from *The Investment in Education Report* at both second and third level (Clancy, in press) would seem warranted by certain economic changes which occurred over the last twenty-five years. In the late 1950s agricultural produce dominated the export trade; in 1958, 68.0 per cent of all exports were agricultural, while only 17.1 per cent were manufactured goods. By 1984 the position had changed radically: manufactured goods now constituted 63.2 per cent of exports, while agricultural produce only accounted for 23.2 per cent (Wickham, 1986: 74). Ireland changed therefore, from being almost entirely dependent on agricultural exports in the 1950s, to being heavily dependent on the export of industrial goods in the 1980s (Central Statistics Office, 1985: 6–7). The shift towards an industrial economy would seem to necessitate a more technical orientation in education.

Problems in the Technological–Functionalist Explanation of Change

The technological–functionalists' argument outlined above does not, however, provide an entirely adequate explanation for the advance of technical education. When we analyse labour-force characteristics in more detail, we find evidence suggesting that Ireland did not require the expansion of technical education (especially at the more specialized levels) to the degree that it has occurred. Wickham's work for example, suggests that the electronics industry (one of the most important of the new manufacturing industries) principally employs semi-skilled assembly workers. He found that 57.4 per cent of the employees in foreign-owned electronics firms were either unskilled or semi-skilled (1983: 170). The Telesis Report makes a similar point about foreign-owned electrical engineering plants. It observes that foreign-owned chemical and pharmaceutical companies do not carry out much research or development work in Ireland (NESC, 1984, Telesis (Summary) Report: 25–9). Neither can it be said that the patterns identified by Wickham and the Telesis group are exceptional, as 56 per cent of all employees in the industrial sector were either semi-skilled or unskilled in 1976 (Wickham, 1983: 170).

To create an export-oriented industrial economy, successive Irish governments in the 1960s and 1970s encouraged (through grants, tax incentives etc.) multinational investment in Ireland. As the industries attracted, however, were often 'capital-intensive and labour-extensive' (Crotty, 1986: 92) what happened in schools or third-level colleges was not as relevant as it might appear: the jobs simply did not materialize despite massive state-investment by the state-controlled Industrial Development Authority (IDA). (The IDA spent around IR£29,000 on every new job it created in the late 1970s (Crotty, 1986: 99, citing NESC *Telesis Report*, 1984: 188).) While 96,026 new jobs were approved for foreign firms between 1970 and 1978 only 28,937 of these actually existed in 1981. In other words, only 30.1 per cent of the approved industrial jobs actually existed in January 1981 (NESC, 1984: 433). Furthermore, employment in indigenous manufacturing industries also declined from the 1950s to the 1980s as did employment nationally. Crotty summarizes the situation well:

> The total number engaged in manufacturing industry in Ireland in 1951...was 212,000. The total had declined to 197,000 by September 1984 and was then still declining. The number engaged in the IDA's enclave industries in 1984 was 80,000. The number continuing to work in Ireland's indigenous manufacturing industry was, therefore, some 117,000 or only about 55% of the pre-Whitaker level [i.e. 1951] level... The total number at work in Ireland declined from 1,217,000 in 1951 to 1,112,000 in 1984, or by 9% (1986: 100).

Given that so-called 'industrial development' has not resulted in a major expansion of technically skilled employment (even international evidence does not suggest that highly technological industries employ large numbers of highly skilled specialists: job forecasts in the US, for example, suggest that only a small proportion of future jobs will be of a skilled variety (Apple, 1986: 157–9), one must ask if new technical skills were greatly required in the services sector.

A brief perusal of contemporary employment patterns in the services sector (which employs *circa* 50 per cent of the labour force (Central Statistics Office, CSO, 1981: Vol. 4, Table 6, p. 20)) does not suggest that high levels of technical skills are in great demand there either. Whether one takes the commercial, insurance, banking, transport or public administration sectors, there is little evidence of large cohorts of specialist technical staff being employed. In the banking and finance area, for example, 11,544 of the 12,214 women employed are clerical workers; 5,483 of the 10,079 men are also in this category (CSO, 1981: Vol. 4, Table 14, pp. 150–1). The same kind of pattern holds true in the insurance area (ibid.). If one examines Government departments (other than the Garda Síochána and Defence) one also finds a preponderance of clerical workers: while 3,043 of the 18,069 men employed are professional or technical workers, 7,699 are clerical; also, 13,759 (87 per cent) of the 15,882 women employed are clerical (ibid., 156–7). Although a majority of those employed in health and education are professionals, they are predominantly teachers and nurses, not exactly new technical occupations (ibid., 158–61).

Perhaps a more plausible explanation for the expansion of technical education in Ireland, therefore, is to see it as preparatory work in the creation of a relatively small technical elite which is required for capital's expansion. By diffusing technical knowledge across a wide base, one undoubtedly increases the level of interest in technical knowledge and subsequently the competition for technical places in both higher education and the job market. Thereby, standards are raised and a sophisticated elite of technical experts and knowledge producers emerges.

> A corporate economy requires the production of high levels of technical knowledge to keep the economic apparatus running effectively and to become more sophisticated in the maximization of opportunities for economic expansion (Apple, 1979: 36–7).

However, as Apple notes, the diffusion of the more sophisticated technical knowledge across the labour force is not required. The fact that large cohorts of pupils fail subjects, or never pursue them to a level at which they become competent within them, is incidental. What matters is that a sophisticated technical elite, which will aid capital's expansion, is produced. Certain features of both the Irish educational system and the current labour market lend credence to this hypothesis.

As both our data (Ch. 2) and that of Hannan *et al.* (1983) shows, not all types of scientific/technological/commercial (technical) subjects are available in all schools. Both the social-class and gender composition of the school influence the type of provision within them. The more academically oriented technical subjects such as physics, chemistry or higher mathematics, for example, are more likely to be found in secondary schools (which have the largest middle-class cohort) than vocational schools (which have the largest proportion of children from working-class and small-farm families). On the other hand, provision in the more practical technical subjects, such as woodwork and metalwork, is best in the vocational sector. While technical knowledge is widely diffused in Irish schools, therefore, the more elite aspects of it are still most available to middle-class pupils, in particular to male middle-class pupils (Hannan *et al.*, 1983).

The expansion of technical knowledge also serves a social control function in our society. At second level, the widespread availability of technical subjects forestalls parental disquiet as to the value of schooling: after all, the subjects taught *seem* to be relevant in an industrial economy. Within-school conflict may also be mitigated by the seeming relevance of commerce and science. The fact that capitalist accumulation is increasingly dependent on capital-intensive rather than labour-intensive means of production (Crotty, 1986: op. cit.) is not visible in the daily life of the schools. Thus, the legitimacy of technical expansion is not called into question. The relevance of the technical conceals the redundancy of technical *labour* in an increasingly *capital* intensive economy.

To understand the increasing orientation of second-level education towards the diffusion of technical knowledge therefore, we must go beyond the functionalist observation that it was necessary because the Irish economy had become increasingly industrialized. Given the relatively small proportion of new jobs requiring technical skills (at least of the kind that require extensive pre-job education and training) the expansion of the technical might be more plausibly explained by the social control functions served by expanding technical knowledge and the role played by small technical elites in capital's expansion.

Competitive Individualism: A Comment

In Chapter 3 we demonstrated how the relational context of learning is both competitive and hierarchical. As the main focus of that chapter has been on the competitive dimension of schooling, and as the question of hierarchical control in schools has been widely addressed elsewhere (cf. the work of Bowles and Gintis, Philip Jackson and Philip Cusick) our focus here will be on examining the competitiveness of school life.

The Universality of Competitive Individualism

Competitiveness in schools is by no means a new educational phenomenon. Competitive examinations were an integral part of the education of the Chinese literati as early as the seventh century BC (Weber, 1946: pp. 422–6). Within Europe, Durkheim notes that the Jesuit schools of the seventeenth century were also highly competitive (1977: 263–4). Indeed, competition of some kind would seem inevitable in any society in which access to finite material resources, power and privileges, is highly dependent on education. In a capitalist society, however, competition is even more likely to be exaggerated than in a feudal society like seventeeth-century France. As Marx observed 'personal relations flow out of relations of production and exchange' (Marx, 1973: 165). Because relations of production and exchange are directed towards accumulation and profit in a capitalist society particularly, competition for money or profit comes to mediate men and women's relationships to each other. 'That which is for me through the medium of *money* — that for which I can pay (i.e. which money can buy) — that I am, the possessor of money' (Marx, 1964: 167). In our society what this means is that relations in school are also mediated by money, as schools currently act as distributors of credentials which give access to money. Competition for credentials therefore merely represents the educational form of monied relationships.

Explaining individual competitiveness in schools as the by-product of a capitalist world system does not explain the nature and degree of educational competitiveness entirely. The high levels of competition in second-level schools is also a function of the unique economic and demographic structures of Irish society at present.

The interplay between the increased orientation of the economy towards employee-type work and the existence of a burgeoning youth cohort with declining emigration options (Rottman and O'Connell, 1982) also explains the high levels of competition in schools. In the immediate post-war period the birth rate was high but so was the emigration rate; internal competition for jobs was thereby greatly reduced. In the last 15–20 years, however, options to emigrate have greatly declined and the employee sector has itself contracted due to the increased dependence on capital-intensive rather than labour-intensive means of production. There is keen demand, therefore, for a declining number of jobs. Levels of competitiveness for jobs has resulted, in turn, in employers using educational credentials to select employees, thus translating the competition for jobs into competition for credentials. As Ireland moves increasingly, therefore, towards an intelligentsia-type society, in which the cultural capital and 'expert' knowledge certified in credentials become the major determinants of power, status and income, schools are likely to become increasingly competitive. In Soviet society for example, where access to power and privilege is already highly dependent on educational credentials, this has indeed happened already (Dobson, 1977; Zajda, 1980).

In Chapter 3 we observed that while competition tends to be universal in schools, it also tends to be rotational in character. Schools which operated selection (competition) at entry were least likely to allocate pupils to classes stratified on the basis of competitive tests (i.e. to stream or band). Those schools which had the most rigid systems of streaming or banding were, in turn, the least likely to have continuous (competitive) assessments and examinations. Thus, while exposure to competition is universal it takes particularistic forms in different types of schools. To comprehend the particularistic aspects of competitiveness one must locate schools within the existing relations of production in society.

The Particularistic Forms of Competition

Schools are collective systems of relationships. As such they develop their collective identity from the character of the relationships within them. In a capitalist society, the relational climate of a given school is strongly influenced by the class competition of its constituent members. In Ireland, the class composition of different types of schools varies considerably; for example, for a variety of political and historical reasons, Irish secondary schools are private institutions: thereby, they can select pupils at entry. Thus, their class composition tends to be more middle-class than that of public schools (cf. Breen, 1984: op. cit). Within the secondary sector itself the class composition of the fee-paying schools differs from that of schools in the 'free scheme' (i.e. non-fee-paying schools). The existence of fees means that the cohort in the fee-paying sector tends to be more bourgeois and upper-middle-class in composition than those in the less selective 'free scheme' sector. Though no school type caters solely for one class, different school types *tend* to cater to different ensembles of classes. We can see, therefore, that the particularistic character of schools can only be understood when one comprehends the class competition of the different types of schools.

In our study we found that fee-paying secondary schools were the least competitive at the class-allocation phase, but the most competitive in the evaluation phase, that is to say, while none of the fee-paying schools operated a total system of streaming, they were the most likely to have frequent assessments or to award prizes for school work. Public schools—particularly vocational schools—occupied an obverse position. They were the least likely to have a strong competitive press in the form of continuous assessments or reports, but they were the most likely to stream or band (Tables 16, 22, A24–A28). These processes reflect the class composition of the school cohorts in question. As both Rutter (1979) and Coleman (1982) have shown, a strong academic climate (in the form of closely monitored and frequently tested work) is associated with good academic outcomes. Consequently, by having high levels of competition for all classes (and little rigid streaming) fee-paying schools are maximizing academic outcomes for *all* pupils. By contrast, streaming and banding—both of which are strongest in the public schools—tend to result in the concentration of resources and interest in the top streams or bands. (Our own data supports this contention as does the work of Hargreaves, 1967; Ball, 1981; Hannan and Boyle, 1987). When resources are concentrated on a few, high academic attainment is only likely to be attained by a minority of the cohort. The widely divergent transfer rates from different types of second-level schools to third-level education would seem to lend support to this hypothesis,[3] though the transfer rates are also undoubtedly a function of factors unrelated to attainment.

What our data implies, therefore, is that, while individual competitiveness is universal in schools, the form of competitiveness reflects the class composition of the school's constituent members. Schools which are predominantly middle-class and upper-class would seem to maximize the consumption of educational resources among the entire cohort within those groups. In contrast with this, the competitive forms which exist in schools with large working-class cohorts only maximize consumption among a minority of the group. Thus, the organizational context within which the distribution of credentials occurs in schools, perpetuates class hierarchies in the consumption relations of the educational system. This does not occur by accident. On the one hand it represents the collective response of the educationally 'wise' to maximize their children's rate of educational consumption. On the other hand it reflects the lack of response of the educationally uninitiated.

As noted above a declining proportion of the Irish work-force are the owners of industrial or agricultural capital. The number of self-employed is an indicator of this type of ownership and this sector has declined steadily since the 1950s (Rottman *et al.*, 1982: Ch. 2). Furthermore, many of the owners of agricultural capital are small farmers who cannot transfer any major status benefit to their children by virtue of what they own.[4] For those who lack productive capital, therefore, the transmission of privilege to children is largely mediated by schools. Unlike the transmission of privilege through material property, the transmission of privilege through cultural property is a highly precarious affair. The child's relationship to the school must be monitored and managed carefully to ensure the safe transmission of educational inheritance. Failure on the school's part to maximize the child's consumption of educational services, or unwillingness on the child's part to consume them, can seriously disrupt the pattern of inheritance. Furthermore, the managerial and monitoring skills involved in transferring cultural property are not 'taught' inside the schools themselves (Bourdieu, 1974). Neither can they be bought easily in the form of professional services in the market. Thus, only those who have had prior access to the school system, or access to informed sources close to it, can manage it successfully. Ability to manage the system to secure one's inheritance is a function of having prior access to the system itself. Hence the perpetuation of existing educational relations of consumption.[5]

While we have suggested above that the specificity of forms of competitiveness ensures particularistic outcomes, neither the specificity of competitiveness or its consequences are readily visible to the educationally unwise observer. Just as consumption abilities are a function of prior knowledge so is one's ability to observe fully the relations of consumption themselves. To see what exists one must be trained to look. Schools appear similar in many ways to the uninitiated: they all do public examinations; they all give tests of various kinds; the subjects taught are broadly similar in all. Furthermore, competition of some kind is universal. It is, in fact, the universality of competition which operates to perpetuate the myth that individual achievement and 'ability' are major determinants of status determination. If everyone is competing then the game must be fair. After all it would be absurd to continue to compete in a game in which the same teams always win. Yet education is a 'game' in which the same social class teams do always tend to win (cf. Clancy, 1988: op. cit.; and Whelan and Whelan, 1984: op. cit.). The meritocratic competitive character of schooling is therefore merely a charade as the dice is always loaded against lower socio-economic groups. While the loading of the dice occurs through a variety of factors (which for obvious reasons of space cannot be discussed in detail here), one very important one is undoubtedly the definition of the game itself. In school, logical-mathematical and linguistic intelligences (cf. Gardner, 1983 for a discussion of these concepts) are equated with 'ability' thereby the academically uninitiated are automatically 'cooled out' by being defined as lacking in ability or intelligence.

Within-school processes are not the only factors which load the dice. Individual competition is only fair if one competes in a world with equally privileged peers. In a materially and culturally hierarchical society, competition between equals is impossible without either handicapping the privileged or compensating the relatively disadvantaged. Such intervention would, of course, threaten the inheritance patterns of those (predominantly middle-class) groups whose superior educational consumption skills now enable them to use schools to perpetuate privilege among their offspring. Given the power of these same groups within the state and within the educational system itself, any intervention to alter the prevailing relations of educational consumption would undoubtedly be strongly opposed.

Competitive individualism in schools must be understood, therefore, at two levels. At the level of ideology it represents a façade concealing the inevitability of educational outcomes. At the level of daily practice it reproduces both the universal monied relations of capitalist society and the particularistic class — and related 'ability' — relations of educational consumption.

Conclusions regarding the Primacy of Individualism in Education

The rise of technical competitive individualism is closely associated with the increasing advancement of industrial capitalism in Ireland since the 1960s. The emphasis on technical competence cannot be adequately explained, however, in terms of the technical requirements of the labour market. The proportion of jobs requiring technical expertise of the type developed in school is still relatively small. Consequently, the increased orientation toward the technical may be more adequately explained by the social-control functions served by expanding technical knowledge and the role played by small technical elites in capital's expansion. Like technical knowledge, the competitive individualism of the school's relational life must also be partly understood in terms of social control. In a competitive system in which 'the same team always tends to win', competition is merely a façade concealing the inevitability of school outcomes. The symbolic significance of competitiveness is distinct, however, from its practical significance. At the level of praxis, competition is a universal quantifiable entity in school life. As such, competitive individualism reproduces — in educational form — the universal monied relations of capitalist society. The unique class-related form which competition also seems to take in schools ensures that the particularistic relations of educational consumption are also reproduced. It should be noted here, of course, that the *form* of technical knowledge (and indeed extra-curricular knowledge) disseminated in different types of schools also reflects their class composition (cf. Ch. 2). Therefore, reproduction occurs both through the formal and informal knowledge systems and the organizational contexts of learning.

What we are suggesting, therefore, is that at the level of both theory and practice, *personal* (individual) development is defined as being synonymous with general social development in education; in the words of Bidwell, it is assumed that 'solving the problem of personal welfare cumulates to solve the problem of social welfare' (1980: 101). Yet there is an inherent contradiction within the individualistic norm itself. The competitive individualism which characterizes the relational context of learning is anathema to the idea that acquired technical expertise will be used to serve collective goals. The learning of technical knowledge takes place in a context in which maximization of self-interest is what is most highly rewarded. In school, one does not just learn expertise through the daily organization of work, one practises at being better than others and at using one's relative advantage to gain access to better and more valuable credentials than one's competitors. The implicit relational norm of school life, therefore, is that knowledge gained is for personal advancement not for public service.

The Implications of Individualism

Introduction

The ideology of individualism pervades educational thought in Ireland and elsewhere at the present time (Bidwell, 1980; Hargreaves, 1980; White 1980; Apple, 1982; Lynch, 1987b). Not alone has individualism been the dominant ideology, it has also taken a particular form. It presupposes an essentialist view of human nature, a consensual understanding of the social system and a belief that solving the problem of personal welfare cumulates to solve the problem of social welfare.[6] Furthermore, the essentialist view of human nature is itself premised on the supposition that the narrowly conceived intellectual development of the person should be given primacy in educational practice. The individual is conceived as an abstract entity whose essential nature is primarily intellectual in the logical-mathematical and linguistic sense. Because psychometricians and educationalists have developed a variety of instruments — albeit scientifically questionable ones — for the measurement of the essentially defined intellectual capabilities mentioned above, this has dialectically reinforced the beliefs (a) that ability is primarily intellectual in the narrow logical-mathematical and linguistic sense; (b) that it can be measured; and (c) that it is an asocial intrinsic quality. The educational intelligensia's most elaborate formulation of the individualist thesis is found in meritocratic ideology. The works of human capital theorists and technological functionalists are suffused with the idea that there is a limited 'pool of talent' which must be encouraged and rewarded if society is to advance economically. Meritocratic ideololgy found sociological expression in the work of Davis and Moore (1945); in Ireland, it found educational expression in the Organisation for Economic Cooperation and Development (OECD) supported *Investment in Education Report* in 1966. The concept of meritocracy in fact, became the guiding principle for educational change in the 1960s (Greaney and Kellaghan, 1984: 22–8). Equality of educational opportunity was defined in meritocratic terms by the policy-makers themselves. The logic was: economic growth depends on educational investment; educational investment means developing the talented few; and the talented are those with narrowly defined intellectual abilities.

Because the educational person had been defined in abstract individual terms, and the individual itself was then defined in terms of narrow intellectual parameters, all problems and solutions in education reflected this abstracted and non-relational concept of the person. As Bidwell notes, for example, school effect studies — which are central to much educational research — interpret social reform as being defined in terms of advancing the individual's life chances for mobility:

> the paramount problem of personal welfare is biased status attainment. The solution of these problems remains an individualistic solution: to give every member of society the means and even the motivation to do well (1980: 101).

In educational terms their reformism is premised on:

> an implicit theory of learning noted for its individualism. It centers on the individual learner; it treats not only his intellectual and motivational capacities, but also his exposure to the resources and social life of the school as if they were his own personal traits (ibid., 102).

What is absent, according to Bidwell, is an examination of how social relations influence social learning or how the school and classroom order affects the distribution and receipt of resources for cognitive learning (ibid., 103). The gaps in sociological understanding which resulted from individualistic assumptions are, of course, not unrelated to the practical social and educational implications emanating from it.

Qualifying, Demeaning and Disqualifying

The meritocratic thesis supposes that those who have ability and who make the effort deserve to be rewarded in society: in the words of Young (1961) that IQ + Effort = Merit. Though undoubtedly a social advance on nepotism, the meritocratic ideal is suffused with ambiguities and highly inegalitarian presuppositions. It is a highly normative concept even when it was paraded as a natural description of the way things work. By defining society as an achieving one 'it makes one particular mechanism of status distribution into the norm' (Offe, 1976: 40). Every social claim which is not based on quantifiable performance is untenable.

> Performance thus counts . . . as the single legitimate measure of every form of social honour. This immediately presupposes the belief that everything humans do is measurable and thus objectively ascertainable (ibid., 41).

The problem with distributing status, or educational credentials, on the basis of individual performance is, of course, that performance must have operational content. Firstly, assuming that the operational content is measurable and visible, there is no logical reason why high performance on one form of content deserves status any more than performance on another form. It is a matter of value–judgement. This is where the meritocratic ideal becomes educationally problematic.

In Ireland, school credentials are distributed primarily on the basis of performance in written academic tests. While a variety of non–academic skills are examined in a limited range of subjects, such as home economics, woodwork, metalwork, mechanical and technical drawing, construction studies and engineering, even within these subjects there is a strong bias towards academic learning. In the Leaving Certificate examination less than a quarter of the marks in the higher level paper in Construction Studies, and only one third of those in Engineering are given for practical skills. There is no practical test in Technical Drawing. Almost all the remaining twenty-eight Leaving Certificate subjects are also assessed by written academic examination. Even languages are primarily assessed in this way (Curriculum and Examinations Board, 1985).

What schools do therefore is not so much to qualify mental labour and disqualify manual labour as Poulantzas (1975: 266) suggests. Rather, they *qualify* certain limited kinds of academic skills — particularly logical mathematical and linguistic intelligences; they *demean* those intelligences Gardner (1983) defined as bodily–kinesthetic, spatial and musical by credentializing only limited aspects of them; and they disqualify and marginalize what I call love labour or solidary labour (the labour required to produce caring relations — supporting, encouraging, listening to others etc.)[7] by not credentializing the intelligences associated with it at all. What Gardner terms interpersonal and intrapersonal intelligences are central to all interpersonal relations including solidary relations. The development of these intelligences is not facilitated in schools.

As schools are the major public institutions ratifying and legitimating cultural forms, those attributes or intelligences which it fails to qualify cease having any formal status in the sociocultural agenda. Whether or not schools could or should credentialize interpersonal or intrapersonal intelligences is undoubtedly a matter for debate. However, by not formally incorporating them into schools, they get relegated to the cultural periphery by default, if not by design.

Although most people are involved in solidary relations of one form or another (such as friendships, parent–child relations, intimate sexual relations), there is no doubt that women's central role in caring (for children, elderly people etc.) has meant that love labour has been a key part of women's work in a way which does not hold true for many men. The marginalization of love labour therefore means that a form of labour in which women have considerable expertise is forced into cultural obscurity. (This could be seen then as another form of the reproduction of gender inequalities by schools.) Indeed, because solidary relations require love–labour–time to be invested in them so that solidary bonds can grow and develop, schools implicitly marginalize love labour in another important way.

The organization of learning is based on the premise that students do homework. The school day, which is already long (usually 9am–4pm), does not end on leaving the school, it ends when homework is completed. Hannan *et al.* (1983) found that senior cycle students spend an average of four hours per night during the week on homework. Consequently, school is organized on the assumption that what little time and energy pupils have left at the end of the school day is further deployed (in part, if not entirely) in the interests of the productive labour of school work. Love labour tasks are implicitly assumed to be of limited importance by virtue of the assumption that time and energy after school is available for long hours of homework. The implicit agenda of school-work organization therefore is that solidary relations are peripheral to productive labour.

Notes

1 In my view, two conceptions of individualism underpin thinking about education in Ireland, much of Europe and North America. Firstly, the individualistic assumption of self-development is a fundamental educational pre-supposition. This implies that the person is in a state of perpetual growth (Lukes, 1973: 67–72). It also assumes that the development of individuals is commensurate with the development of society; that the sum of individual goods constitutes the collective good. This latter assumption is, in my view, quite erroneous. There is no reason why the educated individual should serve the collective good, especially in a capitalist society where profit and gain are appropriated as of right by individuals for their own use regardless of others.

The second individualist assumption underpinning education is the notion of the abstract individual. The latter is a way of conceiving the individual rather than a value or an ideal. It depicts the individual as an abstract entity 'with given interests, wants, purposes, needs' etc.; while society and the state are pictured as 'sets of actual or possible social arrangements which respond...to those individual requirements' (ibid., 73). It finds its most lucid educational expression in traditional IQ theory where the individual is defined as having a fairly fixed amount of intelligence. As recent work by Gould (1981), Gardner (1983) and a variety of others have shown, such pre-suppositions are scientifically untenable. A detailed examination of the above issues is presented in my PhD thesis 'Individualism in Education', UCD, Sociology Department, 1986.

2 'The *Investment in Education Report* published in 1966 is one of the foundation documents of modern Irish education... It was a major analysis of the education system initiated in 1962 by the Department of Education in co-operation with the OECD' (Coolahan, 1981: 165). It recommended a number of changes in education including a greater emphasis on technical knowledge, rationalization in the use of sources and increased participation.

3 Clancy (1988: op.cit., 32) found that 45% of those who did the Leaving Certificate in fee-paying schools in 1985/6 transferred to third level compared with 24% of those in Vocational Schools.

4 In 1981, 78,797 (44%) of the 177,645 farmers in Ireland had less than 50 acres of land (CSO, 1981: Vol. 4, Table 7, p. 21).

5 In emphasizing the crucial role played by cultural processes in reproduction, we are not denying the importance of material resources. Firstly, lack of finance can have a direct bearing on one's ability to acquire cultural capital whether it be by determining one's playmates (by virtue of the type of neighbourhood one can afford to live in) or one's access to cultural products such as art, music, literature etc. Secondly, there are numerous costs associated with schooling even in a so-called free system: the cost of books, trips, equipment, clothes, food etc., all make schooling an expensive business. For those on low income some of these ancillary costs are often prohibitive.

6 These issues are discussed in detail with respect to Irish education in my PhD Thesis (1986) (cf. note 1 of this chapter).

7 In a forthcoming paper in *The Sociological Review* (1989) I specify, in detail, what I mean by love labour and how it is becoming marginalized in our society. What I am arguing in that paper is that the labour involved in producing and reproducing caring relationships is a form of work which takes time. As a time-consuming activity, it is generally in conflict with both productive labour in the material sense, and domestic labour, over the use of time.

Love labour or solidary labour is a discrete social activity which can be distinguished from other forms of human service work, domestic work and economic labour.

Appendix

Table A1. The distribution of the sample in terms of the five major independent variables

		N	% *
Gender Composition:	Female	21	24.4
	Male	20	23.3
	Co-educational	45	52.3
		86	100.0
Administrative Type:	Vocational	27	31.4
	Secondary	54	62.8
	Community/comprehensive	5	5.8
		86	100.0
Size:	≤ 250 small	31	36.0
	251–500 medium	35	40.7
	> 501 large	20	23.3
		86	100.0
Public/private	Public (vocational, community, comprehensive)	32	37.2
	Free–scheme secondary	46	53.5
	Fee–paying secondary	8	9.3
		86	100.0
Location:	City or town > 10,000	27	31.4
	Town ≤ 10,000 but ≥ 1,500	30	34.9
	Rural areas or towns < 1,500	29	33.7
		86	100.0

*Total percentages are presented as rounded numbers throughout the text.

Table A2. The relationship between the size of schools and their gender composition

Gender	Size			N
	Small %	Medium %	Large %	
Female	23.8 (16.1)	57.1 (34.3)	19.0 (20.0)	21
Male	30.0 (19.4)	20.0 (11.4)	50.0 (50.0)	20
Co-Educational	44.4 (64.5)	42.2 (54.3)	13.3 (30.0)	45
Total N	31	35	20	86
%	(36.0)	(40.7)	(23.3)	(100.0)

$P \leq 0.01$ Pearson's $R = -0.18$

Table A3. The relationship between the gender composition of the schools and their location

Gender	Location			N
	City %	Medium towns %	Rural areas + villages %	
Female	52.4 (40.7)	33.3 (23.3)	14.3 (10.3)	21
Male	55.0 (40.7)	30.0 (20.0)	15.0 (10.3)	20
Co-Educational	11.1 (18.5)	37.8 (56.7)	51.1 (79.3)	45
Total N	27	30	29	86
%	(31.4)	(34.9)	(33.7)	(100.0)

$P \leq 0.01$ Pearson's $R = 0.4$

Table A4. The relationship between size of schools and administrative type

Size	Administrative type			N
	Vocational %	Secondary %	Community/ comprehensive %	
Small	38.7 (44.4)	61.3 (35.2)	0.0 (0.0)	31
Medium	34.3 (44.4)	60.0 (38.9)	5.7 (40.0)	35
Large	15.0 (11.1)	70.0 (25.9)	15.0 (60.0)	20
Total N	27	54	5	86
(%)	(31.4)	(62.8)	(5.8)	(100.0)

$P = $ N.S. Pearson's $R = 0.25$
N.S. = Not significant

Table A5. The relationship between the location of the school and administrative type

| Location | Administrative type | | | N |
| | Vocational | Secondary | Community/ comprehensive | |
	%	%	%	
City/large town	14.8	81.5	3.7	27
	(14.8)	(40.7)	(20.0)	
Medium town	33.3	60.0	6.7	30
	(37.0)	(33.3)	(40.0)	
Village/rural	44.8	48.3	6.9	29
	(48.1)	(25.9)	(40.0)	
Total N	27	54	5	86
(%)	(31.4)	(62.8)	(5.8)	(100.0)

P = N.S. Pearson's R = 0.18

Table A6. The relationship between the gender composition of the schools and their administrative character

| Gender | Administrative type | | | N |
| | Vocational | Secondary | Community/ comprehensive | |
	%	%	%	
Female	0.0	100.0	0.0	21
	(0.0)	(38.9)	(0.0)	
Male	10.0	90.0	0.0	20
	(7.4)	(33.3)	(0.0)	
Co-educational	55.6	33.3	11.1	45
	(92.6)	(27.8)	(100.0)	
Total N	27	54	5	86
(%)	(31.4)	(62.8)	(5.8)	(100.0)

P ≤ 0.01 Pearson's R = 0.35

Table A7. The relationship between size of schools and location

| Size | Location | | | N |
	City %	Medium town %	Village + rural %	
Small	19.4	19.4	61.3	31
	(22.2)	(20.0)	(65.5)	
Medium	25.7	48.6	25.7	35
	(33.3)	(56.7)	(31.0)	
Large	60.0	35.0	5.0	20
	(44.4)	(23.3)	(3.4)	
Total N	27	30	29	86
(%)	(31.4)	(34.9)	(33.7)	(100.0)

P ≤ 0.01 Pearson's R = 0.47

Table A8. *Time allocation for non-examination subjects in schools of different sizes: physical education*

J(N = 82)   S(N = 70)

Number of periods per week	Cycle	Size		
		250 or less %	251–500 %	501 + %
1 or 2 per week	Junior	81.5	74.3	85.0
	Senior	82.6	77.4	81.3
3 per week	Junior	7.4	5.7	15.0
	Senior	8.7	3.2	12.5
4–6 per week	Junior	0.0	0.0	0.0
	Senior	0.0	0.0	0.0
Varies for each year	Junior	11.1	20.0	0.0
	Senior	8.7	19.4	6.3

Junior P = N.S.   Senior P = N.S.

Table A9. *Time allocation for non-examination subjects in schools in different areas: physical education*

J(N = 82)   S(N = 70)

Number of periods per week	Cycle	Location		
		City or large town %	Medium size towns + villages ≤ 10,000 + ≥ 1,500 %	Rural area + villages < 1,500 %
1 or 2 per week	Junior	63.0	80.0	96.0
	Senior	59.1	80.8	100.0
3 per week	Junior	18.5	6.7	0.0
	Senior	13.6	7.7	0.0
4–6 per week	Junior	0.0	0.0	0.0
	Senior	0.0	0.0	0.0
Varies for each year	Junior	18.5	13.3	4.0
	Senior	27.3	11.5	0.0

Junior P ≤ 0.05   Senior P ≤ 0.05

Table A10:   Gender differences in subject provision: Intermediate Certificate

Subject	All female N = 21 %	All male N = 20 %	Co-ed. N = 45 %	Statistical significance
Irish (Higher)	100.0	90.0	97.8	N.S.
Irish (Lower)	90.5	100.0	97.8	N.S.
English (Higher)	100.0	95.0	97.8	N.S.
English (Lower)	95.2	100.0	97.8	N.S.
Mathematics (Higher)	100.0	95.0	86.7	N.S.
Mathematics (Lower)	100.0	100.0	100.0	N.S.
History + geography	100.0	95.0	97.8	N.S.
French	100.0	100.0	95.6	N.S.
Commerce	81.0	85.0	93.3	N.S.
Science (A)	95.2	95.0	80.0	$P \le 0.05$
Science (E)	9.5	20.0	44.4	$P \le 0.05$
Home economics	100.0	0.0	93.3	$P \le 0.01$
Art	95.2	60.0	68.9	$P \le 0.01$
Mechanical drawing	0.0	70.0	88.9	$P \le 0.01$
Woodwork	4.8	75.0	84.4	$P \le 0.01$
Music (A)	81.0	35.0	33.3	$P \le 0.01$
Music (B)	57.1	10.0	17.8	$P \le 0.01$
Metalwork	0.0	40.0	64.4	$P \le 0.01$
German	57.1	35.0	11.1	$P \le 0.01$
Latin	4.8	35.0	8.9	$P \le 0.05$
Spanish	9.5	15.0	11.1	N.S.
Italian	14.3	0.0	0.0	N.S.
Greek	0.0	5.0	0.0	N.S.
Hebrew	0.0	0.0	0.0	N.S.
Classical studies	0.0	0.0	0.0	N.S.

Table A11. The proportion of schools of different sizes providing Intermediate
Certificate courses on the timetable

Subject	Small schools N=31 (≤250) %	Medium schools N=35 (251–500) %	Large schools N=20 (501+) %	Statistical significance
Irish (Higher)	96.8	94.3	100.0	N.S.
Irish (Lower)	90.3	100.0	100.0	N.S.
English (Higher)	96.8	97.1	100.0	N.S.
English (Lower)	93.5	100.0	100.0	N.S.
Mathematics (Higher)	83.9	94.3	100.0	N.S.
Mathematics (Lower)	100.0	100.0	100.0	N.S.
History + geography	100.0	94.3	100.0	N.S.
French	96.8	100.0	95.0	N.S.
Commerce	77.4	91.4	100.0	N.S.
Science (A)	74.2	94.3	95.0	P≤0.05
Science (E)	32.3	28.6	30.0	N.S.
Home economics	77.4	82.9	50.0	P≤0.05
Art	54.8	80.0	90.0	P≤0.05
Mechanical drawing	58.1	60.0	75.0	N.S.
Woodwork	64.5	57.1	70.0	N.S.
Music (A)	25.8	51.4	65.0	P≤0.01
Music (B)	19.4	31.4	25.0	N.S.
Metalwork	38.7	42.9	50.0	N.S.
German	16.1	28.6	45.0	N.S.
Latin	6.5	5.7	40.0	P≤0.01
Spanish	6.5	11.4	20.0	N.S.
Italian	3.2	2.9	5.0	N.S.
Greek	0.0	0.0	5.0	N.S.
Hebrew	0.0	0.0	0.0	N.S.
Classical studies	0.0	0.0	0.0	N.S.

Table A12. The proportion of secondary, vocational and community/comprehensive schools offering Intermediate Certificate subjects on the timetable

Subject	Vocational N = 27 %	Secondary N = 54 %	Community/ comprehensive N = 5 %	Statistical significance
Irish (Higher)	88.9	100.0	100.0	N.S.
Irish (Lower)	96.3	96.3	100.0	N.S.
English (Higher)	92.6	100.0	100.0	N.S.
English (Lower)	96.3	98.1	100.0	N.S.
Mathematics (Higher)	74.1	100.0	100.0	$P \leq 0.01$
Mathematics (Lower)	100.0	100.0	100.0	N.S.
History + geography	92.6	100.0	100.0	N.S.
French	92.6	100.0	100.0	N.S.
Commerce	92.6	85.2	100.0	N.S.
Science (A)	63.0	98.1	100.0	$P \leq 0.01$
Science (E)	66.7	11.1	40.0	$P \leq 0.01$
Home economics	92.6	61.1	100.0	$P \leq 0.01$
Art	59.3	77.8	100.0	N.S.
Mechanical drawing	100.0	40.7	100.0	$P \leq 0.01$
Woodwork	100.0	40.7	100.0	$P \leq 0.01$
Music (A)	14.8	59.3	60.0	$P \leq 0.01$
Music (B)	3.7	33.3	60.0	$P \leq 0.01$
Metalwork	92.6	13.0	100.0	$P \leq 0.01$
German	3.7	40.7	20.0	$P \leq 0.01$
Latin	0.0	20.4	20.0	N.S.
Spanish	7.4	14.8	0.0	N.S.
Italian	0.0	5.6	0.0	N.S.
Greek	0.0	1.9	0.0	N.S.
Hebrew	0.0	0.0	0.0	N.S.
Classical studies	0.0	0.0	0.0	N.S.

Table A13. The proportion of schools in cities, towns and rural areas providing Intermediate Certificate subjects on the timetable

Subject	City + towns over 10,000 N = 27 %	Towns + villages ≥ 1,500 + ≤ 10,000 N = 30 %	Rural areas + villages under 1,500 N = 29 %	Statistical significance
Irish (Higher)	92.6	100.0	96.6	N.S.
Irish (Lower)	96.3	100.0	93.1	N.S.
English (Higher)	96.3	100.0	96.6	N.S.
English (Lower)	96.3	100.0	96.6	N.S.
Mathematics (Higher)	92.6	100.0	82.8	N.S.
Mathematics (Lower)	100.0	100.0	100.0	N.S.
History + geography	92.6	100.0	100.0	N.S.
French	100.0	96.7	96.6	N.S.
Commerce	77.8	100.0	86.2	N.S.
Science (A)	92.6	90.0	79.3	N.S.
Science (E)	14.8	30.0	44.8	N.S.
Home economics	59.3	73.3	86.2	N.S.
Art	92.6	70.0	58.6	$P \leq 0.05$
Mechanical drawing	48.1	66.7	72.4	N.S.
Woodwork	48.1	63.3	75.9	N.S.
Music (A)	63.0	50.0	24.1	$P \leq 0.01$
Music (B)	37.0	30.0	10.3	N.S.
Metalwork	33.3	43.3	51.7	$P \leq 0.01$
German	59.3	13.3	13.8	$P \leq 0.01$
Latin	25.9	10.0	6.9	N.S.
Spanish	14.8	16.7	3.4	N.S.
Italian	0.0	6.7	3.4	N.S.
Greek	3.7	0.0	0.0	N.S.
Hebrew	0.0	0.0	0.0	N.S.
Classical studies	0.0	0.0	0.0	N.S.

Table A14.   Gender differences in subject provision: Leaving Certificate

Subject	All female N = 21 %	All male N = 19 %	Co-educational N = 44 %	Statistical significance
Irish	100.0	100.0	95.5	N.S.
English	100.0	100.0	100.0	N.S.
Mathematics	100.0	100.0	100.0	N.S.
French	100.0	94.7	93.2	N.S.
Biology	95.2	78.9	95.5	N.S.
Geography	100.0	94.7	86.4	N.S.
History	100.0	94.7	79.5	$P \leq 0.05$
Business organization	76.2	68.4	75.0	N.S.
Accounting	61.9	84.2	68.2	N.S.
Art	95.2	52.6	56.8	$P \leq 0.01$
Chemistry	76.2	89.5	47.7	$P \leq 0.01$
Home economics (scientific and social)	95.2	0.0	70.5	$P \leq 0.01$
Technical drawing	0.0	63.2	86.4	$P \leq 0.01$
Physics	42.9	89.5	52.3	$P \leq 0.01$
Economics	33.3	78.9	38.6	$P \leq 0.01$
Engineering	0.0	31.6	56.8	$P \leq 0.01$
Home economics (general)	57.1	5.3	40.9	$P \leq 0.01$
Construction studies	0.0	15.8	61.4	$P \leq 0.01$
Music	61.9	26.3	22.7	$P \leq 0.01$
German	61.9	26.3	18.2	$P \leq 0.01$
Physics and chemistry	14.3	26.3	18.2	N.S.
Applied maths	4.8	42.1	9.1	$P \leq 0.01$
Agricultural science	0.0	15.8	20.5	N.S.
Spanish	14.3	15.8	13.6	N.S.
Latin	9.5	21.1	9.1	N.S.
Economic history	14.3	15.8	2.3	N.S.
Italian	19.0	0.0	0.0	$P \leq 0.01$
Mechanics	0.0	0.0	2.3	N.S.
Greek	0.0	5.3	0.0	N.S.
Agricultural economics	0.0	0.0	0.0	N.S.
Hebrew	0.0	0.0	0.0	N.S.

Table A15. The proportion of secondary, vocational and community/
comprehensive schools providing Leaving Certificate subjects on the timetable

Subject	Vocational N = 25 %	Secondary N = 54 %	Community/ comprehensive N = 5 %	Statistical significance
Irish	92.0	100.0	100.0	N.S.
English	100.0	100.0	100.0	N.S.
Mathematics	100.0	100.0	100.0	N.S.
French	84.0	100.0	100.0	P ≤ 0.01
Biology	96.0	88.9	100.0	N.S.
Geography	72.0	100.0	100.0	P ≤ 0.01
History	60.0	100.0	100.0	P ≤ 0.01
Business organization	72.0	72.2	100.0	N.S.
Accounting	60.0	72.2	100.0	N.S.
Art	52.0	68.5	100.0	N.S.
Chemistry	20.0	83.3	80.0	P ≤ 0.01
Home economics (scientific and social)	56.0	59.3	100.0	N.S.
Technical drawing	100.0	37.0	100.0	P ≤ 0.01
Physics	44.0	63.0	80.0	N.S.
Economics	32.0	50.0	80.0	N.S.
Engineering	80.0	13.0	80.0	P ≤ 0.01
Home economics (general)	28.0	40.7	40.0	N.S.
Construction studies	80.0	11.1	80.0	N.S.
Music	4.0	44.4	60.0	P ≤ 0.01
German	4.0	42.6	40.0	P ≤ 0.01
Physics and chemistry	16.0	20.4	20.0	N.S.
Applied maths	4.0	20.4	20.0	N.S.
Agricultural science	20.0	9.3	40.0	N.S.
Spanish	8.0	16.7	20.0	N.S.
Latin	0.0	16.7	20.0	N.S.
Economic history	0.0	11.1	20.0	N.S.
Italian	0.0	7.4	0.0	N.S.
Mechanics	0.0	0.0	20.0	P ≤ 0.01
Greek	0.0	1.9	0.0	N.S.
Agricultural economics	0.0	0.0	0.0	N.S.
Hebrew	0.0	0.0	0.0	N.S.

Table A16. The proportion of schools of different sizes providing Leaving Certificate courses on the timetable

Subject	Small 250 and under N = 30 %	Medium 251–500 N = 34 %	Large 501 + N = 20 %	Statistical significance
Irish	93.3	100.0	100.0	N.S.
English	100.0	100.0	100.0	N.S.
Mathematics	100.0	100.0	100.0	N.S.
French	93.3	97.1	95.0	N.S.
Biology	86.7	94.1	95.0	N.S.
Geography	86.7	91.2	100.0	N.S.
History	80.0	88.2	100.0	N.S.
Business organization	66.7	76.5	80.0	N.S.
Accounting	53.3	70.6	95.0	$P \leq 0.01$
Art	36.7	76.5	90.0	$P \leq 0.01$
Chemistry	53.3	61.8	85.0	N.S.
Home economics (scientific and social)	53.3	76.5	45.0	$P \leq 0.05$
Technical drawing	60.0	52.9	70.0	N.S.
Physics	46.7	52.9	85.0	$P \leq 0.05$
Economics	16.7	58.8	70.0	$P \leq 0.01$
Engineering	33.3	35.3	45.0	N.S.
Home economics (general)	30.0	41.2	40.0	N.S.
Construction studies	33.3	35.3	40.0	N.S.
Music	20.0	44.1	35.0	N.S.
German	16.7	32.4	50.0	$P \leq 0.05$
Physics and chemistry	6.7	26.5	25.0	N.S.
Applied maths	6.7	8.8	40.0	$P \leq 0.01$
Agricultural science	6.7	20.6	15.0	N.S.
Spanish	6.7	8.8	35.0	$P \leq 0.01$
Latin	6.7	5.9	30.0	$P \leq 0.05$
Economic history	0.0	8.8	20.0	$P \leq 0.05$
Italian	3.3	2.9	10.0	N.S.
Mechanics	0.0	0.0	5.0	N.S.
Greek	0.0	0.0	5.0	N.S.
Agricultural economics	0.0	0.0	0.0	N.S.
Hebrew	0.0	0.0	0.0	N.S.

Table A17. The proportion of schools in cities, town and rural areas providing Leaving Certificate courses on the timetable*

Subject	City or town 10,000+ N = 26 %	Towns + villages ≥ 1,500+ ≤ 10,000 N = 30 %	Rural areas + villages < 1,500 N = 28 %	Statistical significance
Irish	100.0	100.0	92.9	N.S.
English	100.0	100.0	100.0	N.S.
Mathematics	100.0	100.0	100.0	N.S.
French	92.3	96.7	96.4	N.S.
Biology	96.2	90.0	89.3	N.S.
Geography	88.5	96.7	89.3	N.S.
History	92.3	90.0	82.1	N.S.
Business organization	73.1	86.7	60.7	N.S.
Accounting	73.1	83.3	53.6	P≤0.05
Art	92.3	63.3	42.9	P≤0.01
Chemistry	80.8	53.3	60.7	N.S.
Home economics (scientific and social)	50.0	60.0	71.4	N.S.
Technical drawing	38.5	66.7	71.4	P≤0.05
Physics	76.9	63.3	35.7	P≤0.01
Economics	46.2	60.0	32.1	N.S.
Engineering	23.1	46.7	39.3	N.S.
Home economics (general)	50.0	33.3	28.6	N.S.
Construction studies	19.2	43.3	42.9	N.S.
Music	53.8	33.3	14.3	P≤0.01
German	53.8	23.3	17.9	P≤0.01
Physics and chemistry	11.5	36.7	7.1	P≤0.01
Applied maths	26.9	10.0	10.7	N.S.
Agricultural science	3.8	20.0	17.9	N.S.
Spanish	26.9	13.3	3.6	P≤0.05
Latin	23.1	6.7	7.1	
Economic history	19.2	6.7	0.0	P≤0.05
Italian	3.8	6.7	3.6	N.S.
Mechanics	0.0	3.3	0.0	N.S.
Greek	3.8	0.0	0.0	N.S.
Agricultural economics	0.0	0.0	0.0	N.S.
Hebrew	0.0	0.0	0.0	N.S.

*Remember that although percentages are based on the whole population (N = 86) two schools have no senior cycle.

Table A18. Frequency of in-house examinations for public examination classes: gender differences

| | Frequency | | | |
Gender	Twice a year %	Once a year %	(Other end of term reports) %	Total no. of schools
Female	85.7 (25.7)	28.6 (35.3)	9.5 (25.0)	21
Male	78.9 (21.4)	21.1 (23.5)	5.3 (12.5)	19
Co-educational	82.2 (52.9)	15.6 (41.2)	11.1 (62.5)	45
Total number of schools with each arrangement	70 (82.4)	17 (20.0)	8 (9.4)	85 100.0

Table A19. Frequency of in-house examinations for public examination classes: school size differences

| | Frequency | | | |
Size	Twice a year %	Once a year %	(Other end of term reports) %	Total no. of schools
250 and under	83.9 (37.1)	16.1 (29.4)	3.2 (12.5)	31
251–500	82.9 (41.4)	22.9 (47.1)	17.1 (75.0)	35
501+	78.9 (21.4)	21.1 (23.5)	5.3 (12.5)	19
Total number of schools with each arrangement	70 (82.4)	17 (20.0)	8 (9.4)	85

Table A20. Frequency of in-house examinations for public examination classes: location differences

	Frequency			
Location	Twice a year %	Once a year %	(Other end of term reports) %	Total no. of schools
Cities and towns >10,000	76.9 (28.6)	23.1 (35.3)	19.2 (62.5)	26
Towns ≤10,000 and ≥1,500	86.7 (37.1)	20.0 (35.3)	6.7 (25.0)	30
Rural areas and villages <1,500	82.8 (34.3)	17.2 (29.4)	3.4 (12.5)	29
Total number of schools with each arrangement	70 82.4	17 20.0	8 9.4	85 100.0

Table A21. Frequency of in-house examinations for public examination classes: differences between vocational, secondary and community/comprehensive schools

	Frequency			
Type	Twice a year %	Once a year %	(Other end of term reports) %	Total no. of schools
Vocational	81.5 (31.4)	18.5 (29.4)	0.0 0.0	27
Secondary	84.9 (64.3)	18.9 (58.8)	13.2 (87.5)	53
Community/ comprehensive	60.0 (4.3)	40.0 (11.8)	20.0 (12.5)	5
Total number of schools with each arrangement	70 82.4	17 20.0	8 9.4	85 100.0

Table A22. Differences between various types of schools in the awarding of prizes for extracurricular activities

School type	% Holding prize-giving ceremonies	N	Total (N)
Gender			
Female	95.2	20	(21)
Male	75.0	15	(20)
Co-educational	86.7	39	(45)
Administrative type			
Vocational	88.9	24	(27)
Secondary	85.2	46	(54)
Community/ comprehensive	80.0	4	(5)
Size			
250 and under	77.4	24	(31)
251–500	88.6	31	(35)
501 +	95.0	19	(20)
Location			
Cities and towns > 10,000	96.3	26	(27)
Towns ≤ 10,000 and ≥ 1,500	80.0	24	(30)
Rural areas and villages < 1,500	82.8	24	(29)

Table A23. Differences between various types of schools in the awarding of prizes for school work

School type	% Awarding prizes	N	Total (N)
Gender			
Female	52.4	11	(21)
Male	40.0	8	(20)
Co-educational	40.0	18	(45)
$P < 0.01$			
Administrative type			
Vocational	40.7	11	(27)
Secondary	40.7	22	(54)
Community/ comprehensive	80.0	4	(5)
Size			
250 and under	29.0	9	(31)
251–500	40.0	14	(35)
501 +	70.0	14	(20)
$P < 0.01$			
Location			
Cities and towns > 10,000	63.0	17	(27)
Towns ≤ 10,000 and ≥ 1,500	46.7	14	(30)
Rural areas and villages < 1,500	20.7	6	(29)
$P < 0.01$			

Table A24. Differences between fee-paying secondary, free-scheme secondary schools and public schools in methods of grouping pupils into classes

Type of school	Methods of grouping						
	Entirely streaming %	Streaming or banding + setting %	Streaming + mixed classes + setting %	Entirely setting %	Setting + mixed classes %	Entirely mixed %	N
Public	42.9	32.1	21.4	3.6	0.0	0.0	28
Free-scheme secondary	24.4	20.0	35.6	2.2	8.9	8.9	45
Fee-paying secondary	0.0	33.3	16.7	0.0	50.0	0.0	6
Total number of schools with each arrangement	23 / 29.1	20 / 25.3	23 / 29.1	2 / 2.5	7 / 8.9	4 / 5.1	79 / 100.0

$P \leq 0.01$

Table A25. Differences between fee-paying secondary, free-scheme secondary and public schools in the frequency of assessments for non-examination classes

School type	Monthly assessments %	Frequency Exams 3 times per year %	Exams twice a year %	Exams once a year %	No. of schools
Public	3.2 (8.3)	37.5 (44.4)	43.8 (27.5)	18.8 (60.0)	32
Free-scheme secondary	19.6 (75.0)	26.1 (44.4)	67.4 (60.8)	6.5 (30.0)	46
Fee-paying secondary	25.0 (16.7)	37.5 (11.1)	75.0 (11.8)	12.5 (10.0)	8
Total number of schools	12 14.0	27 31.4	51 59.3	10 11.6	86 100.0

Table A26. Differences between fee-paying secondary, free-scheme secondary and public schools in the frequency of assessment for both examination classes

School type	Frequency Twice %	Once %	Other arrangement (end-of-term report) %	No. of schools
Public	81.3 (33.8)	21.9 (41.2)	3.1 (9.1)	32
Free-scheme secondary	89.1 (53.2)	19.6 (52.9)	17.4 (72.9)	46
Fee-paying secondary	125.0 (13.0)	12.5 (5.9)	25.0 (18.2)	8
Total number of schools	77 89.5	17 19.8	11 12.8	86 100.0

Table A27.   Differences between fee-paying secondary, free-scheme secondary and public schools in the frequency of in-term assessments

School type	Class tests at teacher's discretion %	Continuous assessment for all %	Continuous assessment for some %	No assessment %	No. of schools
Public	62.5	9.4	6.3	21.9	32
Free-scheme secondary	63.0	21.7	2.2	13.0	46
Fee-paying secondary	50.0	37.5	0.0	12.5	8
Total number of schools	53 61.6	16 18.6	3 3.5	14 16.3	86 100.0

Table A28.   Differences between fee-paying secondary, free-scheme secondary and public schools in the extent to which prizes are awarded for school work

School type	Whether prizes are awarded		No. of schools
	Yes %	No %	
Public	46.9	53.1	32
Free-scheme secondary	34.8	65.2	46
Fee-paying secondary	75.0	25.0	8
Total number of schools	37 43.0	49 57.0	86 100.0

Table A29. *Pupil autonomy and controls within schools: gender differences*

Type of activity	Female %	Male %	Co-educational %	Statistical significance
Extracurricular control: The proportion in which pupils are not involved in introducing extra-curricular activities	76.2	85.0	88.9	N.S.
The proportion in which pupils are not involved in organizing extra-curricular activities	28.6	70.0	73.3	P≤0.01
Prefects/council The proportion with prefects	90.5	55.0	53.3	P≤0.01
The proportion with a student council or union	28.6	15.0	28.9	N.S.
Dress control The proportion with a uniform	100.0	50.0	62.2	P≤0.01
The proportion in which a uniform is compulsory at all times for all pupils	100.0	70.0	57.1	P≤0.01
The proportion with a variety of rules regarding dress (other than those on uniform)	90.5	55.0	48.9	P≤0.01
The proportion with written school rules	57.9	72.7	40.9	N.S.
Subject autonomy The proportion imposing restrictions on pupils' subject choices in the junior cycle	42.9	75.0	51.1	N.S.
The proportion imposing restrictions on pupils' subject choices at senior level	52.4	57.9	58.1	N.S.

Table A30:   Pupil autonomy and controls within schools: differences due to size

Type of activity	Small %	Medium %	Large %	Statistical significance
Extracurricular Control: The proportion in which pupils are not involved in introducing extra-curricular activities	90.3	85.7	75.0	N.S.
The proportion in which pupils are not involved in organising extra-curricular activities	77.4	57.1	45.0	$P \le 0.05$
Prefects' council The proportion with prefects	51.6	74.3	60.0	N.S.
The proportion with a student council or union	9.7	31.4	40.0	$P \le 0.05$
Dress control The proportion with a uniform	54.8	77.1	75.0	N.S.
The proportion in which a uniform is compulsory at all times for all pupils	70.6	77.8	73.3	N.S.
The proportion with a variety of rules regarding dress (other than those on uniform)	45.2	65.7	75.0	N.S.
The proportion with written school rules	35.7	47.8	80.0	$P \le 0.05$
Subject autonomy The proportion imposing restrictions on pupils' subject choices in the junior cycle	38.7	54.3	80.0	$P \le 0.05$
The proportion imposing restrictions on pupils' subject choices at senior level	51.7	60.0	50.0	N.S.

Table A31.   Pupil autonomy and controls within schools: location differences

Type of activity	City or large town %	Medium-sized town %	Villages + rural areas %	Statistical significance
Extracurricular control: The proportion in which pupils are not involved in introducing extra-curricular activities	88.9	73.3	93.1	N.S.
The proportion in which pupils are not involved in organizing extra-curricular activities	40.7	56.7	86.2	$P \leq 0.01$
Prefects/council The proportion with prefects	81.5	56.7	51.7	$P \leq 0.05$
The proportion with a student council or union	25.9	33.3	17.2	N.S.
Dress control The proportion with a uniform	77.8	70.0	58.6	N.S.
The proportion in which a uniform is compulsory at all times for all pupils	81.0	85.7	52.9	$P \leq 0.05$
The proportion with a variety of rules regarding dress (other than those on uniform)	77.8	53.3	51.7	N.S.
The proportion with written school rules	61.9	62.5	33.3	N.S.
Subject autonomy The proportion imposing restrictions on pupils' subject choices in the junior cycle	66.7	46.7	51.7	N.S.
The proportion imposing restrictions on pupils' subject choices at senior level	53.8	56.7	59.3	N.S.

Table A32. *Pupil autonomy and controls within schools: differences between vocational, secondary and community/comprehensive schools*

Type of activity	Vocational %	Secondary %	Community/ comprehensive %	Statistical significance
Extracurricular control: The proportion in which pupils are not involved in introducing extra-curricular activities	92.6	81.5	80.0	N.S.
The proportion in which pupils are not involved in organizing extra-curricular activities	77.8	53.7	60.0	N.S.
Prefects/council The proportion with prefects	44.4	74.1	40.0	P≤0.05
The proportion with a student council or union	29.6	18.5	80.0	P≤0.01
Dress control The proportion with a uniform	40.7	83.3	60.0	P≤0.01
The proportion in which a uniform is compulsory at all times for all pupils	36.4	82.2	100.0	P≤0.01
The proportion with a variety of rules regarding dress (other than those on uniform)	44.4	70.4	40.0	P≤0.05
The proportion with written school rules	50.0	52.6	100.0	N.S.
Subject autonomy The proportion imposing restrictions on pupils' subject choices in the junior cycle	48.1	53.7	100.0	N.S.
The proportion imposing restrictions on pupils' subject choices at senior level	54.2	57.4	60.0	N.S.

Table A33.   Extracurricular activities: gender differences

Name of activity	Female N = 21 %	Male N = 20 %	Co-educational N = 45 %	Statistical significance
Court games				
Basketball	90.5	80.0	91.1	N.S.
Netball	28.6	5.0	17.8	N.S.
Volleyball	61.9	35.0	68.9	$P \leq 0.05$
Badminton/squash	23.8	30.0	22.2	N.S.
Tennis	85.7	40.0	64.4	$P \leq 0.01$
Table-tennis	23.8	55.0	37.8	N.S.
Gymnastics	90.5	30.0	55.6	$P \leq 0.01$
Handball	0.0	25.0	20.0	N.S.
Boxing	0.0	10.0	2.2	N.S.
Art				
Arts and crafts	71.4	25.0	37.8	$P \leq 0.01$
Dancing	14.3	0.0	6.7	N.S.
Musical activities	100.0	55.0	60.0	$P \leq 0.01$
Drama	85.7	40.0	62.2	$P \leq 0.05$
Debating/public speaking	100.0	75.0	73.3	$P \leq 0.05$
Other indoor interests				
Needlework/cookery	14.3	0.0	2.2	$P \leq 0.05$
School magazine	57.1	50.0	46.7	N.S.
Board games	33.3	60.0	48.9	N.S.
Question time/quizzes	23.8	0.0	6.7	$P \leq 0.05$
Radio/CB club	0.0	10.0	4.4	N.S.
Record club	0.0	0.0	2.2	N.S.
Science/astronomy club	4.8	10.0	2.2	N.S.
Business game club	0.0	0.0	2.2	N.S.
Computer society	23.8	20.0	11.1	N.S.
Historical society	4.8	5.0	0.0	N.S.
Irish club	23.8	10.0	2.2	$P \leq 0.05$
Poetry club	0.0	0.0	2.2	N.S.
Film society	4.8	15.0	11.1	N.S.
Photography	19.0	20.0	4.4	N.S.
Field games				
Camogie	47.6	0.0	35.6	$P \leq 0.01$
Hockey	57.1	0.0	17.8	$P \leq 0.01$
Hyrling	4.8	70.0	53.3	$P \leq 0.01$
Gaelic football	4.8	90.0	82.0	$P \leq 0.01$
Soccer	9.5	75.0	64.4	$P \leq 0.01$
Rugby	0.0	25.0	17.8	N.S.
Cricket	0.0	15.0	4.4	N.S.
Golf	4.8	10.0	0.0	N.S.

Table A33.   (contd.)

Name of activity	Female N = 21 %	Male N = 20 %	Co-educational N = 45 %	Statistical significance
Other outdoor				
Athletics	71.4	80.0	84.4	N.S.
Adventure sports	42.9	40.0	33.3	N.S.
Swimming	47.6	40.0	48.9	N.S.
Horse-riding	4.8	0.0	6.7	N.S.
Cycling	9.5	30.0	4.4	N.S.
Fishing	4.8	10.0	4.4	N.S.
Gardening/horticulture	4.8	0.0	4.4	N.S.
Car club	0.0	0.0	2.2	N.S.
Travel/skiing	0.0	0.0	4.4	N.S.
Religious related				
Pioneer society	76.2	40.0	46.7	P≤0.05
Legion of Mary	23.8	5.0	11.1	N.S.
Vincent de Paul	19.0	25.0	8.9	N.S.
Activities for charity	33.3	15.0	17.8	N.S.
Social action group	4.8	10.0	11.1	N.S.

Table A34:   Differences between small, medium and large schools in the proportion offering particular extracurricular activities

Name of activity	Small (≤ 250) N = 31 %	Medium (> 250 & ≤ 500) N = 35 %	Large (> 500) N = 20 %	Statistical significance
Court games				
Basketball	80.6	94.3	90.0	N.S.
Netball	12.9	17.1	25.0	N.S.
Volleyball	51.6	71.4	50.0	N.S.
Badminton/squash	19.4	25.7	30.0	N.S.
Tennis	48.4	74.3	70.0	N.S.
Table-tennis	29.0	37.1	55.0	N.S.
Gymnastics	41.9	68.6	65.0	N.S.
Handball	12.9	20.0	15.0	N.S.
Boxing	0.0	5.7	5.0	N.S.
Art				
Arts and crafts	22.6	62.9	40.0	P≤0.01
Dancing	6.5	8.6	5.0	N.S.
Musical activities	41.9	82.9	85.0	P≤0.01
Drama	61.3	62.9	65.0	N.S.
Debating/public speaking	61.3	88.6	95.0	P≤0.01

Table A34 *(cont)*

Name of activity	Small (≤250) N = 31 %	Medium (>250 & ≤500) N = 35 %	Large (>500) N = 20 %	Statistical significance
Other indoor interests				
Needlework/cookery	0.0	8.6	5.0	N.S.
School magazine	32.3	51.4	75.0	P≤0.05
Board games	38.7	40.0	75.0	P≤0.05
Question time/quizzes	9.7	14.3	0.0	N.S.
Radio/CB club	0.0	5.7	10.0	N.S.
Record club	0.0	2.9	0.0	N.S.
Science/astronomy club	0.0	2.9	15.0	P≤0.05
Business game club	0.0	2.9	0.0	N.S.
Computer society	0.0	22.9	30.0	P≤0.01
Historical society	0.0	2.9	5.0	N.S.
Irish club	3.2	14.3	10.0	N.S.
Poetry club	0.0	2.9	0.0	N.S.
Film society	0.0	11.4	25.0	P≤0.05
Photography	3.2	11.4	25.0	N.S.
Field games				
Camogie	22.6	28.6	45.0	N.S.
Hockey	12.9	31.4	25.0	N.S.
Hurling	41.9	40.0	60.0	N.S.
Gaelic football	67.7	60.0	70.0	N.S.
Soccer	29.0	62.9	75.0	P≤0.01
Rugby	6.5	17.1	25.0	N.S.
Cricket	0.0	2.9	20.0	P≤0.01
Golf	0.0	2.9	10.0	N.S.
Other outdoor				
Athletics	61.3	88.6	95.0	P≤0.05
Adventure sports	12.9	51.4	50.0	P≤0.01
Swimming	25.8	57.1	60.0	P≤0.05
Horse-riding	3.2	8.6	0.0	N.S.
Cycling	3.2	8.6	30.0	P≤0.01
Fishing	9.7	2.9	5.0	N.S.
Gardening/horticulture	0.0	8.6	0.0	N.S.
Car club	0.0	2.9	0.0	N.S.
Travel/skiing	3.2	2.9	0.0	N.S.
Religious related				
Pioneer society	38.7	62.9	55.0	N.S.
Legion of Mary	6.5	14.3	20.0	N.S.
Vincent de Paul	3.2	11.4	40.0	P≤0.01
Activities for charity	19.4	22.9	20.0	N.S.
Social action group	6.5	8.6	15.0	N.S.

Table A35. Differences between vocational, secondary and community/ comprehensive schools in the character of their extracurricular activities

Name of activity	Vocational $N=27$ %	Secondary $N=54$ %	Community/ comprehensive $N=5$ %	Statistical significance
Court games				
Basketball	96.3	83.3	100.0	N.S.
Netball	18.5	18.5	0.0	N.S.
Volleyball	74.1	51.9	60.0	N.S.
Badminton/squash	18.5	27.8	20.0	N.S.
Tennis	51.9	66.7	100.0	N.S.
Table-tennis	37.0	35.2	80.0	N.S.
Gymnastics	44.4	63.0	80.0	N.S.
Handball	22.2	14.8	0.0	N.S.
Boxing	7.4	0.0	20.0	$P \leq 0.05$
Art				
Arts and crafts	29.6	48.1	60.0	N.S.
Dancing	3.7	7.4	20.0	N.S.
Musical activities	40.7	79.6	100.0	$P \leq 0.01$
Drama	44.4	68.5	100.0	N.S.
Debating/public speaking	77.8	81.5	80.0	N.S.
Other indoor interests				
Needlework/cookery	0.0	7.4	0.0	N.S.
School magazine	48.1	50.0	60.0	N.S.
Board games	37.0	51.9	60.0	N.S.
Question time/quizzes	7.4	11.1	0.0	N.S.
Radio/CB club	0.0	5.6	20.0	N.S.
Record club	3.7	0.0	0.0	N.S.
Science/astronomy club	0.0	5.6	20.0	N.S.
Business game club	0.0	1.9	0.0	N.S.
Computer society	3.7	18.5	60.0	$P \leq 0.01$
Historical society	0.0	3.7	0.0	N.S.
Irish club	3.7	13.0	0.0	N.S.
Poetry club	0.0	1.9	0.0	N.S.
Film society	11.1	9.3	20.0	N.S.
Photography	3.7	16.7	0.0	N.S.
Field games				
Camogie	29.6	27.8	60.0	N.S.
Hockey	7.4	27.8	60.0	$P \leq 0.05$
Hurling	63.0	35.2	60.0	$P \leq 0.01$
Gaelic football	96.3	48.1	80.0	$P \leq 0.01$
Soccer	66.7	42.6	100.0	$P \leq 0.01$
Rugby	11.1	16.7	20.0	N.S.
Cricket	0.0	7.4	20.0	N.S.
Golf	0.0	5.6	0.0	N.S.

Table A35 (cont)

Name of activity	Vocational N = 27 %	Secondary N = 54 %	Community/ comprehensive N = 5 %	Statistical significance
Other outdoor				
Athletics	85.2	75.9	100.0	N.S.
Adventure sports	37.0	33.3	80.0	N.S.
Swimming	44.4	44.4	80.0	N.S.
Horse-riding	0.0	7.4	0.0	N.S.
Cycling	7.4	13.0	20.0	N.S.
Fishing	7.4	5.6	0.0	N.S.
Gardening/horticulture	3.7	3.7	0.0	N.S.
Car club	0.0	1.9	0.0	N.S.
Travel/skiing	0.0	3.7	0.0	N.S.
Religious related				
Pioneer society	33.3	59.3	80.0	P ≤ 0.05
Legion of Mary	7.4	14.8	20.0	N.S.
Vincent de Paul	3.7	20.4	20.0	N.S.
Activities for charity	22.2	22.0	0.0	N.S.
Social action group	3.7	9.3	40.0	P ≤ 0.05

Table A36.   Differences between public schools, free-scheme secondary schools and fee-paying secondary schools in the provision of extracurricular activities (selected range)

Activity	School type and % offering the activity in each			
	Public N = 32 %	Free-scheme secondary N = 46 %	Fee-paying secondary N = 8 %	Statistical significance
Hockey	15.6	23.9	50.0	N.S.
Camogie	34.4	30.4	12.5	N.S.
Soccer	71.9	39.1	62.5	P ≤ 0.05
Rugby	12.5	8.7	62.5	P ≤ 0.01
Horse-riding	0.0	4.3	25.0	P ≤ 0.01
Hurling	62.5	39.1	12.5	P ≤ 0.05
Gaelic football	93.8	52.2	25.0	P ≤ 0.01
Cricket	3.1	4.3	25.0	P ≤ 0.05
Arts and crafts	34.4	41.3	87.5	P ≤ 0.05
Musical activities	50.0	76.1	100.0	P ≤ 0.01
Drama	53.1	63.0	100.0	N.S.
School magazine	50.0	43.5	87.5	N.S.
Photography	3.1	13.0	37.5	P ≤ 0.05
Activities to raise money for charity	18.8	13.0	75.0	P ≤ 0.01
Social action group	9.4	4.3	37.5	P ≤ 0.01
Pioneer society	40.6	63.0	37.5	N.S.
Vincent de Paul Society	6.3	21.7	12.5	N.S.

Table A37. *Number of playing fields owned by the school: gender differences*

Gender	One %	Two %	Three %	Four or five %	Six or more %	Rented %	None %	No. of schools
Female	38.1	19.0	4.8	14.3	0.0	9.5	14.3	21
Male	30.0	15.0	5.0	0.0	30.0	20.0	0.0	20
Co-educational	29.5	13.6	4.5	0.0	4.5	31.8	15.9	44
Total number of schools with each arrangement	27	13	4	3	8	20	10	85
	31.8	15.3	4.7	3.5	9.4	23.5	11.8	100.0

P ≤ 0.01

Table A38. *Number of playing fields owned by the school: differences between vocational, secondary and community/ comprehensive schools*

Type	One %	Two %	Three %	Four or five %	Six or more %	Rented %	None %	No. of schools
Vocational	29.6	11.1	0.0	0.0	0.0	40.7	18.5	27
Secondary	34.0	15.1	3.8	5.7	15.1	17.0	9.4	53
Community/ comprehensive	20.0	40.0	40.0	0.0	0.0	0.0	0.0	5
Total number of schools with each arrangement	27	13	4	3	8	20	10	85
								100.0

P ≤ 0.01

Table A39. Number of hard courts in the school: differences between vocational, secondary and community/comprehensive schools

Type	Number of courts							No. of schools
	One %	Two %	Three %	Four or five %	Six or more %	Rented %	None %	
Vocational	40.7	14.8	0.0	0.0	0.0	11.1	33.3	27
Secondary	13.0	25.9	11.1	14.8	11.1	5.6	18.5	53
Community/ comprehensive	60.0	0.0	0.0	20.0	20.0	0.0	0.0	5
Total number of schools with each arrangement	21	18	6	9	7	6	19	86

$P \leq 0.01$

Table A40. Differences between public, fee-paying secondary and free-scheme secondary schools in the number of playing fields in the school

School type	Number of fields							No. of schools
	One %	Two %	Three %	Four or five %	Six or more %	Rented %	None %	
Public	28.1	15.6	6.3	0.0	0.0	34.4	15.6	32
Free-scheme secondary	40.0	17.8	0.0	2.2	11.1	17.8	11.1	45
Fee-paying secondary	0.0	0.0	25.0	25.0	37.5	12.5	0.0	8
Total number of schools	27	13	4	3	8	20	10	85 100.0

$P \leq 0.01$

Table A41. Differences between public, fee-paying secondary and free-scheme secondary in the number of hard courts in the school

School type	Number of courts					Rented %	None %	No. of schools
	One %	Two %	Three %	Four or five %	Six or more %			
Public	43.8	12.5	0.0	3.1	3.1	9.4	28.1	32
Free-scheme secondary	15.2	28.3	10.9	15.2	8.7	4.3	17.4	46
Fee-paying secondary	0.0	12.5	12.5	12.5	25.0	12.5	25.0	8
Total number of schools	21	18	6	9	7	6	19	86 100.0

$P \leq 0.05$

Table A42.   *Differences between public, fee-paying secondary and free-scheme secondary schools in their library facilities*

| Type of school | One % | Two % | Library facilities | | None % | N |
			Use a classroom as a library %	Use the convent/ college one %		
Public	53.1	0.0	3.1	0.0	43.8	32
Free-scheme secondary	84.8	0.0	2.2	2.2	10.9	46
Fee-paying secondary	87.5	12.5	0.0	0.0	0.0	8
Total no. of schools	63	1	2	1	19	86 100.0

$P \leq 0.01$

Table A43.   *Differences between large schools, community schools, free scheme secondary schools and fee-paying secondary schools in the provision of four basic facilities*

| Facility | School type–% with each | | | |
	Community schools	Large schools	Free-scheme schools	Fee-paying schools
3-6 + playing fields	40.0	40.0	13.3	87.5
3-6 + hard court	40.0	40.0	34.8	50.0
Gymnasium	80.0	80.0	63.0	87.5
Library	100.0	90.0	84.8	100.0
N	5	20	46	8

F. L. CALDER CAMPUS

References

ABERCROMBIE, N. and URRY, J. (1983) *Capital, Labour and the Middle Classes*, London, Allen and Unwin.

AHMAD, A. (1985) 'Class, nation and state: Intermediate classes in peripheral societies', in D.L. JOHNSON (Ed.), *Middle Classes in Dependent Countries*, Sage, Beverly Hills, pp. 43–65.

ANYON, J. (1979) 'Ideology and United States history textbooks', *Harvard Educational Review*, **49**, 3, pp. 361–86.

ANYON, J. (1981) 'Social class and school knowledge', *Curriculum Inquiry,* **11**, 1, pp. 3–42.

ANYON, J. (1984) 'Intersections of gender and class: Accommodation and resistance by working-class and affluent females to contradictory sex role ideologies', *Journal of Education,* **166**, 1, pp. 25–48.

APPLE, M.W. (1979) *Ideology and Curriculum*, London, Routledge and Kegan Paul.

APPLE, M.W. (1982) *Education and Power*, London, Routledge and Kegan Paul.

APPLE, M.W., and WEIS, L. (1983) (Eds), *Ideology and Practice in Schooling*, Philadelphia, Temple University Press.

APPLE, M.W. (1986) *Teachers and Texts: A Political Economy of Class and Gender Relations in Education*, London, Routledge and Kegan Paul.

APPLE, M.W. (1988) 'Facing the complexity of power: For a parallelist position in critical educational studies', in M. COLE (Ed.), *Bowles and Gintis Revisited*, Lewes, Falmer Press, pp. 122–30.

ARCHER, M.S. (1979) *Social Origins of Educational Systems*, London, Sage.

ARCHER, M.S. (1982) 'Introduction: Theorising about the expansion of educational systems', in M.S. ARCHER (Ed.), *The Sociology of Educational Expansion*, Beverly Hills, Sage.

ARNOWITZ, S. and GIROUX, H. (1985) *Education Under Siege*, London, Routledge and Kegan Paul.

BALL, S.J. (1981) *Beachside Comprehensive: A Case-Study of Secondary Schooling*, Cambridge, Cambridge University Press.

BECKER, H.S. (1952) 'Social class variations in pupil-teacher relationships', *Journal of Educational Sociology*, **XXV**, 8, pp. 451–65.

BERNSTEIN, B. (1975) 'On the classification and framing of educational knowledge', in B. BERNSTEIN (Ed.), *Class, Codes and Control*, Vol. 3, London, Routledge and Kegan Paul.

BIDWELL, C.E. (1980) 'The sociology of the school and classroom', in H. M. BLALOCK (Ed.), *Sociological Theory and Research*, London, Collier MacMillan.

BILLS, D.B. (1983) 'Social reproduction and the Bowles-Gintis thesis of a correspondence between school and worksettings', *Research in Sociology of Education and Socialization,* **4,** pp. 185–210.

BOURDIEU, P. (1973) 'Cultural reproduction and social reproduction', in R. BROWN (Ed.), *Knowledge, Education and Cultural Change*, London, Tavistock.

BOURDIEU, P. (1974) 'The school as a conservative force: scholastic and cultural inequalities', in J. EGGLESTON (Ed.), *Contemporary Research in The Sociology of Education*, London, Methuen.

BOURDIEU, P. (1977) *Outline of a Theory of Practice*, Cambridge, Cambridge University Press.

BOURDIEU, P. (1979) *Algeria 1960*, Cambridge, Cambridge University Press.

BOURDIEU, P. (1986) 'The forms of capital', in J.G. RICHARDSON (Ed.), *Handbook of Theory and Research for the Sociology of Education*, New York, Greenwood Press.

BOURDIEU, P. and PASSERON, J.C. (1977) *Reproduction in Education, Society and Culture*, Beverly Hills, Sage.

BOWLES, S. and GINTIS, H. (1976) *Schooling in Capitalist America*, New York, Basic Books.

BOWLES, S. and GINTIS, H. (1988) 'The correspondence principle', in M. COLE (Ed.), *Bowles and Gintis Revisited*, Lewes, Falmer Press, pp. 1–4.

BREEN, R. (1984) *Education and the Labour Market*, Dublin, Economic and Social Research Institute (ESRI): Paper No. 119.

BURRIS, V. (1980) Review of *Learning to Labour, Harvard Educational Review,* **50,** 4, November, p. 525.

BYRNE, E. (1978) *Women and Education*, London, Tavistock.

CARLSON, D. (1987) 'Teachers as political actors: From reproductive theory to the crisis of schooling', *Harvard Educational Review,* **57,** 3, August, pp. 283–307.

CENTRAL STATISTICS OFFICE (CSO) (1981) *Census of Population of Ireland,* **4,** Dublin, Government Publications.

(CSO) (1985) *Trade Statistics of Ireland*, Dublin, Government Publications, May.

CHUBB, B. (1982) *The Government and Politics of Ireland*, London, Longman.

CLANCY, P. (1982) *Participation in Higher Education: A National Survey*, Dublin, Higher Education Authority.

CLANCY, P. (1983) 'Religious vocation as a latent identity for school principals', *The Economic and Social Review,* **15,** 1, October, pp. 1–23.

CLANCY, P. (1986) 'Socialisation, selection and reproduction in education', in P. CLANCY, et al. (Eds), *Ireland: A Sociological Profile*, Dublin, Institute of Public Administration.

CLANCY, P. (1989) *Who Goes to College: A Second National Survey of Participation in Higher Education*, Dublin, Higher Education Authority.

CLANCY, P.J., 'The evolution of policy in third level education', in D. O'SULLIVAN and D.G. MULCAHY (Eds), *Irish Educational Policy: Process and Structure*, Dublin, IPA, (in press).

COLEMAN, J.S. et al. (1982) *High School Achievement*, New York, Basic Books.

COLLINS, R. (1979) *The Credential Society*, New York, Academic Press.

COMMINS, P. (1986) 'Rural social change', in P. CLANCY et al. (Eds) *Ireland: A Scoiological Profile*, Dublin, Institute of Public Administration.

COOLAHAN, J. (1981) *Irish Education: History and Structure*, Dublin, Institute of Public Administration.

COOLAHAN, J. (1984) *The ASTI and Post-Primary Education in Ireland 1909–1984*, Dublin, Cumann na Meánmhúinteoirí, Éire.

COUNCIL OF EUROPE (1982) (Ed.), *Sex Stereotyping in Schools: A Report of the Educational Research Workshop held at Honejoss 5–8 May, 1981*, Lisse, Swets and Zeittinger.

COUNCIL OF MANAGERS OF CATHOLIC SECONDARY SCHOOLS (1984) *A Handbook for Managers of Secondary Schools*, Dublin, (Private Circulation only).

CROTTY, R.(1986) *Ireland in Crisis: A Study in Capitalist Colonial Underdevelopment*, Dingle, Co. Kerry, Brandon Book Publishers Ltd.

CURRICULUM AND EXAMINATIONS BOARD (1984) *Issues and Structures in Education*, Dublin, Government Publications, September.

CURRICULUM AND EXAMINATIONS BOARD (CEB) (1985) *Assessment and Certification: A Consultative Document*, Dublin, Government Publications.

CUSICK, P. (1973) *Inside High School*, New York, Holt Rinehart and Winston.

DALE, R. (1982) 'Education and the capitalist state: Contributions and contradictions', in M.W. APPLE (Ed.), *Cultural and Economic Reproduction in Education*, London, Routledge and Kegan Paul.

DAVIES, L. and MEIGHAN, R. (1975) 'A review of schooling and sex roles, with particular reference to the experience of girls in secondary schools', *Education Review*, **27**, 3, pp. 165–78.

DAVIS, K., and MOORE, W.E. (1945) 'Some principles of stratification', *American Sociological Review*, **10**, April, pp. 242–9.

DEMAINE, J. (1981) *Contemporary Theories in the Sociology of Education*, London, Macmillan.

DEPARTMENT OF EDUCATION (1960) *Report of the Council of Education*, Dublin, Government Publications Office.

DEPARTMENT OF EDUCATION (1968) *Investment in Education*, Dublin, Government Publications Office.

DEPARTMENT OF EDUCATION *Statistical Reports 1981/82, 1982/83, 1983/84*, Dublin, Government Publications.

DEPARTMENT OF EDUATION *Rules and Programme for Secondary Schools 1984/85*, Dublin, Government Publications.

DEPARTMENT OF EDUCATION (n.d.) *Rules and Programmes for the Day Vocational Certificate Examination*, Dublin, Government Publications, (Memo V50).

DEPARTMENT OF EDUCATION AND SCIENCE (UK) (1975) *Curricular Differences for Boys and Girls*, Education Survey No. 21, London, HMSO.

DEPARTMENT OF LABOUR (1987) *Economic Status of School-Leavers 1986*, Dublin, Department of Labour.

DI MAGGIO, P. (1979) 'Review essay: On Pierre Bourdieu', *American Journal of Sociology*, **84**, 6, pp. 1460–74.

DOBSON, R.B. (1977) 'Social status and inequality of access to higher education in the USSR', in J. KARABEL, and A.H. HALSEY (Eds), *Power and Ideology in Education*, Oxford, Oxford University Press.

DREEBEN, R. (1968) *On What is Learned in School*, Mass., Addison Wesley.

DURKHEIM, E. (1977) *The Evolution of Educational Thought*, trans. Peter Collins, London, Routledge and Kegan Paul.

EUROSTAT (1987) *Labour Force Survey Results 1985*, Luxembourg, Office des publications officielles des Communautés européenes.

EVERHART, R.B. (1983) *Reading, Writing and Resistance*, Boston, Routledge and Kegan Paul.

FREIRE, P. (1972) *Pedagogy of the Oppressed*, Harmondsworth, Penguin.

FURLONG, V. (1976) 'Interaction sets in the classroom: Towards a study of pupil knowledge', in M. STUBBS, and S. DELAMONT (Eds), *Expolorations in Classroom Observation*, Chichester, Wiley.

GARDNER, H. (1983) *Frames of Mind: The Theory of Multiple Intelligence*, London, Paladin.

GINTIS, H. and BOWLES, S. (1980) 'Contradiction and reproduction in educatinal theory', in *Schooling, Ideology and the Curriculum*, L. BARTON, R. MEIGHAN and S. WALKER (Eds), Lewes, Falmer Press.

GIROUX, H. (1981) *Ideology, Culture and the Politics of Schooling*, Philadelphia, Temple University Press.

GIROUX, H . (1983a) 'Theories of reproduction and resistance in the new sociology of education', *Harvard Educational Review*, **53**, 3, August, pp. 257–93.

GIROUX, H. (1983b) 'Ideology and agency in the process of schooling', *Journal of Education*, Winter, pp. 12–34.

GIROUX, H. (1983c) *Theory and Resistance in Education: A Pedagogy of Opposition*, London, Heinemann.

GIROUX, H. (1984) 'Marxism and schooling: The limits of radical discourse', *Educational Theory,* **34**, 2, pp. 113–35.

GIROUX, H. (1985) 'Critical pedagogy, cultural politics and the discourse of experience', *Journal of Education,* **167**, 2, pp. 22–41.

GIROUX, H. and MCLAREN, P. (1986) 'Teacher education and the politics of engagement: The case for democratic schooling', *Harvard Educational Review,* **56**, 3, August, pp. 213–38.

GOFFMAN, E. (1962) *Asylums*, Chicago, Aldine.

GOODACRE, E.J. (1968) *Teachers and Their Pupils' Home Background*, Slough, National Foundation for Educational Research.

GORDON, L. (1984) 'Paul Willis — Education, cultural reproduction and social reproduction', *British Journal of Sociology of Education,* **5**, 2, pp. 105–15.

GOULD, S.J. (1981) *The Mismeasure of Man*, New York, Norton and Co.

GREANEY, V. and KELLAGHAN, T. (1984) *Equality of Opportunity in Irish Schools*, Dublin, The Educational Company.

HALSEY, A.H., HEATH, A.F., and RIDGE, J.M. (1980) *Origins and Destinations: Family, Class and Education in Modern Britain*, Oxford, Oxford University Press.

HAMMERSLEY, M. (1974) 'The organization of pupil participation', *Sociological Review,* **22**, 3, pp. 355–68.

HANNAN, D. *et al.* (1983) *Schooling and Sex Roles*, Dublin, Economic and Social Research Institute, Paper No. 113, May.

HANNAN, D. and BOYLE, M. (1987) *Schooling Decisions: The Origins and Consequences of Selection and Streaming in Irish Post-Primary Schools*, Dublin, Economic and Social Research Institute, Paper No. 136.

HARGREAVES, A. (1982) 'Resistance and relative autonomy theories: Problems of distortion and incoherence in recent Marxist theories of education', *British Journal of Sociology of Education,* **3**, 2, pp. 107–26.

HARGREAVES, A. (1984) 'Apple crumbles?', *Journal of Curriculum Studies,* **16**, 2, pp. 206–10.

HARGREAVES, D. (1967) *Social Relations in a Secondary School*, London, Routledge and Kegan Paul.

HARGREAVES, D. (1980) 'A sociological critique of individualism in education', *British Journal of Education Studies,* **XXVIII**, 3, pp. 187–98.

HARKER, R.K. (1984) 'On reproduction, habitus, and education', *British Journal of Sociology of Education,* **5**, 2, pp. 117–27.

References

INGLIS, T. (1987) *Moral Monopoly,* Dublin, Gill and Macmillan.

JACKSON, P.W. (1968) *Life in Classrooms,* New York, Holt Rinehart and Winston.

JOYCE, L. (1985) *Administrators or Managers? An Exploratory Study of Public and Private Sector Decision-Making,* Dublin, Institute of Public Administration.

KAMIN, L. (1974) *The Science and Politics of IQ,* Potomac, Md., Erlbaum Associates.

KARABEL, J. and HALSEY, A.H. (1977) 'Educational research: A review and an interpretation', in J. KARABEL and A.H. HALSEY, (Eds), *Power and Ideology in Education,* London, Oxford University Press.

KEDDIE, N. (1971) 'Classroom knowledge', in M.F.D. YOUNG (Ed.), *Knowledge and Control,* London, Collier MacMillan.

KELLY, A. (1980) 'White-collar trade unionism', in D. NEVIN (Ed.), *Trade Unions and Change in Irish Society,* Cork, Mercier Press.

KENNETT, J. (1973) 'The sociology of Pierre Bourdieu', *Educational Review,* **25,** 3, June, pp. 237–49.

LACEY, C. (1970) *Hightown Grammar,* Manchester, Manchester Press.

LIVINGSTONE, D.W. (1983) *Class Ideologies and Educational Futures,* Lewes, Falmer Press.

LORTIE, D.C. (1969) 'The balance of control and autonomy in elementary school teaching', in A. ETZIONI (Ed.), *The Semi-Professions and Their Organization,* New York, Free Press.

LORTIE, D.C. (1975) *The Schoolteacher: A Sociological Study,* Chicago, University of Chicago Press.

LUKES, S. (1973) *Individualism,* Oxford, Basil Blackwell.

LUNN, J.C.B. (1970) *Streaming in the Primary School,* Slough, National Foundation for Educational Research.

LYNCH, K. (1982) 'A sociological analysis of the functions of second-level education', *Irish Educational Studies,* **2,** pp. 32–58.

LYNCH, K. (1985) 'An analysis of some presuppositions underlying the concepts of meritocracy and ability as presented in Greaney and Kellaghan's study', *The Economic and Social Review,* **16,** 2, January, pp. 83–102.

LYNCH, K. (1987a) 'The ethos of girls' schools: An analysis of differences between male and female schools'. Paper presented at the Third International Interdisciplinary Conference on Women, Dublin, 6–10 July.

LYNCH, K. (1987b) 'Dominant ideologies in Irish educational thought: Consensualism, essentialism and meritocratic individualism', *The Economic and Social Review,* **18,** 2, January, pp. 101–22.

LYNCH, K. (1988) 'Streaming and banding in schools: Context and implications', *Institute of Guidance Counsellors Journal,* **14,** Spring, pp. 37–40.

LYNCH, K. (1989) 'Solidary labour: Its nature and marginalisation', *Sociological Review.* February.

MCCARTHY, C. (1973) *The Decade of Upheaval: Irish Trade Unions in the Nineteen Sixties,* Dublin, Institute of Public Administration.

MCDILL, E.L., and RIGSBY, L.C. (1973) *Structure and Process in Secondary Schools,* Baltimore, John Hopkins University Press.

MCDONALD, M. (1980) 'Schooling and the reproduction of class and gender relations', in L. BARTON *et al.* (Eds), *Schooling, Ideology and The Curriculum,* Lewes, Falmer Press, pp. 29–49.

MCDONNELL, A. (1988) 'The perceptions of senior cycle pupils regarding their second level educational experiences' (Unpublished MA Thesis), University College Dublin, Education Department.

McGeeney, P. (1969) *Parents Are Welcome*, London, Longman.

MacGréil, M. (1974) *Educational Opportunity in Dublin*, Dublin Catholic Communications Institute.

McKernan, J. (1981) *Transfer at 14*, Belfast, Northern Ireland Council for Education Research.

McLaren, P. (1986) *Schooling as a Ritual Performance*, London, Routledge and Kegan Paul.

McRobbie, A. (1978) 'Working-class girls and the culture of feminity', in Women's Studies Group, *Women Take Issue*, London, Hutchinson.

Marx, K. (1964) *Economic and Philosophical Manuscripts of 1844*, Ed. with an introduction by D.J. Struik, trans. M. Mulligan, New York, International Publishers.

Marx, K. (1973) *Grundrisse*, Harmondsworth, Penguin.

Marx, K. (1975) *Early Writings*, Harmondsworth, Penguin.

Metz, M.H. (1978) 'Order in the secondary school: Strategies for control and their consequences', *Sociological Inquiry*, **48**, 1, pp. 59–69.

Moore, D. (1984) 'Disparate teacher attention favouring the more able', *The Australian Journal of Education*, **28**, 2, pp. 154–64.

Moore, R. (1988) 'The correspondence principle and the Marxist sociology of education', in M. Cole (Ed.), *Bowles and Gintis Revisited*, Lewes, Falmer Press, pp. 51–85.

NATIONAL COUNCIL OF EDUCATIONAL AWARD (NCEA) (1983) *Directory of Approved Courses in Higher Education*, 3rd ed., Dublin, NCEA.

NATIONAL ECONOMIC AND SOCIAL COUNCIL (1984) *A Review of Industrial Policy (Telesis Report)*, Dublin, NESC.

Newman, O. (1981) *The Challenge of Corporatism*, London, Macmillan.

Offe, C. (1976) *Industry and Inequality*, London, Edward Arnold.

Offe, C. (1984) *Contradictions of the Welfare State*, London, Hutchinson.

Olneck, M. and Bills, D.B. (1980) 'What makes Sammy run? An empirical assessment of the Bowles–Gintis correspondence theory', *American Journal of Education*, **89**, November, pp. 27–61.

Ozga, J. and Lawn, M. (1981) *Teachers, Professionalism and Class*, Lewes, Falmer Press.

Peillon, M. (1982) *Contemporary Irish Society: An Introduction*, Dublin, Gill and MacMillan.

Poulantzas, N. (1975) *Classes in Contemporary Capitalism*, London, New Left Books.

Raftery, A. and Hout, M. (1985) 'Does Irish education approach the meritocratic ideal? A logistic analysis', *The Economic and Social Review*, **16**, 2, January, pp. 115–40.

Ramsay, P. (1983) 'Fresh perspectives on the school transformation–reproduction debate: A response to Anyon from the Antipodes', *Curriculum Inquiry*, **13**, 3, Fall, pp. 295–320.

Raven, J. (1975) 'Teachers' and pupils' perceptions of the objectives of education and examinations, with an interpretation and discussion', Appendix J, in DEPARTMENT OF EDUCATION, *The Intermediate Certificate Examination Report*, Dublin, Government Publications.

Reynolds, D. (1976) 'The delinquent school', in M. Hammersley and P. Woods (Eds), *The Process of Schooling*, London, Routledge and Kegan Paul, pp. 217–29.

Rist, R. (1970) 'Student social class and teacher expectations: The self-fulfilling prophecy and ghetto education', *Harvard Educational Review,* **40,** 3, August, pp. 411–51.

ROTTMAN, D. and O'CONNELL, P.J. (1982) 'The changing social structure', in INSTITUTE OF PUBLIC ADMINISTRATION, *Unequal Achievement,* Dublin, IPA.

ROTTMAN, D. *et al.* (1982) *The Distribution of Income in the Republic of Ireland: A Study in Social Class and Family Cycle Inequalities,* Dublin, ESRI Paper No. 109.

RUTTER, M. *et al.* (1979) *Fifteen Thousand Hours: Secondary Schools and Their Effects on Children,* Somerset, Open Books.

SEXTON, J.J., WHELAN, B.J., and DILLON, M. (1983) 'Some preliminary results from the 1982 ESRI survey of youth employment and transition from education to working life', paper read at ESRI, Dublin, 23 June.

SHARP, R. and GREEN, A. (1975) *Education and Social Control,* London, Routledge and Kegan Paul.

SHAVIT, Y. (1984) 'Tracking and ethnicity in Israeli secondary education', *American Sociological Review,* **49,** 2, pp. 210–20.

SPENDER, D. and SPENDER, E. (Eds) (1980) *Learning to Lose: Sexism and Education,* London, The Women's Press.

STANWORTH, M. (1981) *Gender and Schooling,* London, Hutchinson.

VATICAN COUNCIL (1965) 'The declaration on Christian education', *The Documents of Vatican II,* St Peters, Rome: 28 October, pp. 637–51.

VOGT, W.P. (1981) 'The theory of the credential class', *The Review of Education,* **7,** 2, pp. 135–51.

WEBER, M., *From Max Weber* (1946) H.H. GERTH and C.W. MILLS (Eds), Oxford, Oxford University Press.

WHELAN, C. and WHELAN, B. (1984) *Social Mobility in the Republic of Ireland: A Comparative Perspective,* Dublin, ESRI, Paper No. 116.

WHITE, J. (1980) 'Conceptions of individuality', *British Journal of Educational Studies,* **XXVIII,** 3, June, pp. 173–85.

WICKHAM, A. (1981) 'National education systems and the international context: The case of Ireland', in R. DALE *et al.* (Eds), *Education and The State, Vol. 1,* Lewes, Falmer Press, pp. 321–34.

WICKHAM, J. (1983) 'Dependence and state structure: Foreign firms and industrial policy in the Republic of Ireland', in O. HÖLL (Ed.), *Small States in Europe and Dependence,* The Luxembourg Papers, Vienna, Austrian Institute for International Affairs, pp. 164–83.

WCIKHAM, J. (1986) 'Industrialisation, work and unemployment', in P. CLANCY, *et al.* (Eds), *Ireland: A Sociological Profile,* Dublin, Institute of Public Administration.

WILLIS, P. (1977) *Learning to Labour,* Hampshire, Gower.

WILLIS, P. (1981a) 'Cultural production is different from cultural reproduction is different from social reproduction is different from reproduction', *Interchange,* **12,** 2–3, pp. 48–67.

WILLIS, P. (1981b) 'The class significance of school counter-culture', in R. DALE *et al.* (Eds), *Education and The State, Vol. 1,* Lewes, Falmer Press, pp. 257–73.

WILLIS, P. (1983) 'Cultural production and theories of reproduction', in L. BARTON and S. WALKER (Eds), *Race, Class and Education,* London, Croom Helm.

WOODS, P. (1979) *The Divided School,* London, Routledge and Kegan Paul.

YOUNG, M. (1961) *The Rise of the Meritocracy 1870–2033,* London, Pelican Books.

ZAJDA, J. (1980) 'Education and social stratification in the Soviet Union', *Comparative Education,* **16,** 1, March, pp. 3–11.

Index